BY THE SAME AUTHOR

Ambiguous Africa : Cultures in Collision

Daily Life in the
KINGDOM OF THE KONGO
From the Sixteenth to the Eighteenth Century

TRANSLATED FROM THE FRENCH
BY HELEN WEAVER

PANTHEON BOOKS

A Division of Random House

New York

Daily Life in the

KINGDOM
OF
THE
KONGO

*From the Sixteenth to
the Eighteenth Century*

GEORGES BALANDIER

Foreword

The ancient kingdom of the Kongo endures on the threshold of survival. The glorious sovereigns have ridiculous descendants whose domains are no more than large chieftainries; the ruins of the capital have not yet been entrusted to the preservers of historic monuments; the artistic treasures of the great era have been dispersed or hidden in the homes of aristocrats fallen on evil days. Since the eighteenth century the history of the Kongo has slowly cooled until it has become a mere parody of itself played in the setting of modern Portuguese colonization. The places where it has left its mark are nevertheless places where a living history is being born, where politics are preparing new beginnings; Angolese resistance has established its most active centers on the territory of the defeated kingdom. And some of the disagreements that are weakening the movement for independence stem from the fact that the insurgent Bakongo have achieved preponderance by taking a lead in the struggle. There is nothing accidental about their undertaking: this tribe has not been an active agent of history for centuries without having the potentiality for returning to the role.

One question immediately arises. Within what structure can this people place its collective destiny if it is true that the future of Africa belongs neither to the micronations nor to the solitary nations? The area of Kongolese civilization remains divided despite the vitality which is indicated by cultural associations still active in Congo-Kinshasa. Outside of common historical memories, therefore, there persist a cultural form and content peculiar to the ethnic groups living on either side of the Congo River. This potential unity of civilization constitutes a favorable condition, but it is by no means a sufficient one. It did, however, after the achievement of independence in 1960 and the resulting vicissitudes, justify a plan for the reconstruction of the Kongo which included the formation of a modern state controlling the estuary of the river, its lower course beyond Stanley Pool, and the coastal area bordering its basin. The economic foundation seemed to exist, but the political situation kept the attempt in the realm of intention. The disunited elements could not come together until the two modern Congos were separated, until the

7

Congolese region of Angola had won an actual independence. Recent developments have done little to alter this situation. The Bakongo have lost part of their power in Kinshasa; they have been split over the revolutionary choice of the new regime in Brazzaville; they have become involved in a long war in Angola. Lost kingdoms are rarely rebuilt upon their own ruins. Most often they rise again only on the terrain of the imaginary.

In the course of its history the Kongo has taken its place within a system of relationships which generously overflows its boundaries. To the north its influence has reached the borders of present-day Gabon. To the east, beyond the Kwango River, the mobile and land-hungry Bayaka have posed a permanent threat and have managed to invade the kingdom; mistrust and open hostility have determined the direction of relations between the two 'nations'. To the south the affinities have persisted for a long time, as has the trade network based mainly on cattle and salt, despite the peripeties resulting from a restless history. The states of northern Angola—Ndongo and Matamba—have felt the domination of the Kongo; the kinship of their cultural and political configurations is apparent. Beyond this region certain similarities persist and are particularly evident in the symbolism and conceptions governing royalty. The Bakuba and their original sovereigns appear to have been born of Kongo stock. The Lunda empire has partially turned toward the kingdom of the Kongo, with which it presents certain resemblances. It is clear that the Kongo is located at the hub of a complex that is widely distributed in space; it is the 'crescent' of the western kingdoms hugging the Congo Basin. Modern attempts to establish large political units might find here a foundation forged by history.

History in its peculiarly African form could have been effaced if the creation of the United States of Latin Africa had become a reality. The plan launched in 1958 remained without result. It envisioned the regrouping in a single political structure of the countries marked by Latin and Christian colonization: old French Equatorial Africa, Cameroun, the 'Belgian' Congo, Ruanda-Urundi, and the 'Portuguese provinces' of Africa. It took as its unifying base that laid down by the imported civilization which Catholic Europe had spread according to the hazards of discoveries and conquests. Such a suggestion is revealing. It

8

shows that accession to modernity in this part of Central Africa took identical or parallel paths. Above all it recalls the antiquity of the relations established with the outside world. From Cameroun to Angola, as early as the turn of the sixteenth century, the coastal region was widely open to European enterprise. And here again the Kongo enjoyed a privileged position, since the kingdom was precocious in entering the arena of international relations. It was at the heart of a history productive of Central African states from the fifteenth century on. It was the principal seat of modernization until the eve of the nineteenth century. It certainly has not been summoned to arise from its ashes, but the Kongo complex could play a decisive role at such time as a new political division of Central Africa might be envisaged.

This glorious past raises questions of present interest which in turn must help to illuminate it. The first of these questions seems to be political. Are the current political vicissitudes which the Congo is experiencing rooted in remote history, or are they only the consequence of a decolonization that has failed? No answer can be given without the possibility of error, but one must be formulated if only provisionally. In the Congolese region modern colonial divisions have permanently mutilated political units which were already weakened, notably the Lunda empire in the upper basin of the Congo River and the kingdom of the Kongo established upon its lower course and estuary. The chances for reconstruction were therefore eliminated for a long period of time as early as the end of the nineteenth century. This was all the more true because the traditional powers who had been deprived of their territorial foundation also found themselves placed in a situation of dependence. They became conditional powers subject to colonial bureaucracy. This hardship was added to others accumulated over the preceding two centuries. The slave trade had threatened the very physical existence of the tribes of Central Africa. It caused veritable demographic ravages by the deportation of young people, by 'casualties' arising from the conditions of the traffic in Negroes, and by the numerous wars whose purpose was the hunting of men. An estimate published some thirty years ago fixes the number of Congolese (and Angolese) deported to America at 13,250,000. The figure is excessive, but it nevertheless suggests the magnitude of the human blood-letting performed. Several Kongo sovereigns and a few priests tried vainly to curb the excesses, but labor force remained the most important of the products destined for exportation. It was for this reason that rivalries and economic struggles were multiplied. In this sense, the Negro slave trade contributed considerably to the instability of the region by intensifying competition.

The principal traffic involved men and imported manufactured goods, but this did not exclude a more ancient traffic, which controlled the movement of salt, iron, fabrics, skins, and, to a lesser degree, cattle. It accelerated and quickened commerce, provoked a new distribution of economic centers, caused the multiplication of commercial routes, and increased enforced slavery, inasmuch as caravans of porters constituted the sole means of transport. This economic structure, which included a large part of the Congo Basin, has persisted to a recent period. At the begining of this century, traders were still using the routes that hugged the river on both banks, those that led to the coastal region and those that plunged into the interior of the continent beyond the Kwango River. This trade economy initiated permanent practices and usages. For a long time the units of exchange used in modern transactions remained the *piece* (estimated in quantity of fabric) and the *bundle* (estimated principally in number of guns and quantity of gunpowder). The barter system survived, creating a barrier to the establishment of the so-called monetary economy. The imported *commodities* themselves enjoyed considerable prestige, since they lent prestige to their owners. The colonial archives report that the Bakongo from the Stanley Pool region still kept these treasures in secret places guarded by armed men. In a certain sense these rare goods became 'fetishes'. The psychological obstacles now encountered by professional developers are partly the result of these attitudes, formed in the course of centuries of trade.

Trade has had indirect political consequences as well. The control of centers of trade with European merchants affords a position of power. The episodic forays of the Bayaka in the direction of the coast are partially explained by a desire to return to the source of wealth and instruments of reinforcement (weapons). Too, the shift of trading centers entails a profound modification of the power structure. From the moment that

Portuguese colonization took root in Angola, and Loanda became a commercial center, the kingdom of the Kongo lost part of its vigor. It lost the initiative, and the pole of attraction shifted to the south. Trade creates an economic division of labor which engenders inequality and antagonism between peoples. The peoples of the coastal regions were in competition: Loango, Kongo, Loanda in Angola symbolized this rivalry. Inhabitants of the remote interior regions were not content to be mere providers. The antagonism between the Bateke, settled around the banks of Stanley Pool, and the Bakongo was based partly on this unequal access to the source of wealth. The intermediary groups, on the other hand, occupied an advantageous position. The people of the province of Mbata in the Kongo covered an extensive region with their caravans, and their spirit of enterprise is still evoked in certain popular sayings. They have retained the initiative and the less fortunate groups their resentments, but in both cases the expression of these attitudes today is of a primarily political nature. The recently acquired independence has reactivated ancient political forces.

This observation leads us to examine a problem manifested in all its acuteness by the peripeties of Congo-Kinshasa. Are the difficulties of the modern state also related to the survival of ancient political conceptions and traditions? The Lunda empire, like the kingdom of the Kongo, has remained a loose federation. The existence of a group possessing political power, a capital, and a governmental apparatus should not sustain the illusion of a perfectly realized centralization. The conditions necessary for the establishment of a unified state have been lacking, and empiricism has governed the formation of a system which is a complex amalgam of relations founded on the base of domination and relations resulting from clanic affinities and alliances. The supremacy of the royal power does not exclude the persistence of particularisms; the preponderance of the royal province does not exclude a partially federative organization. Modern political power finds itself confronted with the same problems: it must dominate diversity without crushing it and admit its own coexistence with some of the local powers. The political organization of the present Congo has retained a 'segmentary' aspect, which has just been defined, and a repetitive aspect: the provincial capitals and governments are patterned after Kinshasa and the central government. Throughout this part of the African continent, the struggle between the united and the segmented has been permanent, and the second aspect has often prevailed. It continues to be operative outside the political domain: on the religious level, for example, where it causes the constant multiplication of new churches, and on the professional level, where it determines the proliferation of labor unions.

The facts of permanence take another form. Traditional conceptions of power have not been completely eliminated. In a certain sense the image of the modern president is a retouched copy of the image of the ancient king. The chief must manifest his vigor; he must literally seize the power, and hold it by force in the interest of the collectivity. According to this point of view, recent struggles for the control of the machinery of government are merely a new version of the wars of succession, and military power appears only as the best armed. With the figure of the *strong* chief is associated that of the *lawgiving* chief, who is respected by virtue of the wisdom he possesses and is capable of being the final recourse, of imposing respect for the law and enforcing conciliation. A third figure is associated with the two preceding ones in the traditional representation of royalty: that of the charismatic leader who enjoys a privileged relation with the people, the land, and the system of forces governing fertility and prosperity. Power is still seen under this triple aspect of force, arbitration, and the sacred. The modern Congo since 1960 has not succeeded in reuniting these three faces of the chief in a single individual. In a sense it has possessed them separately in General Mobutu, Joseph Kasavubu, and Patrice Lumumba.

The history of the Kongo and its neighbors throws light on the present situation in a more general way. It makes it possible to assess sociological and cultural conservatisms, to get a clearer idea of the most radical changes. Some of the Kongo villages could still serve to illustrate the old travel accounts, while the cities and the new technological milieu reveal a different society in process of formation. Such a comparison leads to an important observation, that the answer to grave crises has been *constantly* expressed in the language of religion. Since the sixteenth century, in the Kongo, conflicts between the party of the modernists and the party of the conservatives have taken the form of

12

religious wars. From that time on, resistance to foreign inter-
ference has been symbolized by the antagonism between the
missionary (or native priest) and the 'fetisher'. But the most
significant manifestation, occurring in a time of great distress
during the early years of the eighteenth century, was the
Antonian movement. It resulted from the initiative of a young
Kongo woman of aristocratic rank, a mystic tormented by the
misery of the kingdom who took it upon herself to found a
national religion, rekindle hope by announcing a kind of golden
age, and mobilize energies in order to restore the Kongo to its
greatness. She was a heroine even in her martyrdom, a kind of
African Joan of Arc. She predicted the messiahs and prophets
who were to appear much later in various parts of the Congolese
region. It was they who would contribute to the birth of
nationalism, who would establish the so-called new churches and
herald an age of freedom and prosperity. All have been givers of
confidence, *agents provocateurs* of change. Some—especially the
most important, Simon Kimbangu—have become objects of worship in spite of disillusionment. The present crisis of Congolese
society has once again stimulated the forces of religious innovation. Close to five hundred 'religions' have been recorded, some
fifty of which are in Kongo country. At a distance of several
centuries, the same mechanisms are again coming into play
under comparable conditions. And practical rationality continues
to be expressed by being placed in the realm of the sacred.

One last point: relations between the Kongo and Europe foreshadowed those that would be established during the colonial
period and later. They operated to the advantage of the most
powerful partner. The Portuguese sovereigns and their agents
quickly sought the economic advantages, defended their commercial monopoly, exerted pressure on the kings, and even
entered into war in order to reach gold and silver mines that
were largely imaginary. Economic interest engendered political
domination: foreign colonists intervened in the domestic affairs
of the kingdom, advisers from Lisbon took pains to keep the
Kongo in a state of 'obedience', material aid remained within
limits which would not encourage 'disobedience' by virtue of an
apparent reinforcement. The nascent Christianity was com-
promised in these enterprises; it justified them less and less
easily and became one of the elements of misunderstanding. All

policies of modernization were therefore doomed to failure in spite of an openness to outside instruction: the reform of institutions remained in the planning stage, the Kongo élites had difficulty putting their talents to use, attempts at educational and technological advance were unable to achieve lasting results. At several moments in its history the kingdom of the Kongo tried and failed to become a member of the modern age; in this its European partner pushed it forward and held it back at the same time for fear of losing its hold. On another scale, inside other frontiers, by other means, this is the same situation that the leaders of Congolese Africa are experiencing today.

G.B.

Contents

Foreword 7

Introduction 19

Part I: THE FAILURE OF THE KINGS

1. *The Blacksmith King* 27
2. *The Christian King* 42
3. *The Rival Kings* 64

Part II: THE FORGING OF THE KONGO

4. *The Forge and the Palm* 89
5. *The Fragile Towns* 139
6. *The Fabric of Daily Life* 153
7. *Master and Slave* 180

Part III: THE MAKING OF MEN

8. *Education* 213
9. *Language and the Arts* 227
10. *One God Against Many* 244

Notes 264
Bibliographical Suggestions 283
Index 285

Illustrations

between pages 128 and 129

1 Map of the Kongo, dated 1731

From the Collection d'Anville, Bibliothèque Nationale, Paris

2 The sweet potato
The blacksmith

From Cavazzi: *Descrizione storice dei tre regni Congo, Matamba, Angola,* Bologna, 1687

3 View of São Salvador

From Dapper: *Description de l'Afrique,* 1686

4 The King of the Kongo receiving European ambassadors
The royal throne and insignia of power

From Dapper: *Description de l'Afrique,* 1686

5 Angola: modern view of the Cathedral at São Salvador
Congolese crucifix in bronze, from Tungwa

Musée du Congo Belge, Tervuren

6 View of the town of Loanga

From Dapper: *Description de l'Afrique,* 1686

7 The King of Loanga

From Dapper: *Description de l'Afrique,* 1686

8 Two soapstone figurines from Mboma

From the Musée Royal de l'Afrique, Centrale

Introduction

Myth and illusion have long distorted our image of the kingdom of the Kongo. The sixteenth-century Portuguese, elated by the discovery of Diogo Cão, who had reached the mouth of the Congo River in 1482, and excited by the idea of planting the cross in the heart of the dark continent and the hope of a profitable trade, regarded it as an enlarged version of their own kingdom, a kind of negative to be subjected to that developing agent which was Christian and Lusitanian civilization. Writing in about 1556, Camões, in the *Lusiads*, describes the Kongo as 'the greatest of the kingdoms' discovered on the western shores of Africa. Disillusionment came quickly, then discord and the military confrontation which brought about the defeat of the Bakongo at the battle of Ambouila in October 1665, and, following thereupon, the rapid decline of their state.

Glorious memories are slow to die, however. At the turn of the twentieth century the first Africanist ethnologists discovered with joy the ancient chronicles and narrations—testimony bearing witness to vanished splendors. They reconstructed the past with enthusiasm—and precipitousness. They created an imagery that revealed more about the excellence of their sentiments toward the Negro world than it did about the daily life of the peoples in question. But this was to their credit at a time when colonial pride was rampant. Leo Frobenius lent his lyricism to this cause: 'Further south, in the kingdom of the Congo, a seething mass of people dressed in "silk" and "velvet", large States well organized down to the last detail, powerful sovereigns, wealthy industries. Civilized to the very marrow of their bones!' The cry of admiration was taken up by André Breton in his Preface to the poet Aimé Césaire's *Cahier d'un retour au pays natal*, in which he proclaims 'the grandeur of the Africa that was'.

The glorification of the past has recently fed the hope of decolonization. Already weakened in the eighteenth century, the ancient kingdom of the Kongo was definitively broken and subdued at the time of the colonial divisions at the end of the nineteenth century. The chief provinces are in modern Angola; one of them—Mpemba—bears the ruins of Mbanza Kongo, the founding center of the celebrated state, which endured for a while under the name of São Salvador. The two modern Congos, established on either side of the river, include the peripheral provinces and kingdoms now destroyed which had been under Kongo domination. A weakened political and cultural unity was doomed to suffer this mutilation, this division by new boundaries. But nostalgia for vanished unity and glory was to take the form of a demand for liberation. As early as 1920 the Bakongo were to take the initiative in a struggle for independence, their political leaders were to lay symbolic claim to the title of king in order to establish continuity, and the rebirth of a rejuvenated and technologically equipped Kongo would seem possible.

It is a rich history of seven centuries, partly recorded from the late fifteenth century, that is under discussion here. The important dates and changes are known and the basic facts about customs, products of civilization, and beliefs are beginning to be assembled. This does not mean that the task of the historian or sociologist who seeks a historical background for his research is an easy one, but it is less difficult and less hazardous here than it is in regions where only oral tradition remains.

Thus the history of the kingdom of the Kongo is, in certain respects, exceptional for Africa. From the last decade of the fifteenth century—in April 1491 a large party of Portuguese soldiers, missionaries, and laborers worked its way peacefully toward the capital — this history has unfolded in terms of a foreign presence. Whether in agreement with this presence, or in conflict with it after a temporary acceptance of submission, the people of the Kongo have received numerous foreign contributions. One need only name them : Christianity, written knowledge, new principles of government and administration, domesticated plants, goods which have stimulated commerce and unfortunately helped in the establishment of the Negro slave trade. The Kongo has been endowed with a history which does not keep only to African pathways, but also uses the great maritime routes. Indeed, it is no longer the principal agent of its destiny.

Europe has kept its archives, and become its witness and its librarian—a rather disorganized one, to tell the truth. Rome, Portugal, and Angola share this precious documentation. A list of sources and works on the history of the ancient kingdom was published in 1953 by Msgr. Jean Cuvelier; it is long, and seems even more so when one compares it with the documentary inventories of other African histories. From the sixteenth to the eighteenth century travel tales and missionaries' accounts provided more or less detailed 'pictures' of Kongo society and civilization. It is only fair to point out, however, that these 'descriptions' are partly deceptive. First of all, they tend to be repetitive: the observations of the Portuguese 'explorer' Duarte Lopes provided material for the work of Filippo Pigafetta (1591), the translation of the De Bry brothers (1598), and several compilations; the history of the related—and at one time subservient —kingdoms of Loango and Kakongo, edited by Father Liévain Proyart in 1776, utilizes the documents of a short-lived French mission in those countries. Secondly, these accounts are incapable of giving a simple portrait of men, manners, and things. They comment as they describe, and they use a vocabulary that sometimes gets in the way—as when they consider the social hierarchy, political titles or offices, and enumerate 'duchies, earldoms, and marquisates'. Their testimony on the Kongo does not limit itself to the Kongo; unbeknownst to its authors, it reflects the society and thought of their age. Most of the early documentation is of missionary origin. In it the problems and difficulties of evangelization and Kongo reactions to Christianity are considered at length, but the facts about indigenous forms of worship and the 'adoration of idols' are distorted. Nor does it omit the struggle against the heretics: for example, the one which Fathers Bernardo de Gallo and Laurent de Lucques, who belonged to the order of the Capuchins, engaged in from 1705 on, against Dona Beatriz, a young Kongo aristocratic lady and foundress of the Antonian sect.

Inasmuch as the documents and accounts are almost all the work of foreigners, they throw as much light on the history of the first colonization—with its economic goals and rivalries, its greedy colonial minority, its political illusions, and its unsuccessful attempt at Christianization—as they do on the history of the old Kongo kingdom. This means that the difficulties of interpretation remain numerous: it is necessary to 'translate' the information, making allowance for the writers' unsuitable vocabulary, misunderstandings, and prejudices, and to distin-

guish between reliable observations—which usually have to do
with material manifestations of the culture or activities of a
commonplace nature—and those which are less so, which have
to do with activities regarded as extraordinary, customs judged
to be barbarian, or practices referred to as 'superstitious or
diabolical'.

After evaluating the risks, one must immediately acknowledge
the unquestionable utility of most of the 'descriptions': for
example, those of Pigafetta (1591) and of the Italian Capuchin
Giovanni Antonio Cavazzi (1687), published almost a century
apart. The documentary value of these eyewitness accounts is less
surprising when one remembers that the accounts devoted to
China in The Book of Marco Polo very often agree with the facts
in Chinese texts. In this case the test of verification was feasible; it
is far less so in the case of a society in which the researcher has
recourse to an oral rather than a written tradition. Only the
comparison of documents gives any assurance. This becomes
possible as soon as a sufficiently large series has been established.
Since the late nineteenth century this has been the goal of those
historians who are dedicated to a precise knowledge of the kingdom of the Kongo. In 1877, Levy Maria Jordão de Paiva Manso
initiated a publication of Portuguese sources which was completed by Alfredo de Albuquerque Felner in 1933. Then the
research movement accelerated; Father Antonio Brasio brought
out successively the first four volumes of the Monumenta
Missionaria Africana (1953–1954), including original sixteenth-
century texts relating to the Kongo and Angola; Msgr. Jean
Cuvelier edited various accounts, and then, in 1954, in collaboration with Father Louis Jadin, began to publish an enormous
group of documents entitled L'Ancien Congo d'après les archives
romaines (1518–1640).

Naturally the information is not complete, but it does make it
possible to determine the important moments in the history of
the Kongo and to re-create with sufficient accuracy the social
context and the cultural landscape against which the daily life
of the Mukongo must be seen. The period which will concern us
here begins with the sixteenth century and the long reign of
Nzinga Mbemba Afonso (1506–1543) and ends before the
middle of the eighteenth century, when the decline of the Kongo
was coming to an end and outside influences—especially that of

the missionaries—were almost nullified. Its chronology remains unclear, but the facts about the civilization that characterized it are now accessible. Indeed, these facts reveal obvious consistencies despite historical vicissitudes and foreign influences. Thus modern sociological knowledge may be brought to bear on a historical documentation which contains gaps, provided it manages to avoid the dangers of anachronism and accurately reveals changes that have occurred.

There is an undeniable relationship between some of the facts gathered during recent ethnological investigations and those collected by the 'old authors'; this became apparent to me thanks to studies conducted in Kongo country in the vicinity of Stanley Pool, that very ancient site of commercial exchange. The vocabulary of kinship and the clanic mechanism, the precedences associated with seniority, the organization of material life and division of labor follow rules which remain in effect in spite of the passing of centuries. The attributes or symbols of power as Olfert Dapper presents them in his 'description' dating from the seventeenth century reappear in the modern monographs, although the extent and context of that power have changed. These remarks do not mean that the history of the Kongo has been a history of futility. They merely suggest the method to be employed, i.e. that the ancient data be illuminated by modern sociological knowledge, and vice versa. A book of this sort is not the work of a historian. It does not seek to establish a chronology —which is not yet possible for all the kings of the Kongo—nor to set up an inventory of events and their precise location in time, nor to retrace the historical movement of the first colonization. It attempts to reconstruct the picture of a Kongo society and civilization that once were glorious, to show what, in the heart of Africa, the human condition once was, to explore the results of contacts between civilizations which the spirit of discovery brought into sudden juxtaposition.

This book has contemporary meanings despite appearances. It deals directly with the ancient forms of communication between countries whose material development is unequal. Before the disillusionment and the conflicts, the Kongo was long open to the lessons of the outside world. King Dom Afonso, of whom it was said that he studied to the point of exhaustion, symbolizes this receptivity. It seems necessary to emphasize a desire for

23

westernization which anticipates that of the Japanese by three hundred and fifty years, even though it ended in failure. During the age of confidence, a modest technical cooperation was begun. Artisans — blacksmiths, masons, carpenters — peasants, clerks, and even two German printers emigrated to the Kongo, bringing their knowledge and their instruments with them. Some European women went there to teach the household arts to the women of this kingdom—which they seldom managed to do, having to endure certain solicitations. Nor does the picture lack either an attempt at institutional and administrative reform, set forth by the *regimento* of 1512, or the beginning of the formation of an élite class; young Kongo aristocrats received their education in Lisbon, generally at the college of Santo Elói.

The contemporary relevance of knowledge about the kingdom of the Kongo is again revealed by way of political projects which have altered the map drawn by colonization and erased the boundaries of the past century in order to restore the lost unity. Thus history seems to take the form of an effective utopia. It also belongs to the eternal time of myths. For every Mukongo, even one living in the peripheral 'provinces', *Kongo dya Ntotila*—the ancient capital—still exists in the form of a magnificent city where everyone can find relatives who will welcome him and overwhelm him with gifts. The lost kingdom thus becomes the one that every man builds with his hope and his dreams.

NOTE:
In transcribing Kikongo terms and forms in the body of the text, I have used a very simplified system. A single letter represents a sound (u = ou). I have made a distinction between Kongo, meaning the ancient kingdom or the people, and Congo, the river or the two modern states; but in excerpts from the writings of chroniclers I have retained the authors' transcriptions: Congo = Kongo, and Esi-Congo = Esikongo or Bakongo. In general, all Kongo place names and Kikongo terms *appearing in the quotations* are kept in the form adopted by the writers. Lack of codification explains the variants (Soyo = Sogno=Sonho, Mbata = Bata, massa = maza, etc.); these differences are not sufficient to give rise to a false interpretation.

At the outset of this work I should like to thank W. G. Randles and M. Auge, who helped correct the manuscript.

Part I

THE FAILURE
OF THE KINGS

CHAPTER 1

The Blacksmith King

The Kongo eventually gave its name to the river by which the Portuguese caravels reached the kingdom in 1482: that lusty river—*rio poderoso*—which Diogo Cão and his sailors tried to ascend in order to reach 'the central lake' and then the Nile, which leads to the land of the mysterious Prester John. But the bold expedition came to a halt below what is now Matadi: a rock on the left bank has been engraved with symbols, an inscription, and names which attest to the exploit. Beyond the estuary, with its low-lying islands full of a rich vegetation, the Congo grows narrow between the Crystal Mountains; and narrower still near the stretch named the Cauldron of Hell, where its roughness forced the Portuguese to give up.[1] *Nzadi*, the native appellation for the river which the newcomers transformed into Zaïre, overcame the curiosity of the discoverers.

It required, then, an unusual degree of daring to brave, in the words of the geographer Jacques Weulersse, 'the formidable fluvial system of the Congo, the most powerful on the continent, the second most powerful on the globe'. Diogo Cão's plan was based on illusions—both geographical—the search for the basin of the Nile—and political—access to Christian Abyssinia in order to get around the Moslem world; but his successors could not fail to know that the Kongo country as a whole was reached via the river. It was through the estuary, with its port of Mpinda, that access was obtained to the province of Soyo where caravans bound for the capital formed. It was at Mpumbu (Stanley Pool) that communication and trade with the populations of the north, principally the Bateke, were established. Between these two outermost points of Kongo mastery of the

27

river, the latter rushes toward its mouth through falls and rapids, flanked on either bank by plateaus and mountain ranges of medium altitude. The landscape is often harsh in this region; the explorer Stanley, on his journey downstream to the coast in the final stages of his African travels, shows only a lukewarm affection for it. He mentions in his accounts 'places that are antipathetic, even for the aborigine', grey and ugly scenery, and the frequent loneliness of the Congo: 'sad, deserted by men, for not a soul remains to sing the majesty of her great brown tide'.[2]

The Time of the Beginnings

The territory covered by Kongo civilization extends beyond the river. The Kikongo language, which expresses its unity, shows this to be true: 'It is spoken throughout the lower Congo, from Stanley Pool to the Ocean, the length of the coast which stretches north to the Ogooué, in the interior of the country as far as the territory of the Bateke . . . and to the east, beyond the Kwango River'.[3] Throughout this extensive region beliefs, social structures, and customs followed a common pattern. Their kinship is obvious despite the variants, which are comparable to the dialectlike variations of the language.

The generic term Kongo remains generally known, although it is not always claimed today by certain of the tribal groups it includes. During the glorious centuries, however, the inhabitants of Mpemba, the province containing the capital, reserved its use for themselves, proclaimed themselves the only 'pure' and closely related dependents of the sovereign, and never forgot their rank of 'Esikongo'. However that may be, the word was and still is charged with prestige and glory. This does not prevent it from posing an enigma. Many have tried to decipher it, but none has succeeded in winning a decisive consensus. It has been proposed that the term is related to ko-mgo, translated as 'land of the panther',[4] although 'ally of the panther' would be a more accurate translation. Or again, the word has been connected with the word for distinguished hunter: nkongo, or, by a different interpretation, with a hurled weapon called kongo or kong.[5] It has even been suggested that it is the archaic equivalent of the word mfumu which designates the free man, the notable, and the chief.[6] These suggestions, among others, are not unlikely. They refer to power, whether by symbols—like the panther, which is still the animal of nobility—or by themes to be found in the traditions and myths which evoke the founder-hero of the kingdom. Moreover, in the legends, sayings, and proverbs, the word *Kongo* sometimes refers to a powerful and noble personage as opposed to the adventurer or the man of humble rank. It is invested with the magnificence that cloaks supreme power, but its exact etymology, like the original history of the Kongo, has been obliterated by time.

The beginnings seem even more exalted because their memory is dim. The Kongo has never been so vast as it was at the time of its obscure history, at least if we are to believe the list of their states drawn up by the first kings who established relations with Europe. The greatest of these, Afonso the First, set the example by accumulating titles more sonorous than those of the kings of Portugal. He wrote at the beginning of the sixteenth century: 'I, Afonso, by the grace of God King of Kongo, of Loango, of Kakongo, and of Ngoyo, this side of and the other side of the Zaïre, lord of the Ambundu and of Angola, of Aquisima, of Musuru, of Matamba, of Mulilu, of Musuku, and of the Anzico, of the conquest of Pangu-Alumbu,[7] etc.' It is a political unity extending widely on both banks of the river which is described here: reaching northward as far as modern Gabon—for the vassal kingdom of Loango, according to Olfert Dapper,[8] extended to Cape Saint Catherine—and southward even beyond the banks of the Kwanza, and swelling as far as the Bateke plateaus and the Kwango River from the ocean; a *regnum* of more than 300,000 square kilometers which, because of material reasons and other factors unfavorable to any single government, never at any time knew a single law, but which nevertheless received the imprint of a single civilization.

At the end of the fifteenth century, at the time of the discovery, the kingdom did in fact shrink and the Congo River traced its real northern boundary: it included from two to three million subjects, according to the least extravagant subsequent estimates. The Bengo divided it from the kingdom of Angola to the south. To the east, the Kwango continued to represent its approximate border.[9] Six principal provinces formed the structure of the unity: Mpemba, Soyo, Mbamba, Mbata, Nsundi, Mpangu, the first three being the most important. Certain enclosed territories — Wembo, Wando, Nkusu, Matari — and peripheral regions like the 'province of the Ambundu'—were more dependencies than areas subject to the direct control of the king of the Kongo. At no time did the latter succeed in completing the work of unification of all the lands and of absolute centralization of power. This situation is not atypical: all the great national structures in African history have experienced the same difficulties.

At the heart of the political edifice of the Kongo is Mbanza Kongo, founding place of the kingdom, which had become capital city well before the arrival of the Portuguese. The site offers the double advantage of a central position and excellent natural defenses against enemy attack. Jean Cuvelier describes it:

Rising to an altitude of 559 meters, the mountain forms a plateau seven kilometers long from north to south. It slopes from west to east towards the valley. One kilometer away run the sinuous river Luezi, a tributary of the Lunda which makes the neighbouring countryside very pleasant and very fertile. The inhabitants can build fine plantations there. On the plateau itself there are two springs which give a crystal-clear water. The spot has always been considered very healthy.[10]

In Dapper's book, a 'reconstructed' view shows Mbanza Kongo rising above a cliff which overhangs the river Lunda and a narrow valley edged with forest land. Old accounts, for the most part, recall the privileged situation of the town, as in this late sixteenth-century example:

The city is located on the highest mountain in the country, because from the port of Pinda, where you land, to the Congo you walk for ten days rising continually until you arrive at the aforesaid city and the province of Pemba. This province is in the heart and center of the kingdom and is the head of all the other provinces and the origin of the ancient kingdoms.[11]

And at the beginning of the eighteenth century Father Laurent de Lucques still recognizes the qualities of the old city, although decline and ruin are rapidly overtaking it: :

This town occupies the best position in the kingdom on some very fine hills. Thanks to its altitude, the air there is mild. Formerly, it was heavily populated. . . . The inhabitants were wealthy, for it was the metropolis of this very vast kingdom to which the riches of the provinces flowed.[12]

The Bakongo were able to discover and exploit the natural setting in which they built their capital. They succeeded populations long settled, among them, undoubtedly, the Ambundu, whose clans were enslaved, assimilated, or driven to the south. They took over by conquest, and in the process they were compelled to strengthen their political and military organization. All the traditions collected by the chroniclers are in agreement that, as Paiva Manso puts it, 'the nation of the *mashicongo* (king of the Kongo) was always regarded as foreign'; it was composed of 'people from the interior'.[13] Information remains vague as to the place of origin of the conquerors, and various hypotheses have been debated. The myths and the traditional data combine on this point to discourage the historian.

The uncertainties begin as soon as one tries to identify the founder—at once hero, war lord, and bearer of civilization—who created the Kongo by laying down the first laws of the kingdom. He appears under four names—Ntinu, Wene, Nimi, Lukeni—which are sometimes linked in pairs.[14] But these appellations are not contradictory, for they are not of the same order.[35] The last two seem to correspond to clanic names. The other two refer to the conception of power; *ntinu* denotes the sovereign and *(m)wene* signifies possessor of nobility, lord or master. According to Father Joseph van Wing, the names Nimi and Lukeni are those of the respective clans of the father and mother of the first sovereign, whose hypothetical genealogy is represented by the following diagram:

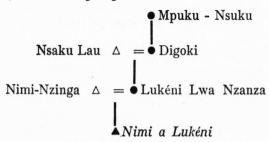

Key: △, male; ●, female; = marriage; | filiation.

The apparent precision of this lineage, however, is misleading. The authors differ as soon as it is necessary to determine the land of origin of the founder-king. For all, the point of departure of the military enterprises is located to *the north* of Mbanza Kongo. For some, it is to the north-east, in the vicinity of the Kwango, which may correspond to the region which later constituted the province of Mbata. For others, it is to the north of the Congo River, in the territory including the Mayombe mountain range. This last theory refers to the name of Bungo—said to be related to Vungu, which indeed designates Yombe country—as birthplace of Kongo ambitions. Moreover, Father Girolamo da Montesarchio, in his travel account, describes the region opposite Vungu on the left bank of the river as the place where the first king 'began to rule'.[16] It was from this beginning that the province of Nsundi grew along the Congo, and acquired a kind of privileged status, becoming the patrimonial domain of the sovereigns, at the head of which the suggested successor was generally placed.

The discrepancy between the two 'versions' just mentioned can undoubtedly be explained by the fact that they refer to different moments in history, to different phases of Kongo expansion, and to royal genealogies which are not connected to a single and identical line. It is still impossible to determine the movement of the conquests precisely. At the terminal spot, a hill near the site on which Mbanza Kongo was to be built, the founder or one of his successors proceeded to divide the territories up among the chiefs who became the revocable representatives of the sovereign. The expression *mongo wa kaila* (hill of partition) recalls this birth of the provincial organization. Cuvelier quotes the story of this memorable event from modern traditions. The passage has greater symbolic interest than historical value :

When they [the relatives and companions of the sovereign and the notables of the conquered tribes] had been assembled, they were greatly pleased to hear the very fine things which the king told them in the enclosure of his residence. When joy had lifted their hearts, they began one after the other to perform a triumphal dance. Seeing this, the king was himself seized by a great joy. He went into his dwelling and returned with the knife which symbolized his dignity, the power of his royalty and his laws. He also took the other symbol of his royalty: the *nsesa*, or buffalo tail. He said to them, 'Dance two by two. . . . ' They began to dance two by two before the king, who was sitting on a seat placed on the royal mat.

After they had danced, they came and knelt before him. As he received their homage, the king moved the middle finger of his right hand, saying, 'Prosper, multiply, live many years'. The king held a second meeting. It was a very great celebration. On that day he divided his power. When all were in the royal enclosure, they felt a great joy. They began to dance again, showing the king the homage which was his due. . . . [17]

The account continues with a description of nine notables who declare their allegiance and proclaim their clanic motto. The latter, which is characterized by pride, does not fail to suggest that the obedience is not unconditional. Thus one of the clan chiefs exclaims, 'I am Mankunku, he who knocks down. I have overthrown the *ndembo*, the drums of the mighty ones!'

Such an account is highly significant. It mentions two of the royal attributes and describes briefly the ceremony of homage and the ritual honoring the sovereign. It recalls the 'pairs' of clans which settled the new provinces and the alliances which united the conquerors and the indigenous conquered tribes. It shows the weakness of a power which remained dependent upon the consent of those notables placed at the head of the founding clans and the territorial unities. But its historical information is negligible.

The growth of the kingdom of the Kongo seems to have been accomplished by successive expansions, by migrations originally undertaken with a view to the acquisition of neighboring lands. Father van Wing has tried through direct inquiry and study of the legends and historic mottos of the clans, to reconstruct the migrations which contributed to the formation of the province of Mpangu. He quotes a legend which an old 'crowned' chief, reputed for his knowledge and wisdom, proudly recited to him after performing the warlike dance of the notables:

At the Kongo of the king
the first man after the king is one who does not yield,

33

> *it is I, Mpangu.*
> *It was old grandmother Nkumba-Nkumba who gave*
> *birth to us all.*
> *When we left the Kongo*
> *there were nine caravans,*
> *nine leaders' staffs.*
> *The bones of our ancestors,*
> *we brought, we use them to anoint the chiefs,*
> *and the grass rings as well.*
> *The roads were sure,*
> *the villages where we slept were peaceful.*
> *We arrived at the ford of Nsimba.*
> *We stayed together,*
> *We did not separate.*
> *We came to many rivers, to waters of all kinds.*
> *A woman, the mother of a clan, stayed*
> *at the ford of the Mfidi.*[18]

The passage thus alludes to the related clans which migrated under a single authority and occupied the region situated northeast of the capital of the Kongo. This migration, which occurred in stages, as it were, seems to have maintained its unity up to the fording of the Inkisi River — referred to as the ford of Nsimba, so named because *nsimba* means 'to stay together'. Subsequently, although retaining a connection with the center where provincial power was established, the clans broke up, dispersed, welcomed newcomers. Slowly they built and expanded the territory, which was subject to the authority of Mpangu and his descendants by royal delegation.

The same process must have taken place in the case of the provinces to the east, the west, and the south. The province of Soyo, whose chiefs played an important role in the history of the old Kongo, is said to owe its existence to the drive of a son born to a woman who was a slave of the first sovereign. This radiating and far-reaching conquest even touched the right bank of the Congo River: Ngoyo and Kakongo, north of the mouth, were incorporated into the kingdom for a short period before acquiring a separate autonomy which the difficulties of communication made 'natural'.

The creation of the kingdom of the Kongo was slow, hampered by internal rivalries and secessions, and never completed to the point where the central power became invulnerable and incontestable. From the moment of birth to that of the Portuguese implantation, several decades passed; it is impossible to determine exactly how many. Father van Wing calculated the time necessary for the 'multiplying of the clans and the populating of six large provinces', leading him to give the end of the fourteenth century as the age of the migrations which gave rise to the province of Mpangu.[19] Various attempts have been made to trace the course of events backward from the time of King Nzinga a Nkuwu, who can be historically located by the fact that he received baptism in May 1491 and became the first of the Christian kings, under the name of João (John). João appears to have been fifth or eighth of the kings of the Kongo, according to an order of succession which is uncertain, but which does, however, reveal that the power did not change generations each time.[20] Despite the statements of the author of the *História do Reino do Congo*, which dates the founding of the kingdom at around 1275, one can hardly maintain a gap of more than one hundred to one hundred and fifty years between this event and the reign of João the First, which necessarily places the activities of the founder-king between 1350 and the final decades of the fourteenth century.

The Civilizing Hero
The first sovereign is best known as Ntinu Wene, *the king*; this is the name that par excellence symbolizes power. Myths and legends still mention him, and it is to this tradition that the first historiographers also referred. Confused historical memories and revealing interpretations of the conception of political power are mingled in this case. Ntinu is a 'youngster', thought to have no hope of acquiring authority and privileges, although he proves to be impatient to 'command', to prove himself as a 'strong and fearless warrior', as Cavazzi puts it. This fact signifies, at least symbolically, that the future king will have to be the sole artisan of *his* kingdom, and this by agreeing to use exceptional means. He takes leave of his family and, followed by his partisans, forms an armed band which collects tolls at the ford of the Congo, or some other indeterminate river. It is then that an event occurs which assures a total 'break', thrusts the young man outside of the normal order, and makes all the resources of magic available

to him. Let us re-read Cavazzi, who mentions the tragic 'exploit' thanks to which a king is born: 'One day he committed a murder upon the person of his aunt, who was going to have a child. Following this "high deed", he was proclaimed chief, *mutinu.*'[21] Here the truth is to be found more on a symbolic level than on the literal level of those changes which make history. By killing his 'kin', Ntinu Wene acquires the state of solitude necessary for the domination of men and the consecration of power. He is comparable to the heroes of Greek legends who seek the royal succession only after they have ceased to respect the prevailing laws.

This defiance of the fundamental principles of any society is the mark of an exceptional being. Sacred violence remains the privilege of a sovereign with two faces: one brutal and tyrannical, the other justice-loving and conciliatory. Ntinu Wene—murderer, powerful warrior, conqueror—is also regarded as the inventor of the art of the forge.[22] He is the blacksmith king who provides his people with the arms of war and the tools of agriculture, in the manner of several sovereigns of Bantu origin. among them the *ngola* of Ndongo who founded the kingdom of Angola. Metalwork therefore became a royal and aristocratic privilege in the Kongo; iron was first produced and worked in the capital under the supervision of the king; the forge was incorporated into various rituals; and until the middle of the eighteenth century the chroniclers observe that 'the art of the blacksmith is practiced by the nobility'.[23] Ntinu Wene also appears in the persona of the wise and just man. One tradition mentions that he was summoned by several tribes because of his sagacity as arbiter of differences. During his early residence in the first conquered region (Mpemba Kazi), he founded a court of justice—*mbasi a nkanu*—which was both respected and feared. Nothing remained but for him to perform the military exploit which would eliminate his rivals and the last rebels and to build his final capital. He was able to furnish proof of his strength and his familiarity with the agents of success. He triumphed over Mabambala, chief of a region known as Mpangala, and 'went to take up his abode on a hill four leagues from a place called Kongo'.[24] Thus did the new king reach the heart of his future kingdom. But the rituals preserve above all the memory of this decisive victory—the defeat of Mpangala's people. Every year

36

the descendants of these people formally, by a female intermediary, protest the usurpation of Ntinu Wene.

This body of information requires critical examination. It
forms less a sequence of poorly dated but nevertheless real historical events than an implicit *theory* of power. One has only to
state the same facts in different language to see the truth of this.
A 'young man', rich in courage, warlike ability, and ambition, is
without future prospects in a society controlled by his 'elders'.
He withdraws, then totally breaks his family ties (murder). Thus
he has denied the ancient order; he has acquired an autonomy
which can be explained only by the possession of extraordinary
powers. It is on the basis of these powers that he will construct
outside the prevailing law a new society subject to *his* law only.
He prevails by inspiring a *sacred* terror. The chronicler Cavazzi
says as much when he describes his first dwellings in conquered
territory : 'Such great respect the inhabitants of the country
have for a place in the forest where . . . he made his home, that
those who passed nearby dared not turn their eyes in that direction. They were convinced that should they do so, they would
die on the spot.'[25]

But the sovereignty of the young founder is full of contradic-
tions, his power is ambivalent: although violent and in certain
respects 'magical' (his arms and his 'touch' killed), it is at the
same time based upon the wisdom and knowledge of the man
who loves justice. Finally, this ambitious 'youngster' is not definitively *qualified* until after a military *exploit*: he has then
destroyed the last obstacle; he has secured the power and the
right to build *his* city—Mbanza Kongo.

One fact becomes clear. The qualities just alluded to—withdrawal from the old society, total rupture of familial bonds,
conquest of power by means of a heroic action, duality of a
power which is both violent and intelligent—are characteristic
of the majority of African kings who created traditional states.
The royal rituals and ceremonial and the myths and symbols
associated with sovereignty 'tell' this unambiguously; so much
so that the facts of the Kongo tradition are less revealing of an
individual history than of a general conception of the traditional
foundations of sovereign power, a theory with which ancient
Africa was widely familiar, but over which she had no monopoly. Georges Dumézil's great studies devoted to Indo-European

representations of sovereignty show that if all kings are kings by nature, some have been so 'by virtue of their creative violence, others by virtue of their organizing wisdom'. Here the ambivalence is between the 'magician-creator' as opposed to the 'law-maker-organizer'.[26] In the Kongo and in other African kingships the founder-sovereign *seems* to assume these two contradictory functions. He abolishes one social order and creates another; he reigns through fear and through wisdom.

But things in their deeper reality do not correspond precisely to this pattern. To be sure, violence and conquest have won Ntinu Wene control of the Kongo. He rules the men, he organizes them and establishes the administration of the territory which contains them. His power encounters religious limitations, however. The conquered land does not contain *his* ancestors; to those who are there, who 'hold' this land and control its fertility, he remains a *stranger*. If he ignores them, he runs the risk of letting disorder overtake his kingdom and bringing it on himself. He must accept the mediation of the first occupants and solicit the ritual cooperation of their representative, Nsaku ne Vunda. This leader serves as intermediary between the living and the ancestors; he controls the rains and the crops; he regulates sowing and reaping; he governs the hunt. The motto of his clan, Nsaku, reveals this privileged relationship to the earth, and hence to the king of the Kongo:

> Lord Nsaku,
> is a man who is second only to the king,
> he lies down
> on the bare earth—he fears nothing.[27]

In contrast to the power based upon creative force and domination, which is political in nature, there is the power based upon the ancestors and tradition, which is essentially sacred in nature. The first derives from the second not only its legitimacy but also the means of converting into durable superiority what was merely vulnerable coercion, transforming into a permanent order what was merely a disorder favorable to innovation.

Because he misunderstood this relationship, the founder of the Kongo was doomed to fail. A legend summarized by Cuvelier is very significant in this connection:

Ntinu Wene failed to make himself known to Nsaku ne

Vunda. One day, he had convulsions: *laukidi*.* His people went
to Nsaku ne Vunda. They knelt down and said, 'Lord, we know
that you are the elder, he who first occupied this region, or
according to the local saying, "who was first at the nostrils of
the universe". Ntinu Wene has fallen into convulsions; bring
him peace again. . . . ' At first Nsaku looked angry and pro-
tested against what he called an intrusion. However, he con-
sented to accompany them to Ntinu Wene. Ntinu Wene said to
him, 'You are the eldest among us. Strike me with the *nsesa*, the
buffalo tail, that my convulsions may cease. . . . ' By this request
he recognized Nsaku's authority and confessed by implication
that the illness from which he suffered resulted from his failure
to comply with an indispensable formality with regard to the
religious leader. Nsaku yielded to Ntinu Wene's entreaties and
sprinkled him with water. This is how we know, the Congolese
still maintain, that for every king who reigns, Nsaku ne Vunda
must be present. If he is not there, the king's authority cannot
be recognized.'[28]

Despite the imperfections of the translation, the meaning is
unmistakable. The new power must be consecrated and legiti-
mized; the cooperation of the conquered is necessary to the conqueror, the 'old-timer' reminds the ambitious, enterprising young
man of tradition; the 'priest' asserts his prerogatives by limiting
the excesses of the political leader. This wedding of the two
powers, which is solemnly acted out at the time of changes of
reign, is sealed by the *compulsory* marriage of the sovereign of
the Kongo to a daughter of the leading family of the Nsaku
clan. It finds political expression in the pre-eminent position of
the two representatives of this clan at the Kongo court and by
the special status of the province of Mbata, where the members
of this clan reside and where the Nsaku Lau family rules.† A

* According to Laman's dictionary, *lauki* refers to a madman, an insane
person.
† *Nsaku Lau* appears (in the hypothetical genealogy) as the maternal grandfather of the founder-sovereign. Two solutions are possible. Either this
genealogy is false and expresses the relationship between the kings of the
Kongo and the Nsaku Laus of the province of Mbata after the fact, the kings
of the Kongo sometimes presenting themselves *symbolically*, as grandsons
(*ntekolo*) of the chiefs of Mbata; or this genealogy is correct, and Ntinu Wene
was an ambitious, power-hungry young man and creator of the state who was
a *native* of the region later known as Mbata.

document dating from the late sixteenth century alludes to this
situation and the relationships which explain it. It states specifically: 'According to a very ancient custom, the king is in the
habit of taking as a wife only a daughter of the Duke of Batta
who, according to tradition, has the privilege of confirming him
in the royal power.' It also observes: 'At the court, there are two
noble chiefs who occupy the first rank. They are called *mani*
Vunda and *mani Lau*.'[29]

Thus the power of the sovereigns of the Kongo appears to
have been founded upon dualisms which were both complemen-
tary and antagonistic: the king represented both violence and
wisdom, despotism and justice; his political power was partially
opposed by the sacred power of the priest, guardian of legitimacy
and guarantor that good relations would be maintained with the
ancestors and the 'earth'; the group of dominators who had
secured the power were opposed by representatives of those
whom power had defeated; the exigencies of the state, which
sought to strengthen itself, was matched by the resistance of the
clans and of the families that controlled them. On this point
Paiva Manso furnishes important clarification in a passage
dating from 1624: it is said that at the time of the accession to
the throne of King Nkuwu a Ntinu ('son' of the founder) the
'lords' (actually, the chiefs of the leading clans) received the
privilege of 'electing the king'.[30] The old clanic order was
insidiously beginning to recover what it had been forced to con-
cede to the state that had been born of the creative conquest.

An analysis of the political vocabulary of the Kongo also suggests an overlapping of powers whose justification and nature
differed. The term *ntotila* seems to have been applied exclusively
to the sovereign, whereas the title of *ntinu* was attributed to the
chiefs of the tribes,[31] and the terms *ne and nnene* evoked either
respect, or superiority and the height of honor. Karl Laman
attributes the title of *ntotila ntinu nekongo*,[32] which may be
translated as 'the king, supreme leader of the great Kongo', to
successors of the founder. The expressions *mwene* and *mwe* (an
abridged form of *mwene*) designate supremacy and the power
inherent in it; they describe the grandeur of God as well as that
of the king. The word *mani*, which occurs very frequently in the
old accounts, has numerous usages: it may be applied 'to all
those who have some authority'.[33] It apparently refers back to

an authoritarian conception of power scarcely indicated by the clanic society; whereas the honorific particle *ma* (abbreviation of *mama*) implicitly recalls the pre-eminence of the ancestress in a matrilinear society in which 'mothers' are the founders of lines. The king of the Kongo claims to be both head of the state and summit of the clanic edifice. But his civilizing function is even today glorified unambiguously by the very title of *Ngangula a Kongo*, Blacksmith of the Kongo.

CHAPTER 2

The Christian King

The union of power and the Christian faith in the Kongo began with a false marriage. This soon became apparent, in spite of the first illusions. In 1490, eight years after the discovery, a veritable 'missionary expedition' was organized at the instigation of João II of Portugal. It set out on the nineteenth of December under the command of Gonçalo de Sousa, and included missionaries—secular priests, Franciscan or Dominican monks, and canons of Saint John the Evangelist[1]—armed soldiers, peasants, artisans—masons and carpenters equipped with tools—and a few women. Its purpose was to reinforce a settlement which, although sparse, had been sufficient to convince the Portuguese that 'trade with the people of the Kongo was very profitable', to quote Pigafetta. Three vessels loaded with men, sacerdotal objects and ornaments, gifts, and even with building materials made up the fleet. Thus it was a microcosm of European society which was exported for the purpose of shaping Kongo society and civilization in its own image.

A False Marriage

Very soon—before the end of the voyage—death struck the apprentice colonists. The plague, which was raging in Lisbon, had been brought on board. It killed first the leader of the expedition who was replaced by his nephew, Rui de Sousa, then Nsaku, first 'ambassador' of the king of the Kongo to the Portuguese sovereign and first Christian convert, João II's representative, and several others. It was not until March 29, 1491, that the caravels arrived at Mpinda, the 'port' of the province of Soyo, where all caravans heading towards the capital were formed. The chief of the province, the *mani* Soyo, who lived a few kilometers from the landing place, had already been in communication with the priests and merchants. He had weighed all the advantages that would result from an active trade with the foreigners. He had expressed his intention of becoming a Christian — anticipating thereby a ritual strengthening of his power, as well as the establishment of a privileged and secure relationship.

The welcome was magnificent. Cuvelier has tried to re-create its atmosphere by describing the processions, the crowds, and the ceremonies, including the war dance executed only by the chiefs. His description is valid as historical reconstruction, not as accurate and verified evidence :

The *mani* Soyo had called his people together. Three thousand warriors, armed with bows and arrows, had gathered at the call of the tom-toms. Another group had been formed by the musicians who carried drums, ivory trumpets, and instruments resembling violas. They were naked to the waist and were painted with white and various coloured paints, a symbol of great joy. On their heads they wore headdresses made of the feathers of parrots and other birds. The chief wore on his head a kind of nightcap decorated with skilful embroidery representing a snake.[2]

There follows a description of the festivities and mention of the display of shooting which Rui de Sousa presented to his host in order to honor him and to impress him with the noise of his own military ceremony.

After receiving (or at least pretending to receive) the consent of the king of the Kongo, the chief of Soyo was baptized on April 3, 1491, Easter Sunday. It is as Dom Manuel that the accounts refer to him. He held a key position in that his province controlled commerce in the Kongo, which put him in direct contact with the European traders. The king of the Kongo, mindful of his relationship with such an indispensable 'intermediary', accorded him a privileged status. He granted him the position by hereditary right in honor of his conversion, reserving, however, the right to confirm his successors. The chronicler of the *História do Reino do Congo* stresses this modification, which differentiated the government of Soyo from that of the other provinces. He states: 'He [the sovereign] made him titled lord, with hereditary transmission, of the whole province of Sonho, which extends many leagues along the coast and ten or twelve leagues into the interior as far as Musaba.'[3]

Such a decision, which granted a certain autonomy in addition to financial advantages to Soyo, obviously was not made without assertion of the royal pre-eminence. Symbolic expression of this featured the regular offering of gifts which indicated recognition of superiority. At the time of the construction of a new home for the *mani*, there was also a ritual recalling the right of the king to the lands of the country, a ritual of such permanence that Father Laurent de Lucques still described it in his account dated 1705.[4]

This relation of dependence was not sufficient to prevent occasional conflicts of interest, antagonisms and, at the end of the process, actual secession. The priority which the chief of Soyo had acquired[5] by his conversion to Christianity seems significant in itself; it put him in first place in the realm of relations with the 'outsiders'.

The Portuguese caravan started off, bound for the capital of the Kongo, during Easter week of 1491. The paths had been cleared and widened as for a royal journey. But insecurity reigned: armed bands of rebels called *mpanzulungu* attacked and plundered travelers. The Portuguese were accompanied therefore not only by numerous porters—for their dignitaries who seem to have travelled upon the famous 'wooden horses' (a small beam supporting an oxhide serving as a saddle in its center), and for their baggage—but also by an armed escort. The journey lasted twenty days.

Here again, Cuvelier has attempted to reconstruct the scene of the arrival, to suggest the excitement and ceremony that accompanied an event which the people of the Kongo recognized as extraordinary since they were unable to consider it historic:

At Mpangala, which is like a suburb of Mbanza Kongo, all the principal men of the kingdom waited for the Whites to welcome them in the name of the king. And the thousands of men, women with their nurslings on their backs, children of every age, jumped, danced, sang, the nobles carrying their

44

shields of buffalo hide and their ironwood swords, the men of the people carrying their bows and arrows. It was with this triumphant train that the Portuguese were led to the large houses which had been prepared for them.[6]

With all due allowance for lyricism, the meeting was auspicious if only because of the rich presents given to the sovereign : brocade and velvet fabrics, lengths of satin, silk, and linen, magnificent garments, horse tails with silver fittings, various trinkets . . . and red pigeons. The king, Nzinga a Knuwu, asked to become a Christian together with certain notables. To give more solemnity and pomp to the event, the Portuguese wanted to wait until the first church (and the first stone building) in the capital was built. The king was all the more impatient because his 'dependent', the mani Soyo, had already received baptism and because rebellion threatened in certain parts of the kingdom. He seems to have been baptized on May 3, 1491,[7] and he adopted the name of João I in deference to the Portuguese sovereign. Also baptized on the same day were several of the 'lords' of the Kongo, among them the chief of the province of Mbata; they did not fail to recall this priority afterward in the honorific wording of their respective motto-songs. The queen or ne mbanda, for her part, had to wait until the 'governor' of the province of Nsundi and future heir to the kingdom, Nzinga Mbemba, had returned to the capital before receiving baptism. This ceremony seems to have taken place on June 4, 1491; the queen adopted the Christian name of the queen of Portugal, Eleanor, and the chief of Nsundi, the Christian name of Afonso, which he was to make glorious. This conversion to Christianity, which was destined to win over the people through the intermediary of the sovereigns and notables, was conducted in haste; as was the edification of the church of Mbanza Kongo which, begun in early May 1491, was almost finished by July of the same year—if one can credit the testimony of late chronicles in the matter of dates.

Even before the benediction of the building, a first test faced the king and nascent Christianity. Nzinga Mbemba had discovered that several tribes were rebelling against the central power; no doubt those living in Mazinga and Nsanga, two of the regions straddling the Congo River which were under the control of the chief of Nsundi. This is the most plausible contention of the author of the *História do Reino do Congo*: 'The king left for the war . . . we must conclude that he waged it in Nsanga and Mazinga, as I heard from some old Mexicongo who learned it from their fathers and they from theirs.'[8] The Portuguese placed this conflict under the sign of Christ—Rui de Sousa gave the sovereign a banner with a cross embroidered on it—and provided military aid. João I was victorious, but the victory was costly for the country, which was ravaged by the armies, and for the Portuguese, who suffered heavy losses.

This war foreshadowed the results of Christianity at the very moment of its introduction. The mechanism in question is easily revealed. The Portuguese, settled in Mbanza Kongo, reinforced the central power materially and spiritually. They altered a precarious balance, *in favor of royalty*. They supplied the advantage of their technology and their manufactured goods, and they introduced incentives to trade. They were the carriers of a new religion, which was all the more warmly welcomed because it seemed to be extremely powerful, as the relative wealth and material power of the people arrived from Europe bore witness. Portuguese reasoning reinforced this impression. When the banner was given to the sovereign, the missionaries reminded him that 'by virtue of this salutary sign, armies had defeated enemies who were superior in number'.[9] The cross justified the crusade against the rebels who were also 'peasants'. *In hoc signo vinces*: like Constantine triumphing over Maxentius and making Christianity the official religion of the Roman Empire, the *mani* of the Kongo must triumph and impose the new faith thanks to his increased power. This interpretation can hardly be debated. There is another proof of it. Cuvelier reports a dream—real or imagined, the significance of the document is in no way changed —of one of the leaders converted along with the king, a dignitary of the first rank, since he was 'governor' of that province of Mbata with which the history of the foundation of the kingdom is associated. The passage in question is as follows:

Dom Jorge [Christian name of Chief Nsaku of Mbata], after greeting the king and the Whites, spoke as follows: 'Listen to the dream I have had. Great is the favor that God has granted us, for know that this night I beheld in a dream a very beautiful lady who commanded me to tell you that now we are invincible. So filled with courage and strength did I feel that I was ready to fight one hundred men.' Addressing himself to the king, he said, 'See that your kingdom becomes Christian, and your power will be increased.'[10]

The conclusion left no room for doubt, especially since it was attributed to authorities who could exert a religious control over the Kongo royalty. Christianity was adopted fundamentally as a source of *ngolo*, or power, which placed it in a political context and laid the foundations of misunderstanding.

Relations between the royalty and the missionaries rapidly deteriorated: the 'defection' of the king took place between 1492 and 1494. Numerous results of his conversion forced themselves on his attention. Elements hostile to the central government, or simply traditionalist, vigorously criticized the abandonment of local customs (*fu kia nsi*). As a consequence, they predicted disorders and calamities, the vengeance of the ancestors who had been betrayed, and increasing danger resulting from a sorcery which the ancient practices formerly held in check. And this was all the more likely because the priests had encouraged the destruction by fire of 'superstitious objects and huts of fetishes'. This is only the first of the vicissitudes which characterize the religious history of the Kongo: a succession of innovations welcomed with fervor, stimulating the burning of 'idols' and quickly disappearing, always to make way for the ancestral gods. In the case of the royal defection, missionary opposition to polygamy played a decisive role. This happened not only because the sovereign thereby lost one of his privileges and one of the instruments of his prestige—for in fact, his wives refused to stop serving him—but also because he destroyed the 'alliances' resulting from his numerous marriages. The precarious balance of the kingdom depended upon these relationships which transformed formidable 'powers' into 'in-laws' of the sovereign; a prime requirement of politics was a skilful matrimonial policy. In this respect, the incompatibility between royal power and Christianity was *total*.

The situation became such that most of the missionaries were obliged to leave the capital (around 1495), and with them, certain of the Portuguese and the converted 'nobles'. They withdrew into the province of Nsundi, where Afonso settled them after resuming control there. The *História do Reino do Congo* mentions this transfer of the religious center: 'He [the king] sent Dom Afonso as governor to Nsundi . . . with him, all the regular and secular priests and the Portuguese whom Rui de Sousa had left in Mbanza Kongo . . . all the *fidalgos* [nobles] who had received holy baptism.'[11]

In a few years, the first attempt at Christianization was ending in semi-failure. Father Joseph van Wing, in his monograph on the Kongo, realistically evaluates the results of this experiment after recalling the dazzling—but short-lived—success of the year 1491:

King John was Christian in name only, and his successors, with a few exceptions, imitated him faithfully. The authors disagree on the question of his formal apostasy. In any case we know that he returned to his fetishes and his harem. When he died in 1500 [sic], the newly established mission had to withstand a general uprising on the part of the *nganga*, the representatives of ancestral religious ideas and customs. They were led by *mani* Mpanza, rival of Afonso, the appointed heir who represented the new ideas.[12]

Rivalries for the power took the form of religious wars. The test of the conquest of power, which created trouble during periods of succession, is a common characteristic of African royalty. The Kongo is no exception. Here Christianity became a weapon to be used by rival parties and by modernists against traditionalists. Hence Dom Afonso, supporter of the missionaries, member of an older family, and candidate chosen by João I, is opposed by Mpanza a Nzinga, member of a younger family and able defender of the threatened traditions. Both had a 'clientele' and an army at their disposal: one ruled at Nsundi, the other at Mpangu. During the last years of the reign of a weakened and hesitant king, the two camps prepared. Afonso strengthened the foundations of the mission and allied himself with the chiefs of strange tribes settled in outlying parts of his province by converting them. Mpanza, whose name means 'attack' or 'quarrel', rallied the majority of the notables and the guardians of the traditional cults. He tried to eliminate his rival from the government of Nsundi—which implied appointment to the royal succession—by comparing the Christians to those sowers of disorder, the *ba-ndoki*, or sorcerers. The kingdom was said to be threatened by drought and sterility because it was in danger of losing the support of the ancestors and of those 'forces' which contributed to its prosperity. Each of the two competitors tried to prove that the supreme God was his ally, in accordance with the saying 'Kongo is a man who comes from God (*Nzambi Mpungu*)'.

The Power and the Miracle

With the death of João I in 1506, the military confrontation could not be avoided: once again, power was conquered rather than inherited. Dom Afonso surrounded the capital with an army composed of 'thirty-seven chiefs and their men'. He was victorious in spite of the number and nature of his adversaries: 'almost all the people and members of his own family'. His victory was attributed to a miracle which is described by several chroniclers. Paiva Manso published a letter dated 1512 which relates the event:

We called upon the blessed apostle Saint James, and as a result [*sic*], miraculously, we saw all our enemies turn their backs and flee as fast as they could, without our knowing the cause of their rout. We followed them, and during this pursuit a great number perished, but not a single one of our men. And after the victory we learned that those who escaped declared as one man that when we invoked the apostle Saint James they all beheld a white cross amid a great number of armed and mounted men which caused them such great dismay that they could not refrain from fleeing at once.[13]

The elements of this tale—intervention of the patron saint of the Portuguese armies, vision of the cross, action of a celestial cavalry—are all foreign to the religious symbolism of the Kongo, whereas they are *typical*, in this or a homologous form, of many accounts explaining victories gained over 'pagans' or 'heretics'. They serve to transform a military victory into a gift of God. They suggest, with the proceedings of the Christian miracle, the innovating ambitions of the conquering king and the new hopes of a colonization which had made a bad start.

49

But the truth, insofar as it can be made out, is otherwise. The conquest of the royalty by Afonso I was less miraculous than it was consistent with ancient practices peculiar to the Kongo and several other African kingdoms. One of the pretenders took the throne by violence. The vanquished were put to death or exiled: Mpanza was executed because, it was said, of his 'obstinate' hostility to the Christian religion. His partisans were obliged to leave the capital; migrations toward Mpangu, Nkusu, and Zombo have been described as consequences of this defeat. There was even the execution of a maternal relative—the sovereign's mother herself, according to certain chronicles[14]—on the pretext of her refusal to renounce 'pagan customs'. The description of this execution shows it to be almost identical with one of which a king of the late nineteenth century was accused under the same circumstances.[15] The 'relative' was led to and laid upon a mat covering a grave, fell into it, and was buried alive. Such continuity suggests that we have here a symbolic ritual associated with the establishment of any new reign. Moreover, the findings of Africanist ethnology support this interpretation; when he takes the throne, the king must often demonstrate in a symbolic manner that he has renounced all family ties, that he has become solitary and is placed over everyone. This is the meaning of the ceremonial murder committed by the sovereign in the Kongo: he 'buries' his lineage—a single word, *ngudi*, designating both lineage and mother—in order to demonstrate solemnly his change of rank and his position outside the common rules.[16]

These remarks have a decisive importance in the interpretation of the history of the Kongo. They remind us that the majority of the documentation is of missionary origin and dates, for the most part, from the period of militant Catholicism. In this documentation the men and events often appear in exaggerated form under the aegis either of edifying literature or of the pagan 'abomination'. A veritable process of translation, guided by modern sociological and ethnological knowledge, is often necessary; not just necessary, but fruitful.

This leads us to consider with sustained critical discipline the reign of the *most Christian* of the kings of the Kongo, Afonso I. Even in his time social and cultural phenomena had a 'two-faced' quality. This ambivalence may be clearly observed in the case of the titles that then designated the principal dignitaries of the kingdom: princes, dukes, counts, marquises, etc. These appelations were intended only for *external* use, for relations with foreigners; they constituted only 'makeshift' equivalences of the Kongo terms and were in no way associated with any modification of functions or responsibilities. In this connection Father van Wing bitterly denounced the dangerous illusion created by the 'trickery of words'. The same process was repeated on other levels. Following his victory over the enemy and the 'miracle'—which was a Portuguese interpretation rather than a conviction of his followers—Afonso I combined the annual military ceremony commemorating his seizure of the power with the feast of Saint James the Greater. It was merely a way of adding a new celebration to an old one, without changing the meaning of the institution as such. At the same time the *ne vunda*, holder of a religious power, traditional priest of the coronation, was given the commission of supervising the construction and maintenance of the churches and furnishing the water necessary for baptisms.[17] Thus he was associated with two forms of the sacred: he had acquired two roles and was obliged to see that each of the two rituals remained in force. Christianity was conceived as a supplementary method of reinforcement, not as a religion exclusive of the old beliefs. From this period began the 'heresies' which were to multiply until the end of the modern colonial period.

One cannot determine with any certainty the degree of belief in the Christian faith of King Afonso I. But it seems evident that when he addressed himself to the Portuguese and the missionaries at the court of Lisbon and the Holy See, he employed words and ideas which belonged to his hearers rather than himself. He did so all the more readily because certain of his foreign advisers encouraged him to model himself upon the Catholic kings. Form can deceive as to the nature of the realities it clothes. At any rate, this sovereign understood better than his predecessor the potential usefulness of the European cultural and technical contribution to an indigenous policy envisioning the consolidation of the state and the renovation of society. He was both the true creator of the Kongo monarchy and a 'modernist' king. In the memories of men his greatness has outlived the miseries of his kingdom: he remains the only one of the historic kings whose name is still known to the common people.[18]

It is impossible to draw a physical and moral portrait of the most glorious of the *ntotila* (kings) of the Kongo with any great assurance of accuracy. Most of the documents have a hagiographic quality; they extol his sanctity and his morals, his devotion to the cause of the Catholic Church, his repeated appeals for an effective missionary activity; they fail to mention the problems of a sovereign whose power rested upon a tradition that was highly incompatible with Christianity. These texts are particularly discreet on the subject of the king's apparent or actual monogamy: a letter from Pope Leo X addressed to a 'prince' Henrique, who was raised to the rank of bishop of Utica, states that this office is not revocable even if it appears that Afonso's son is born of 'an adulterous king or an unmarried mother'. This uncertainty, which is very revealing, was by no means limited to the question of Afonso's matrimonial status; it was more general.

In a report addressed to the King of Portugal in May 1516, the priest Rui d'Aguiar described the sovereign of the Kongo as a lord of faith, learning, and justice. In so doing he established the tone for all those chroniclers who later sang the praises of the apostle king:

May Your Highness be informed that his Christian life is such that he appears to me not as a man but as an angel sent by the Lord to this kingdom to convert it, especially when he speaks and when he preaches. For I assure Your Highness that it is he who instructs us; better than we, he knows the prophets and the Gospel of Our Lord Jesus Christ and all the lives of the saints and all things regarding our Mother the Holy Church, so much so that if Your Highness could observe him himself, he would be filled with admiration.

He expresses things so well and with such accuracy that it seems to me that the Holy Spirit speaks always through his mouth. I must say, Lord, that he does nothing but study and that many times he falls asleep over his books; he forgets when it is time to dine, when he is speaking of the things of God. So delighted is he with the reading of the Scripture that he is as if beside himself. When he gives audience or when he dispenses justice, his words are inspired by God and by the examples of the saints.

He studies the Holy Gospel and when the priest finishes the mass he asks him for benediction. When he has received it, he begins to preach to the people with great skill and great charity, imploring them to be converted and to give themselves to God; in such wise that his people are amazed, and we others even more so, before the virtue and faith of this man. Every day he does this, every day he preaches as I have just said. Your Highness will be pleased to learn also that he is very assiduous in the exercise of justice, that he punishes with rigor those who worship idols and that he has them burned along with these idols. . . . [19]

The eulogy is unreserved; it makes a large allowance for the miraculous; it is closer to *La Légende dorée* than to historical evidence—even with its reference to stakes for idolators. In more or less distorted form, this edifying apology was to be transmitted through the centuries. We find it again in a letter dating from 1622 which also recalls, in altered form, the 'miracle' responsible for the conquest of power:

Dom Afonso . . . the second Christian king who was such a great Catholic that our Portuguese chronicles describe him as the apostle of the Congo, a name he deserved because his holy zeal converted the greater part of his subjects to our holy faith. He himself in his person showed himself to be a model of that evangelical faith which he taught and preached to his people. He was such a great man that he was worthy to see the glorious apostle, Saint James, appear during a battle which he waged against his pagan brother.[20]

The correspondence of Afonso I, a series of letters extending to December 1540 and first published by Païva Manso, is of no help in verifying or correcting the foregoing statements. The letters are the work of royal secretaries, all Portuguese, save one, who is identified as a former pupil of the school of Mbanza Kongo. Their style is conventional and their accuracy in the matter of translation very approximate; so much so that their language has been compared to 'the phraseology which scholars have attributed to kings of the Merovingian period'. They seem distorting, inasmuch as they conform to the customs and language of their intended European recipients.

How, under these circumstances, are we to examine and organize the facts which characterized the reign of Dom Afonso? The *acceptance* of Christianity is evident, but it is not to be explained simply and does not appear to have been a total commitment. The desire to arrive at the knowledge and ritual efficacy which seemed to account for the material power and wealth of the 'foreigners' from *Mputu* (Portugal) can scarcely be questioned. Christianity and useful knowledge seemed inseparable; they were not so much the means of a pact with God— *Nzambi Pungu* is so remote that he seldom intervenes in human affairs—as the instruments of 'reinforcement'; they became part of a system of thought and belief for which 'force was being' and 'being was force', in the words of Placide Tempels.[21]

Afonso I had, in a certain sense, an educational policy. He connected the consolidation of his power and of the state with the creation of a literate class and the establishment of a more bureaucratic government. By 1509 he had built school buildings for four hundred pupils: his brothers (in the classificatory sense of the word), his maternal nephews, his sons, and the children of his 'servants', we are told. He acted first on behalf of those subject to his direct influence, upon his relatives and dependents. The royal lineage was the agent of modernism, and modernism, which was at the time inseparable from the Chrisitian faith, was the instrument of royalty. Cuvelier mentions this first truly revolutionary undertaking:

Dom Afonso, realizing that they [the future pupils] would not easily accustom themselves to discipline and study, ordered them to surround the school with very high walls armed with thorns to prevent all escape. Adjoining the school, another enclosure containing four houses was reserved for the priests responsible for their instruction.[22]

In 1516 Rui d'Aguiar, vicar of the kingdom of the Kongo, notes the presence in the capital of a thousand students, 'sons of noblemen', who were not only learning to read and write but were studying grammar and the humanities 'as well as the things of faith'.[23] More surprisingly, he alludes to the existence of schools for girls, directed by a sister of the king, a woman of some sixty years. He suggests activity in the provinces: 'In all his provinces, he [the king] has distributed a great number of countrymen who keep school and teach our holy faith to the people.'

Thus it would appear that less than a dozen years (the reign of Afonso I began in 1506), and a very limited personnel (the requests for missionaries and technical assistance were quasi-permanent), sufficed to launch the educational revolution. The truth must have been somewhat different. First of all, young men of aristocratic origin had always had to live for a time at the court of the sovereign, where their education was enriched by foreign influences and Christian ideas. So the innovation was not total; it supplemented rather than transformed. As for the introduction of the new teaching to the provinces and to the feminine population, it remained inadequate and precarious. In fact it was the capitals—most notably Mbanza Kongo—and a restricted class — the nobles who supported the king — who reaped the benefits of an enlightened despotism.

Alongside this education provided at home, we must consider that which the cream of the élite acquired in Portugal. In 1506 Henrique, 'son' of Afonso I, and Rodrigo, a maternal nephew of the king, were sent to Lisbon to study. In 1511 it was the turn of a younger brother of the sovereign and some nephews impatient to 'devote themselves for a time to reading and writing'. In 1512, nineteen young people left, then in 1516 a score, some of whom fell victim to the 'rebels' of the lower Congo before they reached the port of Mpinda. But in 1517 the Portuguese put an end to the recruiting of further Kongo scholars because of the mediocrity of the results obtained and the mortality which was decimating Kongo ranks. Two of these pupils, however, were to achieve celebrity: Dom Henrique, who became a bishop, and Dom Afonso, a nephew of the king, who became a professor and directed 'a public school for the humanities in Lisbon'.[24]

The king was proud of this 'overture' to the establishments of learning and universities of Portugal. At the end of his life he still remembered that he had 'sent more than twenty of his children, nephews, and grandchildren' to pursue their studies there,[25] which represented a large fraction of the few dozen pupils and students educated abroad. Thus it appears clearly that learning was reserved for relatives of the sovereign and for the small group of his most powerful supporters. Modern knowledge and Christianity—instruments of power and unity if a state religion could be founded—were the tools of a royal policy that sought to consolidate the central power and control clanic particularisms. Indeed, the enemies of Afonso I saw them as the symbols of a 'party' that threatened tradition and was based upon the power of foreigners.

The sovereign's 'modernist' enterprise and his appeals for an unambitious material aid had economic consequences or provided a pretext for economic interventions. In the interior a state tax, the tithe, was created to provide for the needs of religion and teaching; the collection was assigned to tax collectors who continued to operate into the eighteenth century. In relations with the outside world, there was an obligation to maintain trade with Portugal which would be controlled by her sovereign. The export trade and the traffic in Negroes have their origin and pseudo-justification in this. In 1512, King Manuel of Portugal asked the head of an embassy sent to the Kongo to have the vessels loaded for the return with brass, ivory, and slaves. Cuvelier and Jadin note discreetly in this connection: 'In this way he was able to pay the tuition of the young Congolese and their traveling expenses to Rome.* These objects and the slaves were to serve as payment for all the precious articles, ornaments, arms, clothing, and instruments sent to King Afonso.'[26]

For the moment we must see this as the origin of economic relations which would very soon create antagonism and were to play an important role in the history of the Kongo.

The reign of Afonso I almost coincides with the first period of Christianization. Upon his accession to power this sovereign sought missionaries . . . and 'mortars and muskets' in order to strengthen his side — that is, the modernist party open to Catholicism. In 1508 an expedition left the banks of the Tagus

---

* King Afonso tried to establish more *direct* relations with the Holy See, whereas the privilege of the *padroado* (right of patronage) established the Portuguese crown as its intermediary. The first embassy to Rome seems to have been in 1513, during the time of Pope Leo X.

and sailed toward the Kongo; it included fifteen missionaries, canons of Saint John the Evangelist, and a few secular priests.[27] In 1509 a new convoy was organized, and 'every year the king of Portugal sent several trusted men to the Congo'.[28] In 1512 five more vessels were prepared under the command of Simão da Silva, Knight of the Order of Christ, commissioned by his king to serve as untitled governor of Portuguese subjects living in the Kongo and adviser to Afonso I. A *regimento*, or regulation, defined the purpose of his mission. The 'embassy' included missionaries — apparently Franciscans — and priests, as well as artisans whose chief responsibility was to build churches and a royal palace. But Simão da Silva died on the trail leading to Mbanza Kongo before reaching his destination, and the *feitor*, or steward of the expedition, Alvaro Lopes, replaced him; and the habitation of durable materials intended for the sovereign was still not completed after five years of indolent 'labor' on the part of the imported masons. The work of evangelization hardly seems to have progressed more quickly. Dom Afonso continued to ask for priests who were also teachers, especially for the provinces of Mpangu and Mbata.

Much later, in letters dating from 1526, he again expressed an urgent need for some fifty missionaries and suggested a kind of plan for evangelization. This project is of great interest, for it indirectly reveals the political intentions underlying this excessive support of Christianity. Afonso I intended to consolidate the network of missions operating within the provinces, because he hoped to make Mbanza Kongo the religious capital of the kingdom. He proposed that his town be made the episcopal see and that the Kongo, freeing itself from the tutelage of the bishop of Funchal (Madeira) which had been established in 1514, become a separate diocese. The intention is all the more obvious in that the sovereign anticipated the appointment of his 'son' Henrique, promoted to bishop of Utica at the Consistory of May 5, 1518, as bishop in residence. Even further, on August 25, 1526, he wrote to Portugal expressing his desire that his maternal nephew Afonso 'receive sacerdotal ordination and that he enter the service of this kingdom' by becoming the auxiliary of Dom Henrique.

In this way there might be created a 'national' Christianity, controlled by the nearest relatives of the king, capable of autonomy and adjustment. The religious structure would reinforce the political structure to the maximum; the universality of Christianity would help to control tribal and clanic particularisms; the sacred and the political elements, intimately united, would contribute to the establishment of a theocratic state. Different factors did in fact act in the same direction, that of an increase of the central power.

Afonso I, who had repeatedly to contend with the 'rebels', naturally hoped for this; all the more so because his desire to retain the monopoly on economic relations with the outside world accentuated his centralizing inclinations. Besides, the pattern or organization of the kingdom of Portugal (neatly illustrated in the *regimento* of 1512) and the pattern of organization of the Catholic Church together imposed the conception of a very hierarchical and highly sacralized power. And in a certain sense Dom Henrique, who simultaneously held his ecclesiastical post and the governorship of the province of Mpangu received upon his return from Europe, symbolized by his dual office the evolution taking place. This does not mean that there was a crude imitation of the Christian monarchy or of the 'monarchical' church, but that King Afonso was able to utilize foreign influences effectively in conducting his campaign of reform. As Father van Wing expresses it, his reign 'marks the apogee of centralization'; after him, 'the ties were gradually loosened'.[29]

Kongo of the Bell

Kongo dia Ngunga—Kongo of the Bell—was one of the names of the capital. It alludes to the churches built in the royal city. The first of these, erected by order of João I, seems to have met the same fate as the first attempt at evangelization: it rapidly fell in ruins. Another—perhaps the one known as the Church of the Holy Cross—was built before 1517, the date when King Afonso I describes it. The most important church, São Salvador, which gave its name to Mbanza Kongo in the late sixteenth century, must have been built between 1517 and 1527, according to Cuvelier.[30] Finally, in 1526, the king ordered the construction of 'Our Lady of the Victories', known to the people as *Ambila*, 'the church of the graves', because it was located near the sacred wood where the dead kings lay. Afonso I, 'after ascending the mountain of death' in 1543, was buried there and for several years daily masses for the sake of his soul were celebrated. A document dating from 1595 states that at this time there existed six churches for 'about ten thousand homes'. It would appear, then, that the material growth of Catholicism proceeded steadily after the work of King Afonso.

The truth is otherwise. In a report of 1619, Bishop Manuel Baptista Soares emphasizes the simplicity (and also the extreme poverty) of the churches of the capital. Referring to the most important of these, which had become a cathedral, he says specifically : '[It] is of middle size, but it is very poorly built. It is roofed not with [earthern] tiles but with straw. It has neither choir nor sacristry. . . . The church has a small campanile which is incomplete and for which no funds are promised. It contains only one small bell.'[31]

This description re-establishes the true proportions. It does not deny the facts, but restores their exact and modest measure, here as in the rest of the text, which evaluates the authenticity of Catholicism in the Kongo at the turn of the seventeenth century.

If the reign of Afonso I was the one most favorable to the Christian faith, one must nevertheless beware of being deceived by appearances. Father van Wing was not, for he very soon reported some harsh realities :

The apostolate, according to the documents which have reached us, confined itself solely to administering baptism, preaching, and hearing confessions with the aid of interpreters.* The number of baptisms must have been enormous; the Negroes asked nothing better than to become Christians like their kings and chiefs as long as neither ordeals nor sacrifices were required of them.[32]

And further on, after mentioning the creation of an African bishopric on the island of São Tomé (1534) which would have authority over the Kongo, and the later founding of a chapter in the capital, the author adds :

These two measures, which, in the opinion of their promoters, would strengthen the work of evangelization, were obstacles and

---

* This was still done in the *eighteenth century*; see, for example, the *Relations* of Father Laurent de Lucques.

causes of ruin. The Portuguese canons, who were drawn by the rich prebends, and the Negroes who were later admitted into the chapter, possessed, with few exceptions, none of the virtues of their calling. Haughty and ignorant, inflexible regarding their immunities and prerogatives, eager for profit, above all incapable of resisting the morals of those about them, they scandalized the people, encouraged the chiefs in their dissolute life, and impeded the work of the true missionaries. For two and one half centuries the reports were merely to repeat this sad truth.[33]

Without giving any indication of date, Cuvelier and Jadin make a similar observation: 'Where there should have been missionaries, very often there were only mercenaries of little virtue'. They recall above all the transactions prompted by the conversion of clerical income, consisting of shells — pieces of money called *nzimbu* which were negotiable currency only inside the country—into the only 'money' convertible abroad—slaves. They state:

'The precariousness [of the] methods of payment and the possession of *nzimbu* given by the king and the faithful were often to encourage the clergymen, not only to convert their salaries and the gifts they received into slaves to be sold at São Tomé, which was expected and legal, but also to engage in trade and commerce in order to live. Several, moreover, were accompanied by relatives, nephews, or other persons, who helped and encouraged them to engage in selling.[34]

As early as the first half of the sixteenth century in the Kongo, the expansion of Christianity, trade (above all slave trade) and the clash of civilizations that were different and in some respects antagonistic formed a single complex—one which resembles a crude and exaggerated outline of the one which modern colonization was to create three centuries later. In the mind of the Portuguese sovereign who drafted the *regimento* of 1512, commercial monopoly and spiritual conquest were the ends and means of an unstated policy toward the Kongo. This did not exclude a more insidious influence in the form of the advisors and institutions mentioned.

The economic fact very quickly emerged as decisive. It involved four types of partners: the king of Portugal defending his commercial privileges, the governor and slave dealers of São Tomé, the king of the Kongo and his allies, the Portuguese of the Kongo and their accomplices. Central to the complex relations existing between them was the island of São Tomé, located some distance from the coast of modern Gabon. During the sixteenth century — in 1486 and 1493 its inhabitants had received the privilege of engaging in slave trade on the African coast — it became a very active commercial center. Its position as a stopping point on the route to the Indies and its sugar cane plantations later contributed to an expansion that increased the population to over ten thousand.[35] In 1499, King Manuel of Portugal granted the government of São Tomé to the knight Fernão de Melo on a hereditary basis; but the abuses were such that he had to withdraw the position from his son (1522).

The Kongo was commercially dependent on the island. The control endured and the drains imposed, the smuggling of entire cargos, as well as the intrigues, quickly brought Afonso I and de Melo into conflict. 'Their relations were to become increasingly strained. Of the slaves and merchandise sent . . . even as gifts to the king of Portugal, the governor of São Tomé took as much as half as tax or duty. It reached the point where he would appropriate the entire shipment arbitrarily and sell it at a low price.'[36]

At the time of the 'embassy' of 1512, whose principal purpose was to establish a representative of the Portuguese sovereign at the court of the king of the Kongo, tension reached its highest point. The abusive and profitable transactions seemed threatened: the clan of São Tomé, which was supported by the largest number of Portuguese living in the kingdom (including a priest, Father Nunho) and was led by the 'jurist' Diego Fernandes, was opposed by the party of the two kings, who were temporarily allied in the defence of their monopoly. Indeed, the stake was of increasing magnitude, a matter of dealing in commodities bartered in the Kongo: ivory, brass, raffia fabrics 'fine as velvet or plush', etc.; above all, a matter of taking over a rising slave trade which was soon to reach a minimum of five thousand slaves embarked annually.[37] In this struggle, Afonso I, who had established his reign on 'modernism' and the growth of foreign trade, did not have the advantage. His activities depended largely upon his relations with the outside world. Conscious of this necessity, he tried to acquire a ship and commissioned his nephew Rodrigo to negotiate the matter in Lisbon. King Manual had to weigh the risks of this first attempt at emancipation. He refused, and made a pact with his 'natural allies', the merchants: he granted freedom of trade to the Kongo, but by a decision of November 1519, secured exclusive right of transport, with any infraction entailing the confiscation of the ship used.

With the new Portuguese sovereign, João III (1521), relations worsened and deteriorated, and the conflicting interests asserted themselves. As the exploration of Angola had begun in 1520 under the leadership of Manuel Pacheco, ships began to trade along the coast of the future colony and ceased applying to the port of Mpinda. King Afonso was alarmed, foreseeing the transfer that might take place to the detriment of his capital. Slave trade was now provoking serious conflicts (such as those which occurred in 1526) and was being carried on without effective control; unknown to the authorities of the Kongo, persons of 'noble' rank or even members of the royal family were being deported. Afonso I wrote to João III denouncing the abuses, but in vain, for Brazil was beginning to found her prosperity upon the manpower transported from Africa, and Portuguese commitments in the New World were multiplying beyond all measure. To these reasons for discord was added the greed aroused by a mineral wealth more imaginary than real: the Portuguese believed in the existence of mountains of solid silver; the adventurers predicted profits accruing from the extraction of copper, lead, and silver exceeding the national income of Spain. In 1536, a metallurgist accompanied by smelters landed unexpectedly in the Kongo. His prospecting was a failure. Others repeated the experiment, with equal lack of success. The fabulous metal—there was even talk of gold deposits in the vicinity of Mbanza Kongo—was elusive. The subjects of Afonso I were suspected of fraud or devilry.

It is quite true that the aging king witnessed with anxiety the breaking down of the relationship which had made the Portuguese sovereign his 'beloved brother'. Equality of treatment between two friendly Christian countries seemed more and more like a fiction. Control over the kingdom tightened. At home, the slave traders conspired and plotted to replace Afonso I with a king more amenable to their requirements, less anxious to regulate their activities. During the Easter holiday in 1539 an attempt was made by Europeans upon the life of the 'master' of the Kongo, missed him, but killed one dignitary and wounded two others. Distrust set in. Portugal had now entered the colonial game; she was counting her profits. And Dom Afonso Nzinga Mbemba—of whom it would later be said 'that he was a genius, a great Christian, a hero'[38]—died, without the event even being recorded, sometime between 1541 and 1543; as if his life had become unimportant in comparison with a proud history which now valued only conquests and dominations.

CHAPTER 3

The Rival Kings

The period of disorder resumed after the death of Afonso I, which event, according to tradition, launched the era of competition. The old king had suggested his successor: Nkanga Mbemba, known as Dom Pedro and described by the chroniclers as one of his sons. Such a relationship is doubtful, however, since the Bakongo had established a matrilinear monarchy whereby the power was transmitted either to a uterine brother or to a maternal nephew. The authors of the accounts and chronicles have scrambled the appellations, confused nephews with sons, and failed to distinguish the sons of slave women who managed to accede to the throne, as in the case of Mpanzu a Nimi (Alvaro II). The imbroglio is all the more complete in that succession must have operated from father to son for an ill-defined period,[1] and certain sovereigns tried to establish a dynastic system that would eliminate disorder during interregna. This means that one cannot accept the indications of filiation appearing in most of the documents as they are. These incidental remarks explain the impossibility of accurately determining the family connections of either Nkanga Mbemba, who became king in 1543 under the 'modern' name of Pedro I, or his two rivals for the power, Mpudi a Nzinga Mbemba (Dom Francisco) and Nkumbi Mpudi a Nzinga (Dom Diogo). In spite of the uncertainties, all three seem to have belonged to a single royal lineage, the one that governed the Kongo until 1567 or 1568.[2]

The Struggles for Power

The death of the 'very Christian' king, Afonso I, created exceptional difficulties, difficulties commensurate with his personality.

The traditional ones resulting from the obligation to *conquer* the power were supplemented by those arising from the opposition between 'modernists' and conservatives, between allies or accomplices of the Portuguese and xenophobes. The problem of succession presented itself in terms of a foreign presence : it brought into play economic interests which were for the first time of national importance. The stake was large and the rivalry between pretenders became all the more bitter and persistent. Pedro I had a short reign : after being overthrown by his rivals in 1545, he was taken prisoner and escaped death only by taking refuge in a church where he invoked the right of asylum.[3] Dom Francisco appears (the authors diverge) to have established a short-lived government. In the final analysis it was Dom Diogo, a member of a younger generation, who carried the day : he was to be king from 1545 to 1561. It took two years of conflict and violence to fill the power vacuum. The miracles of the two preceding reigns were not repeated.

It was a bad sign; and this absence of Christian miracles is understood all the better in that relations between Diogo I and the missionaries rapidly deteriorated. The new sovereign quickly demonstrated that he tolerated Christianity only insofar as it served his political plans and economic ambitions; he utilized it as an instrument of power, not as a means of transforming social structures and mentalities. The modernist and conciliatory spirit of King Afonso I had vanished; European cultural contributions coexisted with Kongo civilization without being able to change it profoundly; the vigor of the latter increased proportionately as Portuguese supervision and the cynicism of the slave traders were more bitterly opposed.

Diogo I introduces the era of ambiguity, of contradiction, and of insidious confrontation between the people of Kongo and the 'foreigners'. Very soon (1546) the king sent to Europe an ambassador extraordinary : he was a creole, a priest born and ordained in the Kongo, Diogo Gomes. His apparent mission was to ask for 'a few clergymen and monks of good conscience and good works'.[4] In fact, his two chief objects were to obtain confirmation of the treaty (1517) regulating commercial relations[5] and requiring the Portuguese to restrict themselves to the port of Mpinda, and to establish direct relations with the Holy See by evading the obligations resulting from the *padroado*, or right of patronage. It was an attack on two fronts: to recover initiative in the matter of trade and demand reciprocity of treatment, and to attempt to break the monopoly of Portugal, who was the Kongo's sole intermediary in the area of foreign relations.

The fragile colonial edifice suffered its first jolts. In 1546 the auxiliary bishop of São Tomé 'visited' the kingdom and suggested the construction of a convent where African Dominicans would be trained. But Diogo I intended to limit the sphere of influence of the clergy. The law of the king prevailed over the law of the Church: the bishop was driven out in 1547. The following year, Ambassador Gomes returned to the Kongo accompanied by four Jesuit missionaries. Relations between the sovereign and the priests were at first cordial, the little religious community being more aware of the problems and the attendant disillusionment, as its correspondence shows:

The people of the king's entourage seem good enough to us. . . . As for the things of God, there are very few here who are concerned with religious truth and most are immersed in numerous and stupid errors. With the exception of the king and a few chiefs, they have no stable marriages; they take as many wives as they can afford to feed.[6]

The Jesuits, while continuing to administer mass baptisms, took up the work of education and created a school at Mbanza Kongo:

. . . With the greatest zeal the schoolmaster looks after the children, to whom he teaches the elements of Christian doctrine; he has gathered about six hundred of them in a large place where other masters teach them to read and write; he also has the duty of instructing and guiding these masters.[7]

The mechanisms set in motion during the reign of Dom Afonso seem to have been functioning again. In fact, however, Diogo I meted out his tolerance of Christianity according to the advantages he anticipated or obtained from the Portuguese. After 1549 he limited the activities of the missionaries and denounced a conspiracy directed against his person. The game of intrigue resumed and the Jesuits advised 'King João III [of

Portugal] to have King Diogo, who constituted an obstacle to any progress in the work of evangelization, replaced',[8] which is sufficient to reveal the semicolonial situation of the kingdom. In 1553, after the second failure of his attempt to send an ambassador to Rome to do homage to the pope, the Kongo sovereign increased his pressure on the missionaries and on the white colony in the capital. Since it was impossible to exert a real control over the forces expressing the foreigners' desire for economic and moral domination, Diogo chose to remain sole master of his domain. 'At the end of the year 1555, following new disagreements with the Portuguese merchants, [he] banished all the Europeans from his states with the exception of a few obliging priests.[9] In 1557, five Franciscan missionaries came to the Kongo to replace the Jesuits, their superior having previously composed and had printed a catechism in Kikongo—the first work known to have been published in a language of the Bantu group. They were better tolerated owing to their fuller understanding of the Kongo milieu, acquired through activities in the kingdom which seem to have dated from the discovery. But the fundamental problems remained unsolved.

As for Diogo I, 'the missionaries greatly criticized his immoral and scandalous way of living',[10] which is explained primarily by his unhypocritical observance of the traditional principles regulating royalty. The sovereign's conformity to ancient usages, notably those concerning his choice of wives and his sexual life, was interpreted as evidence of 'licentious' behavior. This particular misunderstanding is typical of all the others. Then there were the conflicts of interest, the maneuvers of factions, the threats that loomed in the outlying provinces and at the frontiers. The reign of Diogo ended in a tragedy in which the Portuguese played their part. On November 4, 1561, the death of the king was announced, as well as the assassination by conspiracy of the pretender who had been appointed to succeed him. The puppet king selected by the colonists was Afonso II; he very soon paid for this compliance with his life, in a generalized insurrection against the foreigners.[11]

The king of the unity that was temporarily restored was Bernardo I, Nzinga Mbemba; he was forced to make an agreement with the Portuguese because his enemies—especially the Bateke and the Yaka—were attacking the kingdom; he died in battle in 1567. His successor for a few months, Henrique I, met the same fatal and glorious destiny late that year. After 1568 the power resided for almost twenty years in the person of Alvaro I, first sovereign of a new lineage, that of Lukeni lua Mbemba. He ascended the throne while the Yaka were overrunning the Kongo, later forcing him to abandon his capital (1569). The chroniclers have preserved the memory of this event, whose consequence was the king's total submission to the Portuguese, who agreed to provide him with military aid.

Certain accounts are unintentionally revealing on this point:

The Yaka entered the kingdom through the province of Bata and very soon made their way toward . . . São Salvador. When the king learned this, he left the town and fled to the Isle of the Horses, which is in the Zaïre, with the Portuguese priests and principal men of the kingdom. Since the Yaka were now the masters, the inhabitants fled into the mountains and deserts. A great number were massacred by the invaders.

Since the Isle of the Horses, where the king had taken refuge, was small and the number of fugitives very great, most of them soon died of the plague and of starvation. They sold one another. Fathers were seen selling their sons. The Portuguese of São Tomé bought them and took them to Portugal. Among them were members of the royal family and of the first families of the kingdom. The king himself received his punishment from God. He contracted dropsy, a disease from which he suffered the rest of his life.

All these misfortunes converted the king. He sent an ambassador to King Dom Sebastião of Portugal to implore his help. The latter immediately dispatched six hundred well-trained soldiers and other adventurers, under the command of Dom Francisco de Gouvea. When he arrived at the Isle of the Horses, King Alvaro joined the Portuguese army with all his people who were capable of fighting. In a year and a half the captain re-established the king in his kingdom and drove out the Yaka after defeating them several times. After four years, Francisco de Gouvea returned to Portugal, leaving the kingdom restored to order and the king more or less calm.[12]

In spite of these disasters and miseries, which were attributed to divine justice, and even taking advantage of the circumstances, the slave traffic, which had corrupted everything in the Kongo for over three centuries, continued. It was the only permanent feature, outside of the traditions which recovered all their vigor in a society threatened by death. Missionary activity was slowly reorganized with the arrival of the Dominicans who accompanied the small band of Portuguese soldiers. And King Alvaro I, in a kingdom ravaged by war, liberated by the foreigners, and plundered by the merchants, followed an uncertain policy. At times he submitted, and seems even to have considered donating a territory to the king of Portugal; the chronicles accordingly praise his skill in governing and his 'more Christian life'. At other times he was elusive, tolerating the traditionalists, limiting the encroachments of the Portuguese, seeking new allies in Europe.

The situation had changed profoundly since the death of Afonso I. The royal power had declined and neighboring tribes, impatient to profit by the slave trade, were increasing their pressure; commerce had declined for reasons of insecurity; the base of the colonization had shifted as soon as the conquest of Angola had been considered and then undertaken in 1575. This kingdom, formerly under the authority of the Kongo, was to become a competing and threatening colonial territory. The position of the Kongo sovereign was to appear increasingly vulnerable: 'The Portuguese, indeed, were more than a few tradesmen and missionaries scattered through his states; they were a military power located at his borders.'[13]

Alvaro I must have foreseen that his reign would be the one during which the fate of the country would slowly be decided. Trapped between two dangers, that of the primitive, warlike, and greedy populations on the internal frontier, and that of the colonists in Loanda on the seacoast, he sought, until the end of his life (1587), the least disastrous solution. He sent repeated embassies to the kings of Portugal and Spain (the latter had been sovereign of Portugal since 1580), and above all to the pope. He requested missionaries—he professed belief in Christianity as the condition of all aid—and help in rebuilding the kingdom. He proposed the transfer of the mines (most of them imaginary) which had been arousing greed for several decades. But his ambassadors were the victims of ill fortune. One died in a shipwreck. Another, Duarte Lopes, having arrived in Mbanza Kongo in 1579 and been made *fidalgo* (gentleman of the royal house) by Alvaro I, left the Congo in 1583 armed with letters of reference and very careful instructions. He too met with extraordinary misadventures:

The ambassador embarked on a caravel which sprung a leak following an accident not far from Cape Vert. Because of adverse winds, it was unable to land, and to escape the danger, they changed direction. Sailing before the wind, they reached the island of Cutagio of New Spain, opposite the island of Santa Margarita where they fish for pearls. The caravel was repaired and they made their way toward the continental port of Cumana, which is in the new kingdom of Grenada in the West Indies. Near this port, the caravel sank. Almost everyone managed to swim to land, but they fell seriously ill from hunger, thirst, and the storms. Lopes was forced to remain there for a whole year and wait for the fleet which sets sail for Spain once a year.[14]

Such a lengthy quotation is justified by the personality of Duarte Lopes, who provided Pigafetta with information resulting in the publication, in 1591, of the celebrated *Relazione del reame di Congo*. This reason would suffice, but the passage contains not only a description of the dangers then associated with extraordinary diplomacy, but evidence of a fatality thwarting all the undertakings of the king of Kongo. Indeed, further quotation is appropriate:

The king of the Congo, receiving no news of his ambassador and believing that he had perished in a shipwreck, entrusted a new embassy to Dom Pedro Antonio, his prime minister. . . . They were captured by English pirates and taken to England. As they were landing, the vessel was smashed and Dom Pedro and his son, who had accompanied him, were drowned.[15]

By the time Duarte Lopes was finally well enough to complete his mission and to go to Rome, King Alvaro I had died. The sovereign had not been able to bring to fruition the great political project cryptically alluded to in the instructions given to his ambassador: 'It probably regarded withdrawing the Congo from the tutelage of Portugal and placing it directly under the obedience of the Holy See.'[16] A donation of 'one hundred leagues of land rich in mines' was to have unambiguously indicated the change of allegiance. The creation of a permanent embassy in Rome, thwarted as it was by the operations of chance and of the protector sovereigns of the Kongo, was delayed by a quarter of a century.

The succession of Alvaro I conformed to the traditions prescribing the conquest of the throne: his son, Mpanzu a Nimi, born of a slave woman, had to defeat the party of one of his rival 'brothers' (who was killed in the battle) and foil the conspiracy of one of his 'sisters' before he could be recognized definitively as king under the name of Alvaro II (1587–1588). Under the circumstances the support of the Portuguese of Angola and of Governor Dias de Novais, who had just founded this colony, was not superfluous.

The new king appeared, however, and very soon, to oppose the authorities of Angola, whom he reproached for their 'encroachments upon Kongo territory'. He was accused of treason and notably of giving aid to the tribes who had attacked the colony in December 1590. In fact, Alvaro II pursued the policy of his predecessor. He tried to preserve the independence of his kingdom, which was very severely threatened. He made repeated efforts to dissociate the Kongo from the Angolese territory, which was of colonial status, and to break the tutelage that had been established with the discovery of the kingdom. The establishment of a bishopric at São Salvador—this was the present name for Mbanza Kongo—and the transformation of the church of São Salvador into a cathedral (1596) were consistent with this intention. Relations between the king and the bishop did not proceed without 'some difficulties', but Christianization recovered a certain vigor with the multiplication of the number of priests.

Alvaro II tried, with a determination equal to that of his predecessor, to establish direct relations with the Holy See. In 1604, he organized an embassy whose concealed purpose was to oppose the protection obtained from the pope for the impertinence of the protector king (the king of Spain, in this instance), who even denied Alvaro the title of majesty. The ambassador

was António Manuel ne Vunda, a man of high rank and traditional religious authority. The instructions given on this occasion
are indicative of the problems and purposes: Alvaro 'claimed the
privileges of the other Christian kings [and] asked that the
bishop remain within the limits of his authority';[17] he asked
that the latter 'not be Portuguese, because if he were, he would
be in full agreement with the governors of Angola';[18] he pro-
tested against the spoliations perpetrated by the latter, who were
claiming possession of lands, making 'concessions of land, dona-
tions which they distribute as they please'.[19] In short, the Kongo
sovereign solicited the intervention and protection of the pope,
whom he wished to transform into a decolonizer before the
appointed time. 'Of all the metal which will be discovered in
this kingdom, he offers some portion to His Holiness for the
apostolic chamber, that it may be recognized as his feudatory
and protected against force and vexations.'[20] Thus the moral
authority of Christianity found itself put to the test, facing the
threats and violence that were justified by the argument of
conquest.

The embassy, like its predecessors under the reign of Alvaro I,
was marked by the sign of fatality. After being robbed at sea by
'pirates' and held at length in Lisbon and Madrid, António
Manuel did not arrive in Rome until January 3, 1608; here he
died two days later, having nevertheless delivered his message to
Pope Paul V. The unfortunate spokesman for the king of the
Kongo, so close to the goal and the honors, succumbed to
exhaustion and despondency after seeing most of his 'familiars'
die. The Kongo at last proved that Rome recognized her as a
Christian kingdom, but by a cruel irony it was on the occasion
of her envoy's funeral services, which were just as magnificent
as those of a former ambassador from France and the prince of
Clèves. The inscription on Dom António Manuel's grave mentions 'funeral ceremonies almost befitting a king', a fresco at the
Vatican depicts a visit which the pope paid the sick man a few
hours before his death, and a bust at the basilica Santa Maria
Maggiore preserves his features. By this position, acquired in the
gallery of past glories, the ambassador from the Kongo cancelled
the 'attacks and offences of bishops and canons' against the king.
his master. The latter continued to seek the support of the
Roman authorities. He obtained the nomination of the cardinal

of Saint Cecilia as protector of his kingdom. He appointed
ambassador to Rome 'by letters dated São Salvador (February 27,
1613), Msgr. Vives, Catalan, referendary of His Holiness, prelate
of great piety and experience in this court'.[21]

The following year, Alvaro II died without being able to carry
any further his policy of 'disengagement' from Portugal and a
Spain which no longer hid their colonial ambitions. His immediate successors were shortlived kings who no longer controlled
the rivalries and intrigues to which the Kongo served as arena.
From 1614 to 1641, the year that marked the beginning of the
long reign of Garcia II Afonso, eight sovereigns occupied the
throne 'forged' by the founder. This accelerated turnover of
kings brought to power some very young men—Garcia I Afonso
(1624–1626) had barely reached his twentieth year when he
took the throne — and even a child — Alvaro IV (1631–1636)
'was no more than thirteen at his accession'. The decline of the
kingdom progressed correspondingly under the assaults of competing forces.

The principal factor in changing the former situation seems to
have been the end of the commercial monopoly of the Portuguese: the French and the English made their appearance and
the Dutch began settling in the province of Soyo at the turn of
the seventeenth century. The travel account of Pieter van den
Broecke, who traded in this region, where he was a pioneer of
the Dutch slave trade, reveals the partial and forced disappearance of the Portuguese and the violent conflicts it provoked.[22]
Besides, the 'colonists' of Angola respected the Kongo
sovereignty less and less; they made territorial appropriations
and, in alliance with the Yaka, repeated raids for the purpose of
rounding up slaves. And under the reign of Pedro II Afonso
(1622–1624), the governor of Loanda even invaded the southern
Kongo with a small troop of Portuguese aided by Yaka! Pressures
of this kind—commercial rivalries and the intrigues they stimulated, and the constant struggle with authoritarian representatives of the Catholic Church—contributed to the debilitation of
a state whose traditional foundations were crumbling and whose
methods of modernization were inadequate. As a consequence,
assaults against the central power were increased: from Mbamba
and Nsundi under Alvaro III (1615–1622), from Nsundi under
Garcia I Afonso and Mbamba under Alvaro V (who was killed

73

in 1636 after a reign of six months), from Soyo under Alvaro VI (1636–1641), who died 'probably as a result of being poisoned'.

All this 'political' activity was less a result of internal impulses than of foreign pressures. It was largely induced, as an important event revealed in 1641. The capture of Loanda by the Dutch brought about a change in internal political relations. First of all, by creating a united front of opposition to the former ruler: 'The chiefs of the Kongo, Angola, and Matamba, who had reason to complain of the Portuguese, rejoiced at their defeat and made common cause with the Dutch.'[23] This enabled the new king of the Kongo, Garcia II Afonso (1641–1661) to reinforce his power with Dutch support and to recover a certain margin of control over the Catholic missions, which were threatened by the introduction of Protestantism. Relations with these missions were reversed: by an ironic turn of fate, the 'Catholic king' of the Kongo became the defender of the Church. He helped the Capuchins to become established in 1645. Taking advantage of the eviction of the Portuguese intermediary, he strengthened direct relations with Rome and tried to 'obtain the support of the pope to make the kingship hereditary within his family'.[24] But in 1648 the defeated Dutch abandoned Angola and the Kongo. 'The Portuguese, aided by the chief of Dongo, punished King Garcia. . . . He was forced to surrender [to them] the island (opposite) Loanda, from which until then he had derived his *nzimbu*, or shell money (1649).'[25] This amounted to exhausting his finances, to seizing, in effect, the treasury of the kingdom —a method of coercion that had been considered since the beginning of the seventeenth century.[26] Garcia II had already strengthened his power sufficiently to meet the test: his was one of the rare long reigns and the last of the dynasties to have governed the great Kongo.

According to Article Twelve of the peace treaty that was suggested in 1649 with the governor of Loanda, Dom Garcia surrendered the mining deposits of the kingdom. 'The king of the Congo will give to the crown of Portugal the mountains in which there are said to be mines of gold and silver', Paiva Manso reports.[27] This was the beginning of the catastrophe that precipitated the decline of the Kongo. The definitive version of the treaty required the surrender of the southern lands of the Kongo, without however altering the ownership of the deposits. Upon the death of Garcia II in 1661, the crown was captured by a new clan, Ki-Nlaza or Ne-Nlaza. António I won it, not for glory, but to launch a period of definitive decline. His relations with the Portuguese were strained to the breaking point. He opposed the prospecting of the mines, which his predecessor had been wise enough to preserve. His resistance acquired a symbolic value and the 'foreigners' made it a pretext for open warfare. The two armies came together, each carrying flags bearing the cross, as is recalled by a commemorative ceramic work depicting the battle which appears in a hermitage in Loanda.[28] The site was Ambouila, beyond the sources of the Bengo; the day, October 25, 1665. The Bakongo suffered a total defeat, and King António was killed and decapitated.

The Great Misery of the Kingdom of the Kongo

This tragic death coincided with the birth of an anguished Kongo. '[It] began the era of rivalries, of double and triple elections. The chiefs, elected by rival clans, lived in São Salvador, Bula, and Kibangu, surrounded by their respective partisans.'[29] It was also the period of the Portuguese withdrawal. After the death of António I, activities aimed at the acquisition of the (imaginary) gold mines resumed, according to the testimony of António de Oliveira de Cadornega, the historian of the Angolese wars;[30] but the evidence could not be denied, and the order to abandon the prospecting was given in 1667. This date marks the withdrawal of the Portuguese colonists; it corresponds approximately to the abandonment of São Salvador. A few years later, the bishop of Loanda was to describe the capital city as nothing but 'a den of savage beasts'.

From 1665 to 1710 the confusion continued to be extreme. 'Separatist' activities contributed to the decline of a royal power that came to have more than a single ruling head due to competing factions: one of the most dangerous of these being that of the chiefs of the province of Soyo, an ocean port without which the sovereigns would be totally dependent on Loanda for intercourse with the outside world. In 1666 troops of the 'count' of Soyo arrived in São Salvador for the purpose of turning the royal election in a direction favorable to their chief. This was the beginning of a series of confrontations which resulted in the *de facto* independence of the province. On several occasions the

Portuguese found themselves engaged in activities aimed at the reunification of the kingdom and the reinforcement of the central power; their military operations, which had been intended to reduce the 'pride' of the people of Soyo, ended in defeat and the massacre of their army.[31] They too had begun to suffer from the symptoms of decline.

By the beginning of the eighteenth century the breakdown of the political unity of the Kongo appears to have been complete. Among the pretenders to the throne, not one had the strength or the means to prevail; the provinces fought among themselves; even the local powers suffered assaults and rebellions. Van Wing describes these disastrous times as a 'revolutionary period', adding:

The royal authority . . . emerged from this period in a very reduced state. The great vassals of Sogno, Mbamba, Mbata, and Nsundi had become completely independent. Mpangu had been so for a long time. Even in the Mpemba, a region adjacent to São Salvador, the king had lost much of his prestige. Also, the Holy See now addressed itself individually to the chiefs of provinces.[32]

The last observation is significant of the fall of the royal power. Laurent de Lucques's accounts, which bear on the first two decades of the seventeenth century, provide precise information on the great misery of the kingdom of the Kongo. They complement the observations of Antonio Zucchelli in his *Relazioni del Viaggio e Missione di Congo*, published in Venice in 1712. Upon his debarkment at Mpinda (1702), the Capuchin missionary notes the ebb of 'foreigners' — the Portuguese had withdrawn at the time of the last war with Soyo—and takes full measure of the disorders. He states: 'In the Congo, owing to ancient rivalries for the crown, the troubles continue. On the eve of Palm Sunday the "Banza" of the duke of Mbamba . . . was attacked by [the] son of a deceased duke of Mbamba. He burned it so completely that only our monastery remains standing. . . . '

The consequence of this total war was to prevent the coronation of King Pedro IV.[33] In 1705 a 'heretical' religious movement expressed the general confusion: its 'ambassadors' taught '[that] according to the will of God, the kingdom of the Congo must be restored and that to this end all the nobles of the kingdom must meet at São Salvador'. The yearning for peace and unity attempted to impose its reasons by any means, including irrational ones.

In an account dated 1701, Laurent de Lucques analyzes the 'intrigues and wars between the sons of the royal house of the Congo and the king'.

One must know that there are two houses which pretend to the crown of the Congo. One is the house of Quimpanzo (Ki-Mpanzu), the other the house of Equimoloza (Ki-Nlaza). Both stem from the same royal lineage. . . . Whence these enmities and wars that exist between them. They are destroying one another, and between the two of them they are destroying the kingdom.

The political picture of the year 1701 bore out this interpretation. It was a sombre one:

The news coming from the Congo is always worse and the enmities between the royal houses are tearing the kingdom further and further apart. At present there are four kings of the Congo. . . . There are also two great dukes of Bamba; three great dukes in Ovando; two great dukes in Batta, and four marquises of Enchus. The authority of each is declining and they are destroying each other by making war among themselves. Each claims to be chief. They make raids on one another in order to steal and to sell their prisoners like animals.[34]

The political decomposition spread. Beginning in 1708, Soyo suffered a severe crisis: a series of revolts against the different *mani* of the province and finally against the 'prince' who died, a victim of the attack of the rebels and the treason of his followers.[35] His two successors seem to have been even less fortunate, if that is possible; before the end of the year 1710 they had died violent deaths.

The weight of evidence indicates that a few years later disorder and insecurity reigned unchallenged and the Christian imprint continued to disappear: 'I shall now discuss the situa-

77

tion of the kingdoms of the Congo. At this time there is no mission and the king is not safe on his throne. The opposing party remains vigorous and plays an active role. . . . Sogno is all in confusion. These populations are divided. . . . '[36]

In spite of the restoration attempted during the reign of Pedro IV, the Kongo was already drifting over the sea of vanished empires. During the eighteenth century its splendor was extinguished to the point where the name of Lower Guinea was beginning to replace a name once glorious to designate Congolese Africa.

This threat of total disappearance and oblivion suggests the gravity of the case. How is one to explain a history thus driven to destroy itself? There are causes relating to the very nature of Kongo society and civilization, the level of technology and the form of government, the weakness of physical communication. It has been said that the Kongo—made up of kingdoms, principalities, fiefs, and provinces—consisted of three great, loosely joined units. A legend recorded at the beginning of the nineteenth century alludes to this idea when it mentions a hypothetical division 'between the three sons of a king'.

The first son is said to have received both banks of the river above Isangila [a place where the Congo bends before its descent to the sea]. The second is said to have had the left bank of the remaining territory and the third the right bank. . . . This division into three parts underlies the organization of the indigenous tribes in the Lower Congo in the nineteenth century.[37]

The kingdoms organized around Loango, the southern provinces of the Kongo in the coastal regions, and the area around Nsundi to the north: such were the component elements. By the time the Portuguese arrived, the loosening process had already begun: the king of Loango no longer recognized the preeminence of the *ntotila* of the Kongo in any but a symbolic sense. At no period, as we have stated, did the latter possess the necessary instruments for the centralized government of a vast political entity.

External forces contributed to the dissolution of this 'empire'. Under the reign of the memorable King Afonso I, foreign intervention initially favored the reinforcement of the central power. Christianity, education, and modernization were not entirely subordinated to mercantile ends and the sovereign derived extra power from Portuguese support. This situation did not last, and the factors of progress all turned into agents of slow destruction.

Christianization itself appears to have been a destructive activity. It was discontinuous, always being started again and never concentrated in any one part of the kingdom. The Franciscans arrived as soon as relations were· established with the Kongo, and their very ancient influence explains the popularity of Saint Anthony. The Dominicans tried to become established on various occasions until the seventeenth century, and they have claimed the first evangelists in the Kongo 'as members of their order'. The regular canons of Santo Elói left their mark during the first evangelization (until about 1530), by their missionaries as well as by the Kongo pupils whose education they provided in Portugal. The Jesuits followed them and from 1548 to 1555 tried to found a mission and a school at Mbanza Kongo; but their disappointments and the new political conditions caused them to turn toward Angola, where they settled in 1561. Loanda was later to become their base of departure for intermittent expeditions into the kingdom of the Kongo. The Carmelites appeared for a short period at the end of the sixteenth century. The Augustinians were even less fortunate in their efforts. As for the Capuchins, they had to storm the gates of the kingdom, but they played an important role during three periods of missionary activity occurring between 1645 and 1765. The list of attempts and undertakings is long, and includes a plan, nursed for almost half a century, to establish a convent in the Kongo. These were, in short, very mediocre results, and obtained at the price of deaths and disasters (whether due to the climate or to sea voyages) which mark the two centuries of evangelization.

Beginning with the reign of Afonso I, the sovereigns were constantly either requesting new missionaries in order to strengthen Christianity, or vigorously opposing a Church which, though its position was precarious, nevertheless exerted pressure on the political and economic life of the country. These reactions only seem to be contradictory. The Catholic faith never at any time found the necessary means for a radical transformation of beliefs and behavior. It was imposed from without and in an authoritarian manner—with an authority that was all the more vulnerable in that the missions, of which there were too few, left it up to the native authorities to provide the defence of Christianity. It had only a superficial influence, which van Wing compares to that of a tropical rain which 'touches the surface without penetrating deep into the soil'.[38] The lack of continuity in the missionary enterprise was aggravated by the weakness or stupidity of the clergy. Although education reached a limited minority, and a plan for the training of Kongo priests appeared late (1660) and came to nothing, evangelization nevertheless retained its statistical character. Baptisms were administered *en masse* and communication with the faithful was generally achieved by means of interpreters—during services as well as during confessions. At the beginning of the eighteenth century, Father Laurent de Lucques was still calling attention to this important function of the *maestri,* or masters, who were always chosen from the aristocracy. By way of contrast, one is amazed at the intransigence of the most virtuous missionaries. In a radical fashion, they sought abolition of *all* the old beliefs, suppression of polygamy—which was interpreted as concubinage— and immediate submission to the Christian ethic; they threatened censure and excommunication and sometimes used the stake. As for the less zealous priests, they were regarded as 'not very respectable' and compared to 'mercenaries'.[39] Father van Wing has recalled their 'dissolute lives' and their worthlessness. Whether by excess or by deficiency, both groups acted improperly. And this was all the more possible because relations with Rome had been indirect for so long and because ecclesiastical authority was located outside the Kongo. It was only in 1596 that São Salvador became a bishopric, and then only for a short period.

Then too, the material conditions of existence of the Church involved the clergy in the game of financial claims and economic speculation. The Portuguese crown partially met the burden of expense resulting from missionary activity by trying to compensate the clergy with a right of priority in the matter of the sale of slaves. The Kongo sovereigns, for their part, had to guarantee the support of the priests at their own expense, and they thus collected a tithe in the form of the local currency, that is to say, in *nzimbu* shells. As these sums, earmarked for the bishops, their representatives, and the clergy were of no use outside the kingdom, they were used to obtain provisions or services, and also to acquire slaves. They created a shameful traffic which made capitalization by means of a restricted currency impossible. Cuvelier and Jadin mention these occupations, which were in theory forbidden to the clergy.[40] King Afonso I had already lamented such practices and must have taken measures toward the expulsion of hypocrites more interested in their personal profit than in the service of the faith.

The Portuguese political hold, the establishment of Christianity, and the Negro slave trade were intimately connected; together they constitute the peculiar structure of the first colonization. We even know of the revealing case of a priest, Father Ribeiro, who sold the sacerdotal objects in order to buy slaves![41] The kingdom of the Kongo provided precious manpower first for Portugal, next for the islands of Cape Vert and São Tomé, and finally for Brazil, the Antilles, and New Castile. Each year between five and ten thousand 'heads' were deported in this way—'besides the infinite number who [died] owing to the lack of ships.'[42] The clergy was involved not only directly by its participation in the slave traffic, but also indirectly, by the pretences of conversion and spiritual protection that obscured the ignoble commerce. It baptized slaves, 'without performing the necessary catechisms', to protect them from 'the greatest dangers'. It defended the Portuguese monopoly and its own economic privileges against the Dutch and the English with the argument of the holy struggle against the heretics. It was not the principle of the selling of men that was called into doubt; all the indignation arose from the fact that it was not *right* 'for persons baptized in the Catholic church to be sold to peoples who are enemies of their faith'.[43] Here spiritual intransigence and material interest coincide.

In the Kongo and Angola the clergy openly participated in the system of slavery. The bishops and missionaries had slaves for their personal service and for their plantations. They patterned their daily lives after the Kongo notables, thus anticipating the forms of agricultural exploitation of Portuguese America: their missions foreshadowed the *casa grande* of colonial Brazil. In 1705 Father Laurent de Lucques described one of these, which was founded by the Jesuits on the banks of the Bengo some distance from Loanda. He observes that 'the fathers have a great deal of property'. He mentions the farming—vegetable gardens, fruit trees, fields of edible plants, tobacco, and sugar cane—and forms of breeding which testify to considerable activity. The sowing of souls and the colonization of lands were not dissociated. Slavery found here an additional stimulus, especially since elements undesirable 'because of misdemeanors or bad conduct' were taken from the plantations to be sold to the Negro slave traders.

The hunting down of men—justified in the name of economic necessity, sanctified, practiced one way or another by all the 'foreigners' and their native agents, was one factor in the destruction of the old Kongo. It perverted social relations. It stimulated the razzias carried out with the aid of the Yaka, the enemies of the kingdom. It wounded the population of the Kongo in its very substance. In a letter addressed to João III, king of Portugal, Afonso I noted these consequences and foretold the inevitable disaster:

We ask grace of Your Highness not to believe the evil said about us by those who have no concern but to sell what they have unjustly acquired, who, by their slave trade, are ruining our kingdom and the Christianity which has been established here for so many years and which cost your predecessors so many sacrifices. Catholic kings and princes like Your Highness are working to provide this great blessing of faith for new peoples. We are anxious to preserve it for those who have acquired it. But this is difficult to do here where European goods exert such a fascination over the simple and the ignorant that they leave God in order to obtain them. The remedy is the suppression of these goods which are a snare of the devil for sellers and buyers alike. The lure of profit and greed lead the people of the land to rob their compatriots, including members of their own families and of ours, without considering whether they are Christians or not. They capture them, sell them, barter them. This abuse is so great that we cannot correct it without striking hard and harder.[44]

The nobility of these remarks obviously was not enough to

change the course of events—nor was the suggestion, naïve or ironic, to put an end to the seduction exerted by the imported goods. The successors of Afonso I often complained of the violence and abuse caused by the Negro slave traffic. Certain priests, like Bishop Manuel Baptista in 1619, also tried to obtain the intervention of the 'protector' kings of the Kongo to curb the excesses. It was in vain; among other reasons, because the royal tax collected by these same Catholic sovereigns amounted to 8,000 reis per slave 'exported'.[45]

One cannot, without risk of misinterpretation, overlook the political significance of Kongo Christianity. It determined internal confrontations and competitions: the struggles for power pitted, at least symbolically, 'modernists', who accepted and utilized the new faith, against defenders of tradition. It engendered those syncretic religions which, at the beginning of the eighteenth century, sought to re-create the political unity of the torn kingdom: for example, the Antonian movement, conducted by the alleged 'ambassadors of Saint Anthony', which demanded the election of a single king and an end to conflict. Finally, in all times and with varying degrees of success, sovereigns of the Kongo tried to use Christianity as an instrument of unification and of reinforcement of the central power. In this dual purpose, they anticipated the decisive role that might be played by a great national religion; they would gladly have imitated the European kings who made the sacred serve absolutism.

The contradiction was total, however, between the idea of a Christianity that would be adapted and, in a sense, nationalized, and the establishment of a missionary Church which was under the authority of a foreign sovereign and contributed to a mercantile expansion. Political preoccupations counted as much as the desire to defend the integrity of Christianity. In fact, thanks to the right of *padroado* which was conferred on them, the kings of Portugal exercised a subtle domination over the Kongo; the vassality was not apparent, but obedience was required; and the missions performed some of the functions of a rudimentary colonial administration. The 'Assembly of the Council of Portugal', in March 1607, opened its recommendations to Philip III with this observation: 'Although he [the Kongo sovereign] is not directly vassal to Your Majesty, he is however subject to the royal patronage.'[46] The spiritual conquest justified and ensured a domination that was less and less disinterested. The kings of Portugal, moreover, defended their privilege with vigor: they opposed the establishment of direct relations between São Salvador and the Holy See. The kings of the Kongo strove to recover their autonomy by following a policy that was rigorously contrary and obstinate in spite of risks and repeated failures.

Their position of dependency can scarcely be questioned. The 'Assembly' of 1607 reveals this clearly: to a request for technical assistance—'a few masons and blacksmiths'—it advises a reply in the negative and suggests that this refusal be expressed by resorting to 'a good respectable method'. Its reasons: 'He [the king of the Kongo] should not be sent workmen; it is not proper that he have in his kingdom someone who knows how to work with stone and lime or with steel, because this would be an occasion for disobedience.'

The argument anticipates one that would be used later to prevent the establishment of industries in the modern colonies. The answer to another request reveals this same preoccupation with maintaining helplessness and inferiority. Alvaro II had hoped to welcome 'white men and their wives to live in [his] kingdom, and young girls, to marry and thus propagate the faith'. With arguments which were not racist but political in nature, the 'Assembly' asked Philip III to reject this claim: 'One ought not to grant this, for it would be prejudicial to the service of Your Majesty if this king had white subjects, because through them he would become so powerful that he would seek to free himself of obedience to Your Majesty.'

The statement leaves no room for doubt; in the absence of conquest, the service of the Christian faith provided justification for the domination of the African kingdom.

The political activity of Portuguese living in the Kongo frequently affected the careers of the kings, whether because the sovereigns found themselves involved in struggles between factions formed within the little 'colony', or because the latter recovered its unity in order to bring a puppet to power. Afonso I experienced this painfully during the last years of his reign. A 'misguided monk', Frei Alvaro, was fomenting rebellion while the slave traders were conspiring in the hope of creating 'a king loyal to them'. In 1539, Dom Afonso 'miraculously' escaped attempted murder. The massacre of the foreigners was in the air. Confidence had been destroyed: 'Mistrust reigned in the minds of the Negroes. They declared that from the Whites they had received many miseries and that if the king of Portugal were as Christian as he was said to be, he would have taken measures.'[47]

The marriage of Europe and Africa had failed. The insidious struggle continued without end. Diogo I opposed the bishop, the Jesuits who tried to have him removed, and the traders—and ended by throwing them all out of his capital. After his death in 1561, the political conspiracy already mentioned almost caused the ruin of the kingdom.[48]

From now on the die was cast. Step by step the decline merely grew out of these events. Beset by rival tribes, subjected to insidious encroachments after the colony of Angola was established, rivalled by ecclesiastical powers (who 'interfere in the affairs of the government of the kingdom'), menaced by ambitions and palace revolutions, caught in the whirlpool of colonial competition, the kings of the Kongo had less and less the ability and the strength to control the evolution of their kingdom. With the fall of Ambouila to the Portuguese troops and the decapitation of the defeated king, António I, a double failure was brought about: that of Christianization and modernism, and that of the dynasties that had shaped the Kongo. After that the royalty split up and a group of separate chronicles became the ironic substitute for history.

Part II

THE FORGING
OF THE KONGO

CHAPTER 4

The Forge and the Palm

The Kongo has built its civilization in the shade of the palm tree. The palm gives the landscape its distinctive appearance, inspires the ingenuity and industry of the villagers, and enriches human intercourse with its sap. In the order of botanical symbolism, this tree is *male* and, in a certain sense, *noble*, which indicates its importance. Pigafetta mentions three varieties of palm in the course of his 'account', and suggests the diversity of uses of this generous plant:

'There is another species of palm tree, analogous to the preceding ones, from which oil, wine, vinegar, fruits, and bread are derived. the oil is made from the pulp of the fruit; its colour and consistency are that of butter, although it is more greenish; it has the same uses as olive oil and butter; it may be burned; it may be used to anoint the body; it is excellent in cooking; it is extracted from the fruit, as oil is extracted from olives; it is preserved by cooking. The bread is made from the kernel of the fruit, which resembles an almond, although it is harder; in the inside there is a pith which is good to eat, healthful, and nourishing. All of this fruit is green, including the pulp, and may be eaten both raw and cooked. The wine is obtained by boring a hole in the top of the tree. A liquid oozes out which is exactly like milk; sweet the first few days, it becomes bitter and in time changes into vinegar, which is used for salad. But the wine is drunk fresh, and is such an effective diuretic that in this country nobody suffers from gravel or stones in the bladder. It intoxicates when drunk in excess; it is very nourishing.[1]

The chronicler's science is approximate, but his account of

the uses of the most important natural resource offered to the Mukongo is significant, if incomplete. A century later, in a description based on direct observation, Cavazzi mentions eight main species of palm tree; he, too, reports its myriad uses; he likens the fruit to the chestnut—'because of its color, shape, and flavor'—and presents it as constituting the ordinary diet, the food of the 'poor'.[2] Early eighteenth-century accounts, such as those of Father Laurent de Lucques, again allude to plantations of palm trees from which the natives 'derive their wine and . . . the oil that provides seasoning for their food'.

Until recently, Kongo ingenuity has contrived to make the most of the palm groves which have always constituted a valued patrimony. *Elaeis guineensis* is primarily used for food. It provides oil—the emulsion in which meat and fish are cooked—and the drink called *malafu ma nsamba*. *Raphia gentilii* furnishes the most esteemed of the palm wines, *malafu ma tombe*, the one needed for communication with the ancestors and solemn moments of collective life. *Raphia laurentii* also produces wine, as well as edible fruits and leaves which are used to cover habitations; above all it furnishes the fibers used in the weaving of cloth money and articles necessary in the making of garments. Thus, the gifts of the palm tree are found everywhere: in the walls and the roofs of houses, in game traps and fishermen's snares, in the public treasury, as well as in clothing, cosmetics, therapeutics, nourishment, and finally, in the system of symbols uniting man with his fellows and with his gods.

The ancient Bakongo were very early regarded as skilled plant growers, since they were able to exploit the fruits of the forest region and domesticate certain species. The collective palm grove attests to this talent, but it is not the only evidence. The *safu*, a fruit with a rosy pulp and a disturbing flavor, produced by *Pachylobus edulis* Don., has the honor of being mentioned in the work of the chronicler Cavazzi, who appreciated its 'very delicate aroma'. Pigafetta, at the end of his botanical inventory, adds, 'Another tree is called *ogheghe*; the fruit it produces resembles a yellow plum, it is excellent to eat and fragrant'; this species was also used to make live hedges or to construct 'a kind of arbor' which 'protects one from the heat'.[3] However, it is the cola, which popular science regards as a 'genus of African mallow' that has received the widest attention. The cola is a plant believed to promote the health of the body and the stimulation of the mind or the emotions. Pigafetta does not fail to mention it:

Another tree produces a fruit called *cola*, which is the size of a pine cone and inside which there are other fruits the shape of chestnuts which in turn contain four separate pulps of a rosy red color. You hold this fruit in your mouth, you chew or eat it to quench your thirst and to flavor water; it is good for the digestion and is particularly effective in diseases of the liver. Lopes* used to say that when a chicken liver or the liver of some other bird that was already spoiled was sprinkled with the juice of this fruit, it became fresh again and almost recovered its former condition. Everyone habitually uses this commodity in very great quantity; it is also a good food.[4]

In the documents compiled by Antonio Brasio, numerous letters and accounts allude to the predilection of the people of the Kongo and Angola for these cola nuts.

Various fruit-bearing trees—the guava, the lemon, and the orange—were introduced by the Portuguese. The Bakongo grew orchards of them in various regions. At the beginning of the seventeenth century, Pieter van den Broecke noted the 'abundance' of oranges and lemons in the villages along the estuary of the Congo. And French missionaries living in Kakongo around 1770 observed, 'There are also found here oranges, lemons, guavas, and other small fruits unknown in Europe'.[5] This arboriculture, which has continued to the present day, introduced a kind of link between the exploitation of non-cultivated plants and the farming which had to provide subsistence. One fact is certain: in Kongo country the gathering of wild foods has occupied an important place in the life of the villagers. Edible roots, tubers, leaves, and fruits are plentiful; in many places the vegetation is rich, and nature has even undertaken to spread and multiply certain imported plants, like the pineapple, 'which grows here without cultivation'. Knowledge of the environment—and of the possibilities for direct utilization

---

* Pigafetta's informant; see W. Bal's Introduction to the *Description* (Louvain, 1963), pp. xi–xx.

of its products—is very advanced. The women and children take part in the search for supplementary foods: the harvesting of mushrooms, of which some twenty species or varieties are commonly known, the collecting of wild greens which are used like spinach, the uprooting of wild yams, the picking of numerous fruits. In this way 'specialists' collect most of the products for medical and veterinary use,[6] as well as the plants necessary to the crafts. The forest constitutes a preserve where man, merely by furnishing the effort of acquisition, finds numerous elements which are indispensable to his everyday existence.

Agriculture

The Bakongo, and even more so their wives, were such skillful farmers that they brought about 'agricultural revolutions' which were less a matter of techniques than of species cultivated. Some of these, which were introduced by the Portuguese, caused a profound transformation of dietary habits: for example, the transition from the consumption of cereals to that of prepared manioc, which, together with the plantain banana, has become the basis of the ordinary diet.

Pigafetta reported that the plateau on which the capital, Mbanza Kongo, stood, was 'fertile and cultivated'. His observations in the late sixteenth century reveal the importance already acquired by the imported cereals:

Grains of various species are produced; the commonest and best is called *luco*. It resembles the mustard seed, although it is a bit thicker. It is ground with a hand mill. The result is a white flour which gives a white bread that is wholesome, agreeable to the taste, and in no way second to wheat bread, albeit only the latter is used to celebrate mass. Grains like these are found in abundance throughout the kingdom of the Congo where they have been growing for a short time. . . . There is also the white millet called *mazza di Kongo*, that is, "grain of the Congo", and corn, which is the least valued and is fed to pigs; rice has not much value either. Corn is called *mazza Manputo*, that is, "grain of Portugal", for Manputo is the name given to Portugal.[7]

Luko (or *luku*) designates *Eleusine coracana*, which is still raised today, especially in Angola, and was first introduced in the eastern regions in very ancient times. This cereal appears to have been one of the most widespread. The chronicles refer to it frequently both before and after Pigafetta: the *História do Reino do Congo* states that *luku* is the principal crop, and Cavazzi mentions it in his agricultural inventory.[8] The former importance of this crop is suggested by the fact that its old Kongo name is now used to refer to manioc meal and bread, that is, the new basic food. The word *masa* (plural of *di-sa* or *ri-sa*) seems to have referred generally to the plants with ears, graminaceous plants. Pigafetta mentions one by the name of 'grain of the Congo', and very probably he is speaking of a sorghum. Cavazzi refers to a second variety. But in both cases these were indigenous plants which formed a large part of the diet of the Kongo. As for corn — *masa ma Mputu*, grain of Portugal—it was imported from America to Europe at the beginning of the sixteenth century and later introduced to Central Africa by the Portuguese.

The *História do Reino do Congo* and Cavazzi indicate the comparative importance of the leguminous plants. In the first place there was *wandu*, a 'species of pea', according to Cuvelier: this was *Cajanus cajan* Druce, a shrub which lives three years and is cultivated for its seeds, which are consumed when half-grown. Cavazzi also mentions *nkasa*, 'a leguminous plant of high yield [whose seeds are] pink in color and resemble our kidney beans';[9] the name *nkasa* is still used to refer to beans, string beans, and various legumes.[10] In fact, the term is used for all the useful plants of the Kongo of the *dolichos* type.

Yams (*Dioscoreaceae*) were part of the everyday diet, no doubt more the wild species—products of gathering—than the cultivated species. The modern Bakongo, who were familiar with a dozen varieties, cultivated barely three, the most widespread being the 'winged yam' whose tubers were eaten boiled or baked. The banana is mentioned by Pigafetta only incidentally: 'Another fruit is the one called *banana*. We believe that this is the *musa* of Egypt and Syria, with the difference that in the Congo the banana plant attains the height of a tree; it is pruned every year to make it produce better.'[11] Cavazzi describes briefly two kinds of bananas: one very thick ('like a man's arm'), the other smaller.[12] At the time of the discovery, these were the only varieties of the type *Musa paradisiaca* L. that had been known since a very remote time, and they were commoner than the chroniclers indicate. These fruits have a mealy pulp and occur frequently in the diet. They have a coarse quality and their modern popular names—bread banana, pig banana, etc.—have banished the poetry of the scientific appellation, which recalls the legend connecting the banana tree with the tree of knowledge. To this plant too, the Bakongo attributed functions which are not only alimentary but also therapeutic and religious. With the Portuguese influence species diversified and the banana tree called *tiba* in Kikongo (*Musa sapientum* L.) multiplied.

This inventory of edible products resulting from cultivation and gathering is still incomplete: tubers, gourds, secondary legumes, condiments, and foreign plants like the peanut, from which an oil is derived, or sugar cane, whose use was limited, should be mentioned. The diversity of produce recognized during the sixteenth century by foreign observers cannot be denied. Indeed, the compiler of the *História do Reino do Congo* seems to perceive in this an amazing harmony with nature: 'They cultivate twelve species of edible plants, each of which ripens during a different month, so that fresh foodstuffs are available throughout the year.'[13]

The introduction of manioc—the *mahiaca* of seventeenth- and eighteenth-century writings—revolutionized the order of things. It was not simply a new addition, but an element that was gradually substituted for the old cereals. It was imported by the slave traders, at what date is not precisely known. None of the sixteenth-century texts mention it; but Bras Correa, writing around 1620, indicates that the Portuguese in the port of Mpinda had been cultivating manioc in the Brazilian manner for several years. According to a tradition of certain Nsaku clans, the ancestor who led the migrations from São Salvador at the time of the Yaka invasion carried away stalks of manioc intended for propagation.[14] If this is not purely a case of symbolically expressed history—a reminder of the foreignness of the plant or its association with the Kongo capital and the birth of a newly formed clan—*mahiaca* must have spread after 1570, and from centers of Portuguese colonization. In his description of the province of Soyo in the early eighteenth century, Father Laurent de Lucques extols the merits of manioc, whose 'root, when roasted over the fire, is very appetizing', and lists some of

94

its culinary uses. He states, moreover, that a flour obtained by grating and drying a root 'similar to the turnip' is produced 'in great quantity' in the region of the Bengo, near Loanda.[15] French missionaries living in the kingdom of Kakongo in the middle of the eighteenth century comment that manioc is 'the commonest food of these tribes'; they describe how it is prepared after being steeped for three or four days, and note that its market price is one *lubongo* (the unit of cloth currency) for a daily ration in times of abundance.[16] In actuality, the spread of manioc and its substitution for the former staple foods occurred at different times and in different proportions in different regions of the ancient kingdom. But so greatly did the Bakongo excel in the cultivation of manioc that eventually they contributed the exportation of new varieties to neighboring countries—to Gabon, for example, which received maniocs very significantly named *matadi* and *bakongo*.[17]

If it is possible to form a historical picture of agricultural production, it is much harder to find detailed accounts of the techniques and organization of farm labor. All the accounts agree in emphasizing the responsibility that lay with the Kongo women : 'They take charge of cultivating the land, sowing, and reaping, in order to obtain sufficient food for their husbands'; or, even more emphatically, 'only the women are concerned with working'. The *História do Reino do Congo* reports the same observation and adds unnecessarily, 'the men never work'. As for Cavazzi, he is disturbed when he contemplates 'the incredible sufferings of the women', who dropped with fatigue in the field, especially when they were pregnant or taking care of a very young child.[18] There are various indications, however, that the men did not devote themselves solely to military, artistic, or commercial tasks : as is still the case today, they at least took care of the preparation of the farmland by the felling of trees and the clearing of shrubs.[19] Extensive agriculture with fallow periods of variable duration was, as early as the ancient kingdom, the commonest form of agricultural exploitation. However, it was not the only one.

Certain remarks made by Laurent de Lucques in his discussion of the 'principality' of Soyo are of interest. He notes :

[The women] have the duty of preparing the food and working the land at specified times, and this is quickly done. At the first rains they go with their little hoes and loosen the top soil and plant their beans or other legumes on top of it. If the rain favors the crops, they are marvellously productive. The fields are not fertilized here; the rain alone suffices. After the women have planted, they do not return to the fields (except for the two annual weedings to prevent the plants from being choked) until harvest time. There are two harvests per year, one in January, the other in May. Afterward they again harvest the beans, which yield in great abundance, and the very copious dew is enough to make them continue to thrive and be fruitful.[20]

This brief description undoubtedly refers to the peculiarly Kongo technique of cultivation on hills or ridges, although no mention is made of the clearing and burning of stubble, a labor which is done even today in these kinds of fields. Speaking of the latter, a geographer has stressed the existence in Kongo country of 'humanized landscapes [which] form a real country-side'.[21] In the old villages, which were much more spread out than those of the modern era, small cultivated patches (of Indian peas, corn, etc.) were scattered among the habitations;[22] gardens, occasional fruit-bearing trees, and adjacent palm groves thus formed, in several regions, an original rural pattern.

Observations relating to the system of land ownership are few and inaccurate. They suggest that labor upon the land is equal to the right of ownership—'nobody can take it away from the man who first worked it'—and that family fields represent the limit of effective exploitation. They reveal the communal nature of the ownership of uncultivated lands, whether fallow fields, preserves, or hunting zones. Incidentally, there are indications concerning methods of magical protection against thieves : broken branches or 'superstitious wands', as a missionary expresses it.

Agricultural techniques combined the rite and the tool, and depended upon a system of practices, beliefs, and symbols whose ends were fertility and prosperity. In spite of his indignation against superstition, Laurent de Lucques provides valuable testimony on the rituals that accompanied sowing and were intended to bring about a fertilizing rainfall. I shall quote it in its entirety, in spite of its irritating value judgments :

I shall describe a practice that takes place every year in December. It is during this month that the people of these regions prepare to plant beans, millet, and other kinds of plants which we do not have in our countries. In December, then, custom requires that the count and countess [the chief of the province of Soyo and his wife] and the other principal dignitaries prepare a certain dish every day. On the Tuesday before Christmas week, they place this preparation in a vessel especially reserved for this purpose and used only for this. This vessel is held in very great esteem, more so than treasures or relics. The aforementioned dish consists of mushrooms and other ingredients which even pigs would refuse to eat. When this conglomeration is ready, the count sits on a leather seat placed on a mat. All those present sit in a circle on the bare ground. When they have taken their places, the ceremony begins. The countess comes forward accompanied by two of the eldest matrons and two of the principal dignitaries. They empty their vessels into the count's. Next they invoke the devil. They say that they believe in him, and that they are offering him these things as a sacrifice so that he will grant them rain and an abundant harvest, etc. After this, they all go one at a time and receive a portion of this food from the hands of the count. After eating this manna of the devil, they begin to shout and leap in front of the count. When this diabolical ceremony is over, they return to their huts content.

The following Tuesday another ceremony takes place. This day of the week is the count's day, for he never performs any public function except on Tuesday. Others also have specified days for their diabolical practices. On Monday evening, drums and other instruments are played to announce that the usual ceremony will take place the next day. On Tuesday morning, another signal from the instruments summons the people. When all have assembled, the count reclines in a hammock which is carried by several of the principal men. Other notables walk before, one carrying the parasol, another the seat, another the mat, etc. They repair to a field where other invocations and ceremonies take place. You would think the devil and all his crew had been raised, as much by the uncouthness and the dingy color of this mob as by the confusion of voices, instruments, and gestures. When he has arrived, the count sits down and receives the customary homage of his subjects. They kneel before him and clap their hands together, etc. All have their knives, which resemble the one with which Saint Peter cut off Malchus' ear, for they are crudely made. The count has his knife too. At a certain moment he rises from his seat, and when he and all the people begin to move it looks again as if all hell has broken loose because of the shouting multitude. The count makes his way toward a tree, where he says a few words accompanied by various gestures. He strikes the tree with his knife, which he then throws into the field. The man who can take it and offer it to the prince is considered fortunate. He will have earned permission to drink one more time than the others, which he regards as a very great favor. After this, every man comes and strikes this tree with his knife. Then all, uttering cries, accompany the prince to his abode.

On another Tuesday, everyone returns to work this field, which they call in their language Uri. They say and believe that in this field there is a devil in the form of a snake whom they call Uri, and it is for this reason that they give the field the same name. In the middle of this field they leave a thicket to provide shelter for the snake whom they falsely suppose to be there. They never cultivate this spot. When they have cultivated the field, all go and stand around the thicket. They speak to the snake and say, 'Uri, Uri, we have offered you sacrifices, we have honored you by our ceremonies; be good enough, therefore, to grant us much rain and abundance in all things'. Having offered this prayer full of diabolical faith, they utter cries as they accompany the count to his home. Here they all joyously drink their *malafo* [*malafu*—palm wine] and then return to their huts. Until these superstitions are performed, they cannot cultivate; now all go or send members of their families to the fields or clearings.[23]

This passage is accurate, and it can be useful if one ignores the comments denouncing the 'diabolical practices'. Two separate rituals with a single meaning—the opening of the farming season and the search for good harvests—are described here. These rituals show the central position of the chief, who was sometimes specially designated for these sacred functions and referred to as 'chief of the land' by the early authors,[24] with

98

respect to the clanic territory and the ancestors who own it, and to the forces that determine fertility. The first ceremony units the chief, his feminine counterpart, the 'eldresses' who represent the women and the heads of lineages, and the 'notables' symbolizing the clans and lineages in question. By a communal and sacrificial feast, communication with the ancestors is established. This communication provides the representatives with a reinforcement which is necessary to all those members of the lineages whom they represent. This is a technique which is found in other circumstances, notably in the context of the initiation rites of the Kongo.

The second group of ceremonies has to do with the farming of a sacred field; in return for cultivating on behalf of the invisible powers, the men expect the generosity of nature to be provoked and certain abundance to follow. The interesting element is the observation of the worship of a snake, which is quite certainly the python. In a large part of the Bantu world, as far as Gabon, this creature seems to have been associated with the rainbow, which in turn is a symbol of glory and power, a means of communication between the earth and the gods, and an emblem of life-giving moisture and femininity. The python and the rainbow have together occupied a central position in those traditions concerned with agricultural abundance and fertility. The Kongo ritual described by Laurent de Lucques reveals one form of this symbolism of fecundity and creative power. In its own way it expresses an old dream: the dream of seeing fields labored by men as rich with fruits as the gardens of the gods.

The Bakongo regard nature as a source of vital products whose acquisition requires knowledge, skill, and the consent of the generative or guardian 'forces'. Indeed, the ordeals of the initiatory schools in which young people arrive at maturity require training in the gathering of wild plants and those small bush animals used in the preparation of certain dishes. The savannah rat, the lizard, the snake, the caterpillar, the palm worm, and various insects appear in the diet. Cavazzi observes this and notes that they are consumed when craving for meat is prolonged.[25] This is only small game. The pursuit of big game, which provides the foundation of the meat diet, requires greater skill and ritual precautions—for it involves death by strategy. Pigafetta has described the hunting of elephants with traps:

99

To capture the elephants, you dig very deep ditches in the places where they are accustomed to graze. These ditches are narrow at the bottom and widen at the top, so that there is no way for the beasts who have fallen into them to escape. So the elephants will not notice the trap the ditches are covered with earth, grass, and leaves: when the animal walks over them he falls into the hole.[26]

The chronicler also mentions a technique of direct attack whose purpose was to cut off the animal's tail, 'the hairs [of which] are sought after'. Actually, the description evokes a method of hunting which was very audacious and is still practised in the Congolese region: the hunter in ambush, after smearing himself with elephant's urine or excrement, leaps upon the animal and cuts off his trunk or hamstrings him. The meat, as much as the tusks (which were valued 'only after the Portuguese began to engage in trade') or the hairs ('a single one of which could be exchanged for two or three slaves'),[27] was a motive of this rash undertaking. Pigafetta also alludes to the hunting of dangerous wild animals ('tigers') by poisoning and the setting of traps 'with a kid as bait', and the hunting of buffalo, antelope, and wart hogs; in this connection he calls attention to the use of the bow, the 'pike' (assagai), and the arquebus.

Pieter van den Broecke, during his travels in Soyo in the early seventeenth century, commented on the abundance of game, especially 'large and small antelope' and 'wild boar'. But again it is Laurent de Lucques who offers the most significant ethnographic observations. He explains the meaning of the prohibitions affecting certain categories of animals, although he fails to remark that these categories were associated with specific social groups of which they were the emblems. He notes:

There are in these regions large numbers of roe [antelope]. They [the villagers] say that they are sent by the devil to provide food for their fetishers; for if anyone else ate of them, he would become leprous. There are others, however, who have more judgment and who, ignoring such foolishness, catch and eat them if they can.[28]

This remarkable chronicler, despite his obsession with superstition, recognized the social importance of the hunt, which was associated with power (the *mani* or chiefs) in the ancient Kongo, as well as its religious implications. Once again I must quote him at length:

Among the numerous *mani* there are some who have their [own] hunters of elephants, leopards, and other animals. Before sending them to the hunt, they summon them. The hunter kneels and holds out his hands. The *mani* rubs them vigorously and hits them many times, meanwhile promising him a good hunt. The hunter leaves full of hope, but not contenting himself with this, he goes to see a fetisher, from whom he receives a bundle of straws which he will scatter on all the paths in the forest so that neither man nor beast can harm him. The fetisher also gives him some pouches containing hairs from an elephant's tail. The hunter always keeps this hanging around his neck so the elephants cannot harm him and so he will be strong enough to kill them. Thus armed with superstitious objects, he leaves, full of faith and with the sure hope of having a good hunt. But very often these hunters are killed by wild beasts. Although they are obviously aware of this, in spite of everything they retain their conviction and remain in the hands of the devil.[29]

Thus there are two kinds of procedures which still obtain in several regions of Kongo country. The *mani*, in rapport with the clanic territory and the ancestors—those masters of pacifying and fecundating forces—must provide the ritual protection of the hunter and of the clan. He protects the others from the dangers of an unregulated violence, an unleashing of death which would strike men after harming the animals of the bush. Even today the hunt involves the risk of sterility and collective misfortune, according to Kongo beliefs. Moreover, the hunter ensures his own security and seeks the success of his undertakings by means of personal rituals and a specific magic. He has his private altars; Father de Lucques has described one of these: 'I passed the house of a hunter. I saw a very large elephant skull and other bones of savage animals together with a number of superstitious and diabolical objects over the door of his hut. The hunters use these in the hope of having a good hunt.'[30]

And elsewhere the missionary again expresses his indignation upon discovering the cross among the instruments intended to secure protection and reinforcement:

In one place there was a pile of horns of wild animals surrounded by branches. In the middle, the holy cross had been planted. . . . I found a similar superstition in the country of Bamba. This one I destroyed. I broke the cross and burned the pieces. The use of horns in fetishist assemblages is a hunter's superstition. The devil leads them to believe that this is the way to kill many wild beasts. But it often happens that the wild beasts themselves (by divine permission) make a cruel slaughter of the hunters.'[31]

These observations, though accurate, give an incomplete picture of techniques used—weapons, various traps, nets, bird-lime —and of preparatory practices like abstinence from sexual relations or suppression of all social relations before departure for hunting expeditions. Nor do they provide any information on either the organization of these expeditions or the rules of distribution of the take. Among the Bakongo the hunter no longer occupies the eminent position—justified in terms of a mythical lore which elevates him to the level of the civilizing hero— which he enjoys in other Central African civilizations.* And generally speaking, the chroniclers have neglected him in their 'descriptions'.

Bras Correa, confessor to the king of the Kongo in the early seventeenth century and presumed author of a history of the kingdom, attempted to make a general inventory. So complete did he wish it to be that he carefully listed all oceanic and freshwater fish then known to the Bakongo, thus suggesting the importance of fishing. Pigafetta refers to places abounding in fish—the lagoon of Loanda and the mouth of the Zaïre, for example—and after mentioning the royal privileges attached to various fish, adds, 'People also fish the river for other species . . . whose names we judge it unnecessary to give here.' Like certain meats—elephant and buffalo meat, for example—the flesh of

* Although the distinction certainly is not strict, as a proverb quoted by Cuvelier indicates: 'Of the Kongo of the hunter the most powerful takes possession.'

large fish was smoked and sold in the markets. Here again, the accounts neglect to accurately describe fishing techniques (those used at night to dazzle the fish and those resorting to poison appear to have been very ancient) and equipment (nets, snares, harpoons, etc.), no doubt because such activities were the privilege of specialized groups. The prohibitions, obligations, and rituals involved in fishing have more strongly aroused the curiosity of the chroniclers.

Pigafetta has stressed the unusual characteristics of the manatee — the *Trichechus senegalensis* Desmaret described by Georges de Buffon, the French naturalist—and its position as royal animal, sought after for its flesh and its fat:

In this river there live various animals: ... [one species] has two handlike organs and a tail in the shape of a shield and is called *ambize angulo*, or 'pig fish', because it is fatty like the pig and because its flesh is excellent. The fat is rendered and preserved. Although it is a fish, this animal does not taste like one. It never leaves fresh water, feeds on the grass of the banks, and has a snout like an ox. This fish may weigh five hundred pounds. The fishermen go after it in their boats. They watch the places where it feeds, and spear it with harpoons or forks, then they drag it out of the water, cut it up, and take it to the king, for otherwise they would be put to death. ... Certain other fish, called royal fish, must also be taken to the king; any fisherman who did not observe this rule would be severely punished.[32]

One fact is clear: power exerts its influence over the products of fishing, and some of these products are reserved for the exclusive use of the sovereign and notables. This is not a simple aristocratic privilege. Once again Laurent de Lucques provides a key to the explanation when he describes the election and enthronement of the 'count' of Soyo. During one stage of the ceremony, 'the' fisherman and 'the' blacksmith appear symbolically:

On the night following his election, he [the count] sends for a fishing net and an axe. These instruments are always carefully kept. The fisherman who has charge of the net and the carpenter [?] who has charge of the axe are nobles to the count. ... When the net and the axe have arrived, the men enter a house under construction where together they destroy the net with the axe inside the house. Afterward they leap and dance until, exhausted, they accompany the count to the palace, full of hope and certainty that this ceremony will ensure them long life and good fortune in everything. The fisherman takes his net, convinced that the catch will be abundant, and the carpenter [?] his axe, with like conviction that he will make a large profit and enjoy the strength necessary for work.[33]

This part of the ritual suggests one of those myriad rites relating to fertility, reinforcement, or material wealth. Our evidence remains meager and largely inaccurate if we limit ourselves to this reference. We must also go to that body of beliefs and symbols having to do with water and aquatic life. The spirits were associated with water—according to a statement reported by Joseph van Wing, 'they are men of the water as we are men of the land'[34]—and some of them were precisely localized around springs, pools, and rivers. They controlled nature in flux, whereas the ancestors (bakulu) were masters of the earth, of that ordered nature whose cycles and regularities are known to men. They manipulated countless and dangerous forces; magic tried to recover these forces, power sought ways to capture, domesticate, or neutralize them. From another standpoint, water symbolically represented the time of genesis, of beginning, birth, and rebirth; it identified with the life that comes and goes; it evoked femininity and renewal. This can be clearly understood in connection with a Kongo initiation rite in which a ritual fishing for sheatfish (bangola) followed the 'resurrection' of the initiates.[35]

A context of this kind illuminates the rituals required by the accession of a new chief. The beginning of each new reign referred back to the origins, to the first moments of the world and of the order created by man; it was the occasion for a symbolic reconstruction, a reinforcement. This gives meaning to the extracts from de Lucques's accounts. During the ceremonies accompanying 'the election of the count' (of Soyo), the symbolism of water and fishing operated several times:

A few days after his election, the count [participates] in a fishing expedition which takes place near the mouth of the river

Zaïre. . . . Here there is a great quantity of fish of different species, some of considerable size. I myself have seen them, especially one which the Portuguese call *Peixe mulher,* or woman fish. It has a very good taste, and might be mistaken for veal. . . .

This fish is broader than a man and the same height. It has no feet, but it does have arms. Its eyes are so small that one can barely distinguish them. It has no ears, only two openings so small that you could put into them nothing thicker than a stout needle. It has teeth like us and its mouth is similar to a man's. When you try to catch it, it defends itself very well with its arms. . . . This fish ordinarily lives at the bottom of the river, where it searches for its food in the mire. For this reason when you want to catch it, you explore the bottom of the water. When you see it, you throw at it a shaft tipped with steel like an arrow, the other end of which is attached to a very long cord. If it is hit, you release this cord while it struggles; but soon the great loss of blood immobilizes it. Then you pull it onto the ground and take it to the prince with songs and shouts of joy. . . . This fish is always reserved for the count because it is flavorful, rare, and difficult to capture. . . .

In this place . . . the new count will take possession of the power. . . . All the men go fishing together. From the beginning they reveal their wicked superstition, for the first fish they catch is immediately sent to the countess, who must prepare it with her own hands; if she entrusted its preparation to someone else, they would not eat it, for if they did, they believe they would all die before the end of the year. . . . When they reach their village, they eat the fish cooked by the countess, after which they abandon themselves to their customary leaping and rejoicing. After these ceremonies they look forward to a great abundance of fish and the enjoyment of all prosperity.[36]

Fishing for manatee and the ritual consumption of the first fish caught are related to those solemn acts which accompany the taking of power. They suggest the chief's position at the conjunction of the natural order and the social order, at the point of convergence of those forces which give life to the creation. They also attest to a civilization in which the need for fertility, fecundity, and prosperity occupies a central position. Beyond this is perceived a mode of thinking which regards every human activity under the twin aspect of the practical and the symbolic, of utility and ritual. Thus, fishing is part of the Kongo system of symbols as well as one of a group of techniques of acquisition learned from a very distant cultural heritage.

This double function, which eludes ordinary utilitarian conceptions, is also observed in the case of breeding. Before presenting it, we must examine the traditional context of this activity, for the evidence often appears exaggerated. First Pigafetta: 'There are many herds of domestic cows and oxen, domestic pigs and wild boars, flocks of sheep and goats . . . The pasturages are so rich . . . that the mothers can nurse all their young. . . .'[37] A description dated November 1595 similarly declares: 'They [the people of the Congo] possess a countless multitude of sheep, oxen, and other domestic animals of this kind, not to mention birds of different species.'[38] The História do Reino do Congo, a compilation of the same period, offers a more modest inventory: 'The Negroes have a few domestic animals (pigs, goats, sheep, chickens). They plant legumes beside their huts. This is all their wealth.'[39] The uncertainty persists into the seventeenth century. Pieter van den Broecke, writing between 1608 and 1612, suggests considerable cattle-breeding activty: 'We saw in particular a great many oxen, cows, sheep, and goats who, in large flocks of one hundred, were led to pasture by shepherds. . . . These sheep have short hair and long manes like the horses in our country.'[40]

But Cavazzi, whose chronicles were published in 1687, specified that most flocks rarely had more than twenty head, and often of smaller livestock. In the eighteenth century Father de Lucques confined himself to a mere mention on this subject: 'These animals [pigs, oxen, sheep, chickens] are found in these regions.' And the French missionaries of Kakongo were amazed at the slight extent of breeding: 'They breed few domestic animals. There is only a small number of goats, sheep, pigs, ducks, chickens, etc.'[41]

The quotations and uncertainties could be multiplied. They reveal excesses of judgment, and above all, local differences. Cattle were encountered only in limited regions, notably in the district of Pombo, according to Cuvelier, in Soyo, and in small numbers outside the capital. This breeding seems to have regressed, possibly in proportion to the decline of power, for only the king and the chiefs had the right to possess cows. The latter were used to indicate social status and express a hierarchy of prestige, rather than to satisfy economic ends. Cavazzi noted this fact in his own way when he observed that the number of heads owned and the composition of the flocks (only 'sons of the king' or 'governors of provinces' possessed several 'kinds' of domestic animals) revealed certain social discriminations. The addition of meat or fish to the daily diet had the same distinctive meaning: 'Persons of high rank sometimes supplemented their *infundi* [boiled cereal] and beans with a bit of fish, chicken, pork or beef, or lamb.'[42] The symbolic functions of the flock were not restricted to the indication of hierarchies or the display of the prestige and wealth of the aristocrats—the 'principals' in the language of the old accounts. Cattle were part of the matrimonial compensation given in exchange for a wife. They were used in the service of the sacred; domestic animals were immolated during sacrifices. A few, like the he-goat, were central to specialized cults: in Soyo, the people worshipped 'goats with very long beards which are the object of superstition and idolatry'.[43]

Techniques

For the Bakongo people the order of nature and the order of civilization were closely interwoven; but this intimate association did not exclude the desire to make natural resources available to men by transforming them, by turning them over to the artisan. The Promethean intention was not absent and possessors of material techniques were honored, a fact which provoked the amazement of Father de Lucques: 'All . . . artisans are always persons regarded differently than they are in our part of the world.'

The highest position was occupied by the profession of ironwork. The myths presented the founder of the Kongo in the guise of a blacksmith king, and 'the art of the blacksmith is carried on by the nobility'.[44] Iron metallurgy must have spread through the region starting with Eastern Africa, around the fourteenth century,[45] or at about the time the kingdom was forming; which implies a relationship between the two processes and explains the skill attributed to the semi-mythical sovereign who was the creator of the Kongo. Political vigor and comparative material strength seem, therefore, to have been closely related. The people of the Kongo are not unaware of this, as Robert Wannyn recalls in his book on the ancient art of metal in the region of the Kongo:

Ironwork has always been honored among the Bakongo. . . . Historians are inclined to believe that this is a myth, and yet the answers to our hundreds of interrogations agree: the first *ntotila* (king) was an 'ironmaster', if not a blacksmith.

The most authoritative dignitaries agree in admitting that ironwork was never the exclusive prerogative of the king or some other dignitary. All free men of the clan could engage in it, provided they fulfilled certain initiatory conditions. But the same notables readily emphasize the great interest the king has shown, from heroic times, in the numerous blacksmiths' shops located on the hills adjacent to the capital. These workshops produced the weapons necessary, first, to the defence of the country, and next, to its territorial expansion. They also produced those domestic implements, particularly axes and hoes, which permitted what was in those days a more rational exploitation of the land and the forests. . . . The Bakongo claim that it is to the art of ironwork that they owe their early greatness and prosperity before the arrival of the Europeans.[46]

Ore in the form of ferruginous rock abounds on the surface in several parts of the Kongo, and has been the object of a very widespread industry, as is evidenced by the scoriae resulting from the old founderies. These were more numerous in the vicinity of the capital and, according to Cuvelier, in the privileged province of Nsundi. The early descriptions, however, tell us very little about this metallurgy. Pigafetta alludes to copper mines, the bartering of iron, and transactions involving metals, particularly silver. Of the region situated to the north of Mbanza Kongo, he writes simply: 'It is a heavily populated territory with many mountains which produce various metals.' He emphasizes the position occupied by ironwork in the province of Nsundi: 'It is above all iron that is sought after by the inhabitants, for from it they make knives, weapons, axes, and other instruments of this kind which are necessary and useful to man.'[47] Cavazzi is more precise, and the information he gives has unquestionable ethnographic value. He briefly describes smelting from iron rock, and an engraving shows that the blacksmith's craft was then very similar, with respect to techniques and tools, to what was reported by nineteenth-century observers like Dom Antonio Barroso.[48]

In Loango the metal was quarried by a primitive method : alternate layers of ore and charcoal filled a vast hole dug in the ground; all around, large bellows controlled the intake of air. In Nsundi country, better made ovens seem to have been used to treat laterite.[49] But the most detailed documentation concerns the blacksmith and the making of iron; there is very little information regarding the process of smelting. Here again, Laurent de Lucques provides some useful observations :

There are blacksmiths who work the iron in a very curious way, both in the method and in the instruments they employ. They light a fire on the ground and sitting nearby, they practice their art with tranquillity. The instruments they use amaze us. They have neither hammer nor anvil, nor other instruments which we use. In place of a hammer they use a large piece of iron stout enough to fill the hand, and whose shape resembles that of a nail. The anvil is a piece of iron weighing about ten pounds which is placed on the ground like a log. On this they do their forging. The bellows is made of hollow logs over which a hide has been stretched. They raise and lower this hide by hand, and in this way blow air on the fire; this serves them very well and without difficulty. With these three instruments they make everything.

These blacksmiths also have their special skills. With their bellows they blow into people's faces. If someone is suffering from a disease, he goes to the blacksmith, gives him some payment, and has his face blown on three times by the bellows. When you ask them why they do this, they reply that the air that comes out of the bellows drives the evil out of the body and preserves their health for a long time. Despite experience to the contrary, they remain immersed in their errors. These blacksmiths are ordinarily fidalghi [fidalgos], that is, nobles.[50]

The equipment of the forge—the hammer, whose manufacture required presentation of offerings to the ancestors and mobilization of specialized spirits, the anvil, and the wooden bellows with its membrane of hide and clay pipes—is commonplace. The exalted status accorded to specialists in the art of metals is much less so. The sovereign owned the mines and was regarded as the first of the 'masters of the forge', according to the accurate statement quoted above. Notables of high rank who qualified as blacksmiths intervened ritually on various occasions in the lives of the chiefs responsible for governing the provinces. Thus, in Soyo, at the time of an election or construction of the house of the 'count': 'The *mani* Masongo, who is a blacksmith, walks all around the site of the house, manipulating his bellows. He also sprinkles the water that is used to cool the iron, so no harmful thing may approach this place and so the count and countess may remain in good health.'[51]

The blacksmith, master of iron, fire and water and maker of arms and tools, possessed a power which ranked him with the chiefs (and he sometimes was one), as well as with the priests and magicians (as is suggested by his title of *nganga lufu*). He was subject to numerous prohibitions; he had special spiritual 'protectors' at his disposal; he was capable of warding off insidious dangers just as the weapons produced by his industry kept off the enemy. His magic, which was necessary to all and especially to the guardians of political power, was beneficent. The usual term which designates him — *ngangula* — is derived from *ngangu*, which has several meanings (intelligence, talent, skill), and both terms seem related to the word *nganga*, which was applied to the priest and the magician and signifies, etymologically, he who has the ability to make.

Three tools were said to be of ancient fabrication. According to the traditions of several clans, the knife was the first object forged: 'at the time of the first *ntotila*, at the time of the creation of the world', some authorities even claim.[52] After knives in the shape of three-sided rectangles, 'the royal blacksmiths must have produced axes of the African type, with the wrong end of the cutting edge fitted into a wooden handle with an eye'; next, *nzundu* are said to have been made, 'little pestles of solid iron' which were used to pound the heated ore and shape the metal.[53] These are three very highly valued instruments which evoked a mythical and legendary context. They were associated with the period of origins: separation of the first human (knife), birth of a political power (ceremonial axe), beginning of the manual techniques and arts (hammer and anvil), and they remain objects of veneration and symbols of tradition in several Kongo communities. As for the other tools in common use, they raise a question of 'nationality': the hoe does not appear to be indigenous, and the machete must have been introduced during the last four centuries. The same is true of the weapons employed by a people whose military qualities are nevertheless undeniable; the lances tipped with iron, copper, or brass seem to have been produced from borrowed models,[54] and the first swords, which were designed primarily to indicate the rank of chiefs and to appear in rituals glorifying the political power, were imported from Europe, as Dapper does not fail to recall.

The double bell (ngonge), known not only in the Kongo but in many other regions of Africa, had been produced locally before the fifteenth century. It had the general shape of a horseshoe; its two brims were flattened and it had no clapper: its two elements were struck alternately with a hardwood stick, producing two rather distinct sounds. The ngonge were ranked among the badges of chieftainry. They were used 'to announce the news of investiture, as well as to accompany the chief as he made his way solemnly to the court of justice'; they were used 'to summon to duty, council, or official gatherings, and to communicate decisions of the higher authority'; they appeared at every important moment of public life, to announce a death, to provide rhythm for the dancing required by funerary etiquette, and to announce the opening and closing of the markets.[55] The double bell attested to the constant presence of power, the ubiquitousness of the ancestors who were the founders of an order of which the chief was the protector and interpreter. Indeed, one of the archaic emblems of royalty shown by Dapper in one of the fine engravings illustrating his Description de l'Afrique is a group of three iron bracelets, called nlunga, which figuratively signifies union, symbol of alliance; it suggests the system of relations and alliances of which the sovereign or the chief was the center.

The Bakongo knew how to forge copper and, no doubt, how to melt lead. Wannyn rightly emphasizes the position accorded to the first of these metals: 'Copper is to be found throughout the Bas-Congo, as it is customarily called. It is from the Nkanda

Mountains, located on the road to Maquela do Zombo, or from the vicinity of Bembé, that the raw material from which crucifixes and rings are made is derived.'[56]

The 'christs' — klistu (from Christus) or nkangi (more frequently used) — imitated, with various degrees of freedom of interpretation, the objects introduced by the missionaries. They were cast by the lost-wax process or by the process known as 'open at the top', with reserves formed on the reverse. They had many uses, but seem mainly to have been symbols of judiciary authority. As for the rings and bracelets, which increased from the seventeenth century on, they served at once as ornaments, clanic treasures, and marks of social importance.

[Women of rank] wore the greatest possible number on their forearms and ankles, with one at the neck which gave them a haughty bearing. . . . All travellers from ancient times have been impressed by these heavy ornaments, and they never fail to speak of them in their accounts. It has been estimated that a single woman might carry a dozen kilograms of copper on her person. But in the past the Bakongo regarded the non-ferrous metals—copper, lead, and tin—as very precious substances. One wonders whether the bracelets did not actually represent the wealth of the clan chief rather than mere ornaments indicative of rank.[57]

The lighter arm bands—they were less than five millimeters thick—constituted the distinctive symbol of masculine dignity. They were called ma-dyenge a mfumu, the chief's bracelets. They were decorated with chased geometrical motifs which were male symbols, especially the centered circle or solar disc which was found on ceremonial arms and certain male garments.

All these pieces of the slave-bracelet type testify to the knowledge of elaborate techniques. A number of them must have been cast by the lost-wax process or in a two-part mold. Others, like the masculine arm bands, seem to have been cut out of a flat piece forged by hand and curved and polished on both sides.[58] The decorative themes that they received after being shaped were engraved with an awl. There is no doubting, as these examples and the ironwork attest, the existence of an expert metallurgic art in the ancient Kongo; only the competition of objects from abroad and the slow cultural deterioration brought about its decline. A further proof is provided by recent ethnographic documents. The Bakongo were aware of the toxicity of lead vapors. They devised preventive and curative methods, both pharmacological (massive doses of pawpaw and palm oil) and mechanical (exerting of pressure to free the digestive tract), for combatting lead poisoning.[59] Technology and rational knowledge tried to keep in step.

Metals ranked first, but the artisans worked with the most varied materials. Earth, in the form of clay, belonged to the domain of the potters. These women worked either by placing one on top of the other rings of clay which were carefully joined and polished, or by hollowing out a lump of clay with their fingers. Immersion in water in which bark had been steeped or a hasty daubing gave the pieces their dark tone or their patina. Potsherds found in the excavations do not indicate inventive workmanship, although these are objects widely and commonly used: household receptacles, for the most part—salt strainers, perhaps, and vessels for the treating of brine, 'banks' in which shell money was kept. From the fifteenth to the nineteenth century the soft stone permitted the appearance and development of a statuary of great artistic value which took the form of numerous *mintadi*, figurines which served as familiar or collective 'guardians'. Wood, in the hands of sculptors, was used to make various figurines of ritual, magical, or protective use; it was also used to make the drums—'large and small, which were played at celebrations, in time of war, and on other occasions'[60] —which were associated with political power, as they were in certain ancient royalties of eastern Africa, and rudimentary furniture or domestic articles—trays, saucers, and the like—for aristocratic houses. Finally, quickly cured hides were widely used, from those symbolizing the king and the chiefs (leopard skins for their seats, skins for the royal drums) and those indicating persons of exalted rank (civet, otter, wildcat), to the leather used for shields.

But it was by their excellence as basketmakers and their considerable talent in clothmaking that the Bakongo first attracted the attention of the chroniclers to their arts and crafts. The wicker articles were made of vines that had been split; generally speaking, they consisted of baskets designed for the carrying or storing of certain products, and in some regions, fishing implements (special baskets and nets). Like weaving, this activity seems to have been primarily masculine; the French missionaries of Kakongo numbered among the artisans those who 'make baskets' and those who 'make the local cloth'.[61] In the daily life of the Kongo mats were widely used; when they were dyed they served to decorate 'noble' houses, to which they lent 'a fine appearance'; above all they were universally used as beds, their number depending on the social status of the owner.

The art of weaving here did not rely on the classic raw materials such as cotton, wool, or silk, but on vegetable fibers obtained primarily from the raffia palm. In his description of the eastern provinces and frontiers of the Kongo, Pigafetta devotes a long passage to this industry, which successfully combined technical skill with aesthetic requirements:

I must describe the extraordinary art with which the inhabitants of this country and the neighboring regions weave various types of fabric, such as velvets with and without nap, brocades, satins, taffetas, damasks, sarsenets, and other similar fabrics, which are not, to be sure, made of silk, since the silkworm is unknown; if certain persons are dressed in silk, it is silk imported from Europe. But the fabrics which have just been named are derived from the palm leaf. The trees must be kept low, and to this end they must be pruned every year so that tenderer leaves will grow next season.

After treating these leaves in their fashion, they extract from them threads which are all equally fine and delicate; the longer the thread, the more it is valued, for it may be used to weave larger pieces of cloth. By using different methods, they make velvetlike fabrics with nap on both sides and those cloths known as damasks with decorative motifs and varied textures, as well as those brocades which are referred to as high or low, and are finer than our brocade. Only the king and those on whom he decides to confer this favor may wear this fabric. The largest pieces are of brocade, and attain four or five handbreadths in length, and three or four in width. Brocade is called *incorimbas* from the name of the region where it is made, which is in the vicinity of the river Vumba. The velvets are the same width; they are called *enzacas*, the damasks are called *infulas*, the satins *maricas*, the taffetas *tangas*, and the sarsenets *engombos*. . . . It is these fabrics that the people ordinarily wear, each according to his means. Besides, they are light and withstand water very well.[62]

The textile art is described and praised in a number of ancient texts: Cavazzi discusses it and alludes to the technique of weaving which utilizes a somewhat primitive vertical loom;[63] various documents in Father Antonio Brasio's *Monumenta* mention the fabrics of the Kongo. And Father Laurent de Lucques, while usually very critical in his evaluation of Kongo culture, does not conceal his astonishment at this activity which was still flourishing in the early eighteenth century. He notes in his sixth *Relation*:

[The prince of Soyo] made us a gift of some fabrics of these regions which are made of the leaves of trees and of which his own clothing is made. No one else can wear them without his permission. These fabrics are called *libonghi* [*lubongo* or *mbongo* in the plural]. There are different kinds. They are truly beautiful and curiously wrought. Some of them closely resemble velvet, others are so richly adorned with various decorations and arabesques that it is a wonder that anyone working with leaves from the palm and other trees could make such fine and beautiful fabrics, which are every bit as good as silk. In these regions cloth is used for money.'[64]

These beautiful and noble fabrics were made with fibers obtained from *Raphia textilis* Welw., a palm tree which seems to have been the object of very careful cultivation according to observations recorded by Pigafetta. Other botanical species were used in the manufacture of ordinary cloths: *Adansonia digitata* L. and *Ficus psilopoga* Welw., a tree called *nsanda* in Kikongo language; these trees furnished a tough fiber which was also used, after beating and retting of the bark, to make cords, nets, and sacks. This, then, was a case of a more archaic technique— the unrolling and beating of 'the outside bark, which contained a kind of fiber'—which the chroniclers Pigafetta and Cavazzi have identified accurately. In the ancient Kongo society with its rigorous and clear-cut hierarchies, the order of men and the order of things were intertwined: the palm tree and weaving were associated in a sense with royal privileges and with the aristocratic condition.

The fabrics woven were differentiated according to their origin and workmanship, but also according to their dimensions, their quality, their use, and their exchange value when they were regarded as money. The vocabulary of textiles included numerous expressions, all subject to precise usage: the *nkorimba*, which resembled brocade, came from the province of Mbamba; the *ma-dikula* were dyed shades of red; the *ntanga* were large pieces which have given their name (in Portuguese too) to the loincloths which they were used to make; the *ngombo* were pieces of woven raffia and also garments or coverings made from these pieces. The *mpusu* and the *(m)bongo*, often in strips of a dozen, were cloth money, the first being the size of a napkin and the second the size of a 'large sheet of paper', according to the missionaries of Kakongo: 'Little pieces of cloth made of grass (and also of raffia) take the place of money in this region. Each of these little pieces, which they call *bongo*, is the size of a large sheet of paper and is worth more than a sou.'[65]

A rich and specialized lexicon was thus associated with one of the kingdom's major industries, whose productions were diverse and were, in certain cases, works of art as well as of skill. The analogies to which the chroniclers resort in describing the brocades, velvets, satins, and taffetas are revealing. An industry which had become necessary for the preservation of the foundations of Kongo society and civilization, it supported taxation and consequently the economic privileges of the aristocracy, it permitted transaction, it created the conditions for the art of dress, it provided an education—the decorative motifs of the fabrics had meaning—and an aesthetic which certain of the early travellers sensed.

Communication

The Kongo in the seventeenth and eighteenth centuries possessed diversified techniques, flourishing arts, and extensive learning—even in the realm of medical science and therapeutics—but it seems to have been inadequately equipped when it came to conquering space and to intensifying social intercourse. A network of communications controlled by the capital nevertheless existed. Wannyn writes:

The 'royal' routes, traces of which still remain, were trails wider than ordinary paths with sturdy bridges of vines spanning bodies of water difficult to ford. Even today we have seen some of these bridges which are constructed in the ancestral manner and bear witness to a proven technique and an undeniable concern for architectural elegance. Some were about two meters wide and had spans of over twenty meters, Maintenance of bridges, clearing of trails, and upkeep of fords, which required a considerable manpower, have always been the responsibility of the regional authority. The little trails of local use have never been cared for, either now or in the past.'[66]

These remarks confirm an observation already made by Pigafetta: 'In these regions, when the king and the principal lords travel, the custom is to repair and clear the paths.'[67]

Methods of transportation remained primitive, despite the conception of a public service responsible for large roads, the importance accorded to long-distance transactions, and recognition of the strategic role of communication routes. No domesticated animal was used to bear burdens, no vehicle with wheels had been devised. Carrying was done on the backs of men; the caravan replaced the freight train. Persons of quality—beginning with the sovereign and the chiefs—moved from place to place by using the 'wooden horses of the Kongo'. The reference is to the *tipoye*, as described in the *História do Reino do Congo*:

The people of the Congo take a round, thickish stick three handsbreadths long which is capable of bearing a man's weight. In the middle they nail a hide so as to form a seat on which the traveler sits. He holds on with his hands to keep from falling. A man in front and another in back hoist the stick to their shoulders and walk eight to ten leagues a day.[68]

Besides this rudimentary version of the vehicle there were litters, originally made of skin, which were modified and enhanced with imported fabrics and ornaments under the influence of the Portuguese, as Cavazzi suggests.[69] Religious requirements —the king had to avoid direct contact with the earth—and the desire to indicate social status operated in this area as well as reasons of convenience and speed, if it is true that the bearers ran 'as fast as post horses at the gallop'.

The Bakongo were not renowned sailors, even in the coastal regions of the kingdom. Their canoe (*lungu*) was monoxylous, that is, made of a single piece of timber. The *mfuma* (or kapok tree, *Ceiba thonningii*) and the *nkondo amfinda* (*Sterculia ambocensis*) were used for this purpose and permitted the manufacture of large-sized boats. According to Father Giuseppe Monari da Modena, some of these had a capacity of sixty persons or five hundred sacks of merchandise.[70] The traffic between the islands in the mouth of the Congo River, especially the Isle of the Horses, and the port of Mpinda necessitated the maintenance of a small fleet of similar units until the end of the seventeenth century. Otherwise, the raft continued to serve: floats made of oiled raffia navigating on the river Inkisi, or more complicated crafts made of palm-tree trunks 'moved by oar and sail' and employed for coastal fishing, according to Pigafetta. The same author mentions the military use of large canoes during conflicts between chiefs who lived on islands:

Sometimes these chiefs, out of enmity, make war on each other, riding in small crafts hollowed out of tree trunks of enormous size. . . . The oars are not attached to tholepins, but are free and are simply held in the hand and used to beat the water vigorously. Each warrior is armed with his oar and his bow, and in battle they drop their oars and take up their bows. To maneuver and steer the craft they use no rudder, but only oars.[71]

These 'conflicts resembling civil wars' noted in several old accounts resulted not only from rivalries for the power but also from economic competition, which was intense in a region where the Negro slave trade found its outlet and where centers of exchange with European slave traders were established.

War

The Kongo was born of violence; down through successive reigns power had always been taken by force; force had remained a fundamental value, and the first 'miracles' attributed to the Christian God and his saints were performed on fields of battle. *Vita ntu, ka mabundu ko*; war is the business of the chief, not of the subjects. The drums, symbols of royalty and power, guarantees of vigor and fecundity, upholders of the very existence of kings and political leaders—also gave out the 'word' of war.

Better than other chroniclers, Laurent de Lucques has observed this:

There are here many drums both large and small, which are played at holidays, in time of war, and on other occasions. The largest ones are used to give military signals, other drums serve other predetermined ends. . . . The drums of the Congo do not have the same shape as the drums of Europe; they are made of a single piece of wood, very thick and well hollowed out; the upper part is covered with a skin which they beat not with drumsticks but with their hands. . . . When the skin of one of these drums breaks, the count [of Soyo] must give the man who is beating it a fish and a measure of millet or beans. The count discharges this obligation immediately, for otherwise he would be afraid that someone would smash his skull.[72]

There was also a wartime ritual, a dance called the dance of the sword (from the verb *sanga* which refers to it), which only chiefs and aristocrats could perform. It took the place of military training for those who had the responsibility to fight. De Lucques describes it in an ironic tone:

Sangare is nothing less than a military drill which these Blacks are accustomed to perform, in which they brandish their swords as if they were fighting against their enemies. It is very curious and laughable to see them, some with swords and shields, others with muskets or clubs, running here and there in a disorderly manner or making grotesque grimaces or contortions. He who distorts himself most violently is most highly praised.[73]

The national holiday associated with Saint James, the apostle who was said to have contributed to the success of King Afonso I, required the same ritual together with a magnificent ceremony and renewed all allegiance due the sovereign and his 'governors'. A report by de Lucques on the province of Soyo describes this demonstration, which lasted eight days, or two Kongo weeks:

On the feast of the saint, before coming to church to hear mass the count goes to see the countess, from whom he receives the bow and arrows. In the presence of his wife, who sits on the ground, and together with two of his principal chiefs, *mani* Pangala and *mani* Quime, he immediately begins to perform a private *sangamento*, that is, to leap about and flourish the bow. After this military drill, he returns to his palace and attends mass, giving satisfaction first to the devil and then to God. He performs this ceremony to protect himself from being assassinated at this time. On another day there is a public *sangamento* outside the church; to see so many Blacks shouting and screaming, you would think you were witnessing a scene from Hell.[74]

This gives us some sense of how closely the capacity to govern and physical vigor, which the war dance expressed and maintained, were related. A decline of power was regarded as contagious: it threatened the 'health' of the kingdom and that of the people, so that it was the duty of any inadequate power to disappear. Again it is Laurent de Lucques who best reveals the religious imperatives and the rules that traditionally regulated military operations. One cannot refrain from quoting this accurate observer:

When the count [of Soyo] wishes to make war on a prince, he gathers his council and makes known his intentions. Having obtained the consent of the principal men, on the following day he orders the drums of war played while certain persons shout tumultuously. This is the familiar signal. The people who hear it give answering shouts from all sides. The men all take their arms and run to the house of the prince. In a short time a great number of armed men are assembled. Then the count comes out of his house, also armed, and before this multitude he proceeds to leap about, flourishing the bow and arrows in sham combat, and then sits on a seat.

His officers and the *mani* do the same thing (that is, feign combat), and so do all the people. Merely to see them is terrifying. This ceremony or military exercise having ended, all listen silently to the count, who reveals his intention to make war on such and such a prince. When the people have heard him, all resume their warlike shouting and skirmishing, They decide on the day of departure, which is ordinarily the third day after the proclamation of war. They leave without provisions taking only their weapons. When they meet the enemy, they contend for an hour or two; they are either victors or vanquished, for if they are weak they flee and the stronger side gives chase and takes prisoners. They kill the oldest men and keep the young men. When the battle is over they return home, shouting all the while, 'We have won the war'. When he has returned to his *(m)banza* [capital], the count has the prisoners counted and determines how many each man has captured. If someone has captured four, for example, he lets him keep one. If they have taken objects such as mats, seats, or the like, these are given to the count, who leaves them only the ordinary things. The slaves (prisoners) are sold to the Dutch, when they come to these parts, or to other nations. This count [of Soyo] is highly regarded by his subjects because of his power, as well as by the neighboring princes and all the kingdom of the Congo.[75]

Military operations required not only a preliminary ritual, a training of combatants and people, but also the intervention of priests, who shook wooden bells (the *ndingi*) during the battle to obtain the assistance of the ancestors. Thus they required the magic of protection. Laurent de Lucques, who visited the Kongo during troubled times, observed the phenomenon on several occasions:

When the people [of Soyo] go to war, they ordinary take their fetishers with them. The latter carry bells made of wood which they rattle, saying that there is nothing to fear because the devil is with them. These bells are cup-shaped. Some have two cups, others one; the clappers are also wooden. In spite of this, they make a rather loud noise. The fetisher rattles them as he walks, invoking the devil the while. Those who go to war unarmed with superstitious things are few in number, for before leaving they go to see their fetishers. They are given a few leaves of the *matteba*, a tree similar to the palm, whose leaves, however, are stronger. They are used to make cord which is as strong as ours. They wrap their bodies in these leaves in the belief that this will protect them against the enemy.[76]

The magical interpretation does not exclude rational conceptions: thus, the *matteba* leaves actually provided a camouflage for the combatants. The place accorded to ceremony, rite, and magic—which for that matter are always present in all armies and in all human enterprises where there is the risk of death— nevertheless left room for military art and for a technology which the Portuguese, although better equipped, paid for more than once by suffering defeat.

The towns were built in defensive positions. By choice of location, first of all: this was true of the capital, which was built on an 'eminence' dominating the surrounding hills, and was subsequently fortified to the south (according to Dapper) by a wall of stones and lime; it was also true, in the early eighteenth century, of the seat of the province of Mbamba which was defended 'as if by a fortress, thanks to the density of the underbrush and the confusion of the forest vegetation';[77] and humble villages were often located away from communication routes used for the movement of troops. The Bakongo also made use of primitive techniques of fortification. The royal palace, the palaces of provincial governors, and the houses of dignitaries were isolated by palisades—lumbu—which formed a number of internal yards and passageways. In Mbanza Kongo this enclosure, which was made of stakes tied together with vines, had an outer circumference of over a thousand meters. It constituted a veritable stronghold where an armed guard was permanently stationed. The great chiefs who governed the provinces maintained a similar protection, notably in Soyo, which very quickly became a state within the state of the Kongo:

Along the road leading to the prince's enclosure . . . about five hundred soldiers armed with bows and arrows were stationed. Having passed this first guard, one entered the yard, where there were also a great many soldiers, positioned like the previous ones. Here there were also muskets, and seven cannons. Toward the back of the yard there was a *corps de garde* and some musicians playing drums and other barbaric instruments. From this yard one passed through a second and a third, all full of armed men, as above [description dating from the early eighteenth century].[78]

In the capital, where the royal enclosure was more extensive and included more than one entrance (*mavitu*), there lived large troops of several thousand men, some of them foreigners, who were subject to a strict military discipline. But even the villages had their defences: the chief's enclosure, where the women gathered in time of danger, paths armed with thorns and stakes tipped with ironwood (*nsako*), traps consisting of ditches covered with branches and earth.[79] The Kongo fighter seems to have relied more on cunning than on direct confrontation, more on the defensive and the surprise element than on the pitched battle, which was generally of brief duration.

Pigafetta made a painstaking study of the military organization and fighting techniques of the Bakongo. He accurately described the order of the troops, the sonorous methods used to inspire courage and inform the soldiers, and the armament and strategy leading to a decisive engagement. He discusses these matters in several parts of his account, especially in the chapter devoted to the southern regions of the kingdom:

> The battle order of the Mocicongo [Esikongo] . . . and of the people of Angola is almost the same. They fight only on foot, they divide their armies into several units, adapting themselves to the terrain and brandishing their emblems. . . . The movements of the combat are regulated by various auditory signals. It is the general who, marching in the middle of his army, gives the signal for the movements he wishes executed: join the battle, retreat, advance, turn right or turn left, or perform some other maneuver. The general's orders are transmitted by means of sounds which are agreed upon and precisely determined, as is done in our own armies by different ways of beating the drum and sounding the trumpet.[80]

And further on in this description, Pigafetta discusses the fighting of the battle:

> In front of the fighters march valiant, sturdy men who leap about, beating their bells with wooden sticks, firing the courage of the soldiers, and warning them of the weapons being launched against them and the dangers they face. When the fighting begins, they the ordinary [soldiers] run into the fray in scattered formation, shooting their arrows from afar, turning and dodging this way and that, darting in all directions to avoid being hit. . . . When [they] have fought a certain length of time and the captain decides they are tired, the signal for retreat is

given by the ringing of bells; when they hear this, they retrace their steps and other soldiers take their place in combat, until the armies are engaged with all their forces in a general melee.[81]

Pigafetta declares, 'These people understand military strategy and a certain battle order'. The troops were divided into several divisions and included a cadre of officers. According to a document of 1595, the king of the Kongo has at his disposal an army of 100,000 men who, 'out of good will and affection for him and without receiving payment, are at his service'. And further on there is a very useful statement: 'The king has a guard which is commanded by four nobles selected from the principal men of the kingdom. Each of these has under his command four to five thousand men subject to military discipline. There was no lack of these garrison soldiers either at home or abroad.'[82] Indeed, there seems to have existed at the time the equivalent of a standing army — hence the 'guards' surrounding the sovereign and governors of provinces, and the possibility of carrying out a kind of mass levy in the event of large-scale conflicts. The provincial armies were bound to the sovereign insofar as governors and local chiefs had declared their allegiance (tambuka) and received the royal favor. However, certain of these notables enjoyed a privileged status by virtue of their political ability. The mani Mbamba was 'general captain of the army', ne tuma; for his province continued to be 'the key and fortress of the kingdom', by resisting many rebellious neighbors, and his subjects were 'great warriors' on whose aid the king was constantly calling.[83] The mani Mbata, second authority in the kingdom, 'had the privilege of having harquebusiers', which showed great confidence in his loyalty, and the duty of forming a shield with his troops to withstand the incursions of the Yaka. As for the chief of Nsundi, he had the capacity to raise a large troop composed of men who were 'agile, strong, tall, warlike, [and who] did nothing else'.[84] These facts are useful but incomplete. One can have no certainty on the subject of either permanent or provisional forces. Armies numbering a minimum of twenty to thirty thousand soldiers appear to have been raised on several occasions: this same figure defined the royal army organized under Pedro IV in February 1709, when the latter undertook to reconquer and reunite the torn kingdom.

Kongo troops were 'mobilized' without possessing those services which permit hostilities of long duration. They had no
means of transportation and no commissariat: food supplies
transported by slave caravans were rapidly exhausted. They had
therefore to find provisions on the spot, ravaging the crops and
livestock of the villagers despite the frugality of the combatants:
'The soldiers procured food and drink, each man for himself.
They could survive on very little in case of necessity, and they
could even go without eating for three or four days without
suffering a great deal.'[85] Nevertheless, it was not unknown for
famine to force the warriors to return to their own country.

From the sixteenth to the eighteenth century armament was
modified under the influence of the Portuguese. The bow and its
arrows with barbed iron tips and feathering and the ironwood
branch used as a club were the most widely used of the traditional offensive weapons. These were supplemented by the
dagger made with a handle 'like a knife', the lance, whose
length 'exceeded the height of a man', and the assagai, and,
according to Bishop Manuel Baptista (in a letter dated 1619),
the dirk, the billhook, the small axe, and the sword—in other
words, objects primarily made in Europe according to specifica-
tions suggested by the traders. The sword, whether imported or
copied by the Kongo blacksmith, was more of an honorific attribute—*mbele a lulendo* (knife of dignity)—held by kings and
notables, than a weapon of battle. To ensure their personal protection in hand-to-hand fighting, some of the Kongo fighters
armed themselves with shields of bark or buffalo hide. Such an
inventory does not reveal unusual or more powerful weapons
than those frequently encountered in Africa. It was, in fact,
contact with the Europeans that increased the offensive capacity
of the people of the Kongo. From them they received firearms:
as gifts, by capture on fields of battle, and above all through
trade: 'Since the sixteenth century Portuguese, French, Dutch,
and other commercial vessels have steadily brought to the
Atlantic coast percussion guns, spears, lances, and instruments
of all kinds manufactured especially for this market.'[86] The
power of the kingdom in comparison to its neighbors, but also
the disastrous violence of internal rivalries, were the consequence
of this reinforcement.

Little is known about the organization of the armies. Officers and common soldiers wore distinctive uniforms. The latter 'had only the lower part of the body covered'. The former were more encumbered with clothing and special insignia, according to Pigafetta:

This was . . . the military dress of the Mocicongo [Esikongo] lords: on their heads they wore headdresses decorated with feathers . . . which made them look taller and gave them a fearful aspect; about their necks and hanging down on both sides, they wore iron chains whose links were as thick as the little finger. . . . They wore breeches of linen or taffeta and over these a garment that fell to their heels; they raised its ends and attached them to their belts. These belts, as we have said, were finely wrought; on them they hung little bells . . . which rang when the warriors moved about and fought, giving them courage to strike the enemy. On their feet they wore laceboots in the Portuguese style.[87]

The description must be partially inaccurate. It suggests, however, the existence of an obvious military hierarchy which may have been specialized (the chronicler distinguishes officers with bows and daggers from those who carried swords and shields), but in any case was effective, judging from accounts of the important battles. The military leaders aroused the ardor of the soldiers and transmitted their orders by means of resounding signals. This code required the use of three kinds of instruments, or noisemakers: the drum (ngoma), carved from the trunk of Ricinodendron africanum and featuring a single piece of leather which was beaten with little ivory mallets; the clapperless bell or ngonge, which was struck with wooden sticks; and finally, the transverse horn of ivory (mpungi) which, according to Pigafetta, 'produced a martial sound, full of harmony and joy'. The sizes of the instruments differed according to the position in the hierarchy of the chief who controlled them. Pigafetta has noted this and showed that these variations made it possible to diversify the messages:

[The] three kinds of instruments may be of various sizes: the general carries large ones, so that his signal will carry all over the field of battle; in the various units which make up the army, instruments of lesser size are used in the same way, and each individual officer uses even smaller instruments within his company. . . . In this way, when the sound of the master drum, or of the horn, or of the other instrument is heard, each division of the army responds with its own instrument, thus indicating that it has heard the signal, and then the officers of inferior rank do likewise.[88]

This system of telecommunication suggests the differentiation and order of the elements constituting an army on the field, as well as the unity of command that was maintained during the operations, thanks to this system.

'The people of the Kongo are inclined toward war,' states the author of the *História do Reino do Congo*. What are the reasons for this inclination? First of all, we must distinguish war from all those conflicts which, though violent, were strictly regulated and of limited extent, whose purpose was to terminate a serious dispute which eluded habitual methods of conciliation. These are classified today as feuds by English-speaking ethnologists; no doubt they correspond to what Girolamo da Montesarchio has called 'village wars'. Van Wing mentions them in his *Études bakongo*:

An insult received at the neighboring market, a wound caused unintentionally at a dancing celebration, the burning of a hunting preserve or a piece of land reserved for a nursery, and other accidents of this kind were so many occasions or motives for war between two villages. The injured party stirred up his relatives and friends, vengeance was taken immediately in the form of very violent injuries or of damage to the opposing side. . . . When the blood had flowed—death was not even necessary—peace negotiations could be discussed.[89]

Beyond these confrontations between villages, war fitted some essential functions in the ancient Kongo. It was imposed by restless and ambitious neighbors, notably by the Yaka, whose occasional allies the Portuguese became during their quarrels with the kings of São Salvador; beginning with the reign of Afonso I, defence of the frontiers necessitated campaigns of long duration.

But it is those struggles whose motives were, properly speaking, political that appear most significant. Of primary importance were the wars of succession, inevitable result of the principle according to which each new sovereign must take the power and the kingdom by force. Rivalries resulted in interregna during which war sometimes lasted for several years; and even in an endemic state after the defeat of Ambouila, which brought about the ruin of the Kongo: 'The civil wars were at that time so cruel and implacable . . . that in fifty years, more or less, more than thirty kings were massacred.'[90] Moreover, the vulnerability of the central power often left the field open to attempts at rebellion and refusals to pay the tax. The religious argument, which was used to defend tradition, provided an excuse to contest the authority of sovereigns who were denounced as friends of the foreigners and of the imported religion: Cuvelier has mentioned the 'danger of war' created by the influence of 'fetishers' or 'revolutionaries' who claimed to be 'possessed by the spirit of a deceased ancestor'. In fact, these people served as pretexts for the ambitions of the local powers and fed a certain popular distrust of the aristocrats of the capital and their modernism. Tension frequently existed between the royal power and the provincial powers, one of whom—the governor of Soyo found himself in such a position of strength that he could harbor a desire to conquer the regions on the right bank of the river, Ngoyo (1631) and Kakongo, and pose a threat to the kings of the Kongo during the last decades of the seventeenth century. Finally, it must be said that a number of the wars had economic causes: they provided occasions to steal merchandise and objects of value and to capture young men destined for deportation by the slave traders or for domestic slavery.

Economic Life

War is only the last resort of politics and economics; violence is no stranger to either the administration of goods or the management of business. In the Kongo too, political and economic conflicts and dynamisms were intimately related. The king required of his immediate subordinates homage and tribute, loyalty, and a material contribution to the support of the state. He was the master of men and of things. He controlled the wealth (notably the mines) and, to a large extent, its distribution. He possessed that capital instrument, money.

Without money the kingdom could not have arrived at the

1 · Map of the Kongo, dated 1731.

2 · The sweet potato

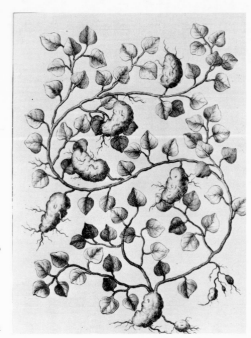

The blacksmith

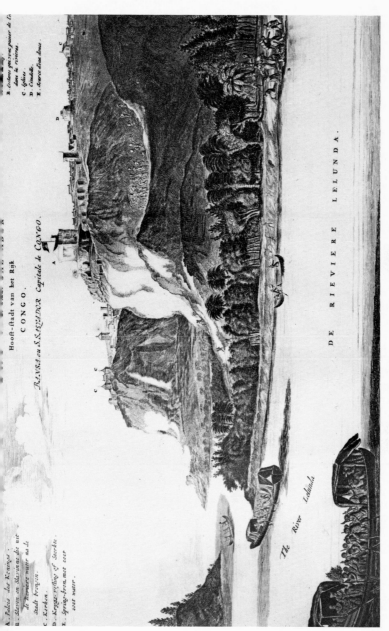

3 · View of São Salvador

4 · The King of the Kongo receiving European ambassadors

The royal throne and insignia of power

5 · Angola: modern view of
the cathedral at São Salvador

Congolese crucifix in
bronze, from Tungwa

6 · View of the town of Loanga

7 · The King of Loanga

8 · Two soapstone figurines from Mboma

level of development attained during the sixteenth century. The sovereigns had been attentive to the good operation of the monetary system and to the good results of the fiscal mechanisms supplying the royal treasury. They were not then 'poor and naked', as a nineteenth-century missionary report states. Their chief sources of revenue were slaves, native fabrics, ivory and skins, the shell money of which they had a monopoly, various taxes and duties, and tolls, according to Dapper. A specialized administration took care of the payment and recording of this revenue. Cuvelier mentions three orders of functionaries responsible primarily for fiscal policy: the *mfutila* (from *futa, futila*, to pay), the *mani mpanza* (from *mpanza*, money[?]), and the *mani samba*, who were responsible for the collection of tolls and other taxes, the management of monetary contributions, and the levying of duties on the slaves, respectively.[91] It is impossible to gather adequate data regarding the yield of the fiscal policy and the various types of monetary restrictions applied. The *História do Reino do Congo* suggests that the principle of 'maximum revenue' reigned supreme; it determined royal favor and the advantages anticipated by those in power:

The first obligation of the village chiefs is to collect from their inferiors those duties which are paid to the king and which they take to the viceroy [governor] of their province. This governor goes twice every year to the capital to take the tribute. If the king is satisfied with it, he replies this word, *uote*, which means 'You have done well. . . . ' But if the king does not say *uote*, he [the governor] returns very crestfallen and next time he makes certain to bring a larger tribute. This tribute is not fixed as to quantity: they bring as much as they can. If the governor does not do better, the king reprimands him severely and takes away his functions. . . . What the king does to the viceroys, the latter do to the chiefs and the chiefs to their inferiors, who pay by the head.[92]

One of the most important sources of wealth for the king and for officials of the bureaucracy was the exclusive exploitation of the shell money gathered on the shores of the island of Loanda, which the Portuguese called *Ilha do Dinheiro* or *Ilha de Moeda*, after this function. Duarte Pacheco Pereira already mentioned the fact in some observations recorded around 1505. Pigafetta refers to it in his description:

> This island is the money mine used by the king of the Congo and the peoples of the surrounding regions. This is why women are seen on the beaches working at depths of two fathoms and more to fill baskets with sand and bring up little shells. . . . These shells are found up and down the coastline of the kingdom of the Congo, but the best ones are those of Luanda. . . . Note that gold, silver, and other metals are not regarded or utilized as money in these countries, but shells are . . . with these one can even obtain gold and silver.[93]

The collection, which was inspected and recorded by royal functionaries, was accomplished under the direction of the *mani* Loanda, the governor of the island, who was also responsible for its transfer to the capital.

The shell coins were known in Kikongo as *nzimbu*: *nzimbu kitombe* and *nzimbu a mbudi*. According to the classification of naturalists, they were of the species *Olivancillaria nana* Lamarck; there existed several varieties, which had received different values, but their geographical distribution seems to have been limited to the coast of Angola. They must be distinguished from the cowries (*Cypraea moneta*), very common in Western Africa, which were circulated in the kingdom of the Kongo only by intervention of the slave traders; indeed, these new monetary elements, called *mbesi*, ended by supplanting the money produced locally.[94] The *nzimbu* were standardized: by means of a calibrated strainer the 'little ones' were sorted from the 'big ones', which had ten times their value. Vessels serving as measures contained a precise number of money shells: 40, 100, 250, 400, 500, and in the case of superior units: 1,000 (the *funda*), 10,000 (the *lufuku*), and 20,000 (the *kofo*, which corresponded to a weight of thirty kilograms). And although the *nzimbu* were used only domestically, the European equivalent of these units has been estimated. Working from missionary correspondence, Cuvelier establishes the following conversions for the year 1575:

> one *funda* = 1,000 big shells = 100 reis
> one *lufuku* = 10,000 big shells = 1,000 reis
> one *kofo* = 20,000 big shells = 2,000 reis

This currency has depreciated over the centuries: economic and political causes and, above all, the competition of new currencies have contributed to this devaluation. Under the reign of Afonso I, at the beginning of and during the golden age of relations between Europeans and people of the Kongo, the *kofo* must have been worth 50 cruzados, or 20,000 reis; in the last decades of the sixteenth century and up to the middle of the seventeenth, it was worth only 2,000 reis; it seems to have settled at about 1,000 reis after 1650, and remained at that figure until the last quarter of the eighteenth century.[95] These facts are fallible, but the indication of a trend is undeniable. Afonso I had exceptional monetary means at his disposal:

He could without difficulty support a large clergy and hire many artisans. To the masons, in spite of their almost worthless work, he gave collectively one *lufuku* or one *kofo* per day. All of which, at the time, represented considerable buying power. Indeed, these masons purchased slaves.[96]

The depreciation became very apparent and continued throughout subsequent reigns.

The *nzimbu* had essentially a monetary function: they standardized exchanges; they formed the major part of the 'tribute'; and they met the expenses of the state, and enabled sovereigns to contribute to the support of the Church of the Kongo and honor with endowments those foreigners who had won their confidence. The importance of the shell money, which had become the basis of the economy and the instrument of the administration, was clearly recognized by the Portuguese. Toward the middle of the seventeenth century, in order to exert pressure on the king, they cut off the source of the treasury by seizing the island of Loanda and restoring it to the authority of João IV of Portugal, annexing it definitively after the battle of Ambouila. This forced surrender put an end to a long, insidious war: at the turn of the seventeenth century, the inspector Domingos do Abreu de Brito was already proposing to seize the money 'fisheries' and to treat the *mani* Kongo as a vassal king.[97] Such a recommendation reveals the monetary character of the *nzimbu* (as 'coin of the realm' they were indispensable to any ideas of conquest then entertained) and their dominant role in the area of public finance. The precious shells had a secondary symbolic function : they were used in clothing, amulets, and charms and in the making of certain magical objects, and they appeared during ordeals.

All of the kingdom and the territories associated with it did not form a single monetary zone. In several regions—Mbata, Mpangu, Nsundi, for example—it was cloth of local manufacture that provided the principal currency. According to a criterion of size, as we have seen, at least two units were frequently used : the *lubongo*, the size of a sheet of paper, and the *mpusu*, the size of a napkin; these pieces of cloth, in strips of ten, were known as *kuta* or *dikuta*.

In Angola, Soyo, and Kakongo, the cloth money was in competition with other media of exchange. Until recently in the latter kingdom, the *lubongo* was used in the markets for purchases of an ordinary nature. In 1770 the French missionaries estimated its value at 'a little over a sou'. An observation of this kind arouses curiosity as to the value of these currencies which were produced in great quantity and were so well incorporated into the economic system of the Kongo that the term *mbongo* (plural of *lubongo*) came to refer to property, wealth, money. Around 1640, Cadornega evaluated the *mpusu* at 50 reis and the *lubongo* at 12 reis (or more). He observed that 'the power of the king of the Kongo is so great' at the time, that he was able to honor the Portuguese living in São Salvador by granting them an annual pension paid in cloth money, and to meet the peace treaty of 1649, which required payment of 1,500 loads of cloth worth approximately forty million reis. Toward the end of the seventeenth century, Marcellino d'Atri noted that one hundred *mpusu* corresponded to 4,000 reis and represented the purchase price of one slave in the province of Nsundi.[98] The value of the cloth money varied from the sixteenth century on; it appears to have depreciated slowly, but it is still difficult to estimate this devaluation, owing to lack of information.

The domestic market functioned, well before the economic results of Portuguese colonization had appeared, either by direct exchange or by recourse to monetary species. In the first case, it was *nsolo* — particularly highly valued and sought-after merchandise—that appeared, and first of all salt, object of long-distance transactions, greed, and even pride, since the *mani* Soyo included in the list of his titles a reminder of 'his conquest of the salt mines'. In the second, it was first little pieces of forged iron, then the *nzimbu* and the cloths, that were used; and, at an unknown date, the *misanga*, or necklaces of blue pearls obtained by importation. The 'foreigners' had a profound influence on the old system. They introduced goods of superior exchange value: fabrics (Indian or Guinean), even 'parasols of red silk the color of fire', as in Kakongo, brass hairpins, etc. They put their own currencies into circulation. They created a new and powerful foreign market which necessitated the use of a wealth that was definite and convertible outside the frontiers of the kingdom; this 'currency' was unfortunately the slave. The missionary clergy itself did not fail to convert royal allocations earmarked for its support into this commodity.

The author of the *História do Reino do Congo* says of the people of this kingdom, 'They give evidence of good judgment, particularly in business. They cheat astutely.' A description dating from 1595 completes the observation: 'There are among them some very busy markets where there is a heavy traffic in the things we have mentioned.' The invasion of the Portuguese and their products at the end of the fifteenth century merely stimulated talents already well trained and commercial mechanisms already in effect. On these mechanisms, however, the *História* offers only brief indications, but they are useful in that they reveal the economic function of slavery:

The slaves alone work and serve. Those who are powerful have a large number of slaves, whom they have captured at war or bought. They do business through these slaves, by sending them to the markets, where they buy and sell according to their master's orders. Colorful shells the size of chick-peas are used as money. . . . In other regions, this shell money does not exist. Here they exchange fabrics of the type used for clothing, cocks, or salt, according to what they want to buy.[99]

The slave, besides being an object of transaction, was the necessary condition of economic life. He acted on behalf of his 'lord'; he formed the caravans without which merchandise would not circulate.

Pigafetta's account not only evokes the briskness of trade as a result of the foreign economic impetus, but also suggests the traditional nature of certain exchanges. Nsundi sought 'palm cloth, belts made of palm leaves, which are highly valued', skins, and more recently, ivory. In the south, especially in the allied kingdom of Loango, iron gave rise to profitable exchanges for those who imported it. To the north of the kingdom of the Kongo, the Bateke engaged in an occasional trade which enabled them to acquire salt and shells for ornamental purposes. But it was in the province of Mbata, so closely associated with the royal province, that barter seems to have been most profitable. Pigafetta observes: 'Commerce is identical to that of the provinces we have just described, but income, the profit which the king derives from Batta, amounts to double what he derives from the two provinces previously mentioned [Nsundi and Mpangu].'[100] In short, salt, iron, cloth, skins, and shells used as money and as ornament occupied a large place in the trade of the Kongo.

Recent ethnographic investigations have clarified the role of the products of craftsmanship in this system of exchange, pointed out regional specializations, and elucidated the role of the capital as a stimulus. Wannyn reports his own observations and remarks:

The Manianga of Lunga and of Dunga [in the province of Nsundi] still recall with pride that . . . their earthen pots and water jugs were highly valued at the great market of Salvador, which was one of their principal buyers. The other centers of craftsmanship scattered through the kingdom very probably also directed a large part of their production [toward this market], which had in a sense become a center of trade and redistribution, as well as an arbiter of fashion, as it were. For it appears that numerous traditional objects of various kinds had never been made in Salvador or in its environs. . . . Traditionally, iron has been produced and forged first in the capital under the control of the ntotila, and next in the provinces. The same thing may have been true of wood: seats, carved staffs, and domestic implements such as combs, ladles, and bowls. But the fine brass ware must have been produced in the south, the fine pottery in the north, and the mats and woven raffia in the northeast.[101]

The extent of communication may be verified in another way:

by studying the institution of the market cornerstone of the socioeconomic edifice in the Kongo. The *nzandu* (market) introduced both peace and commerce; within its limits, violence lost its rights and the rules promulgated by its founders absolutely ensured the security of persons and freedom of trade. It brought a regularity to commerce, and the name attributed to it may simply have referred to the day of the week on which it was open. It imposed a certain standardization of prices. In the large markets, the merchandise offered was displayed in a predetermined place (or *mbangu*); for instance, there was one section reserved for blacksmiths, another for the display of slaves. All business was done under the surveillance of the directors of the market and with the protection of the notables (chiefs of the villages in question) who had created the *nzandu* and placed it in neutral territory defended against possible attack. But the market was much more than a commercial center. It was a place of asylum, a favorable spot for political and matrimonial negotiations, a convenient place for the dissemination of news and fashions. It was also a religious center where the solemn execution of 'criminals' and sorcerers was performed and the final rituals of the great initiations took place. The *nzandu* testified to the vigor of the economy and the severity of the laws in the ancient Kongo.

The intervention of the Portuguese and later of other European slave traders affected commercial life so profoundly from the sixteenth century on that politics and economics became even more closely connected. The most obvious consequence of this connection with an outside market was the liveliness of commerce—imported goods were seductive—and the multiplication of routes open to commercial caravans. It is impossible today to discover the exact pattern of this network, but the principal routes are known. They converge toward the capital. The best one, which was maintained up to the modern era, since Stanley used it in part, ran toward the Mpumbu (the Pool); it was the Mount Bangu road. It went through Kimpese, now on the railroad line, and Dunga; but an offshoot went right through the mountain and left the region to the south of Lunga. The main road, the one most frequented, linked São Salvador with the port of Mpinda; it was about three hundred kilometers long, which represented a minimum of six days on foot; it saw considerable traffic, and the rich caravans that used it needed a military escort for protection from plunderers like the *mpanzulungu*, who exploited travellers in the late fifteenth century. Leading toward Ambrizete on the coast there was a road that passed through some busy centers of craftsmanship: Bembe and Tomboko. To the east, the Makela (Zombo) road went as far as the valley of the Inkisi. 'In addition, there were certainly several routes to the south and the southeast, and at least one running to the mouth of the Congo River which tradition tells us it crossed.'[102] These communication routes, which were maintained by means of a kind of compulsory labor force, were a source of revenue, through the collection of tolls, and a way of strengthening the political and economic domination of the capital by ensuring customers for the provincial capitals and the important markets. Their deterioration and the decline of the central power were to follow the same course.

The foreigners from Mputu (Portugal, Europe) introduced new goods, represented a new demand, and imposed the rules of mercantilism: brutal competition and the ruthless pursuit of profit. They transformed an economy partly geared to survival and partly to the service of the state and the aristocracy, into an economy that was mercantile and essentially inhuman, since the prime commodity became the slave destined for exportation. The exchanges followed a pattern: imports included fabrics, rugs which were found in the homes of the king and the chiefs, glassware and crockery also destined for aristocratic houses, alcoholic beverages, and, transported by a private route, weapons; exports included ivory, certain raffia fabrics, hides, copper, *tukula* wood which was used to make a cosmetic powder, medicine, stimulants, and above all, slaves originating from the outlying regions, from Mpumbu (vicinity of the Pool) and Kwango.

The mechanism of barter and trade has been described in the *História do Reino do Congo*:

The [European] merchants were of two kinds. The first were called *Pombeiros*, who went into the interior of the country and traded with pagans and Christians alike. They bought and sold the merchandise which they had brought with them. What they bought were slaves whom they sent to the Congo [São Salvador] and Pinda, or to colleagues who put them on board vessels bound for the port of the island of São Tomé. . . . The second were inhabitants of the city of the Congo or the port of Pinda, and their function was to receive the slaves whom the *Pombeiros* sent them. They had slaves of their own, and they sent those with whom they were pleased, with merchandise, into the interior of the country to buy and sell like the *Pombeiros*.[103]

The bold travellers who crossed the frontiers of the Kongo travelled Africa from west to east, and had native defendents and rivals resorted to the most profitable methods — 'albeit against morality'. They were denounced by their contemporaries for their 'frauds' and for 'the exorbitant prices they asked for the things they sold'.

This long-range commerce not only created a merchant class, but also strengthened the economic position of those tribes who played the role of intermediaries. This was true of the people of the province of Mbata, who lived east of the capital in the regions of Ndamba and Makela (Zombo), and were often described as *Bazombo*, the general term for traders. They drained an extensive region—as far as Kwango to the east and the Congo River to the north—and their caravans were so numerous and their audacity so impressive that the Milky Way, located along one of the axes of their movements, was given the name of *Nzila Bazombo*, or Bazombo Way. A recent study describes them as 'the great intermediaries of trade and the principal disseminators, of the cultural elements introduced by the Portuguese'.[104] They were undeniably agents of modernization, which partially explains the central role of their modern descendants in the movement for independence.

Van Wing states that 'external trade with the *Pombeiros* and *Bazombo* was the exclusive right of the chief' in most clans; besides being 'very lucrative', it also provided an opportunity 'to rid oneself easily of undesirable subjects by selling them as slaves'. On the other hand, 'internal trade was open to everyone, without exception'.[105] It is certain that the kings and the aristocracy tried to maintain a monopoly over those profitable relationships established with the outside world. This was merely an extension of their economic domination to a new domain: real masters of the agrarian rituals, privileged beneficiaries of certain products, owners of slaves, creators of markets, collectors of duties, taxes, and tolls, they could not allow this commerce stimulated from without to operate outside their control and, eventually, to their disadvantage. The economic routes were all forced to take the hierarchic path. This situation also obtained, for the same reasons, in the little allied kingdom of Loango. Here, two high-ranking dignitaries were in charge of relations with the foreign traders: the *ma-fuka,* a kind of 'minister of commerce' who kept in constant contact with the European businesses; and the *ma-ngovo,* a kind of 'minister of foreign affairs' who served as intermediary to the sovereign.[106]

In spite of the precautions taken, the control of king, chiefs, and aristocracy rapidly diminished. Greed sharpened competition, especially in the search for slaves for the slave trade, the old rules were no longer respected, and even Afonso I severely criticized the abuses. Besides, Portuguese traders and their accomplices wanted to operate with the greatest independence and the highest profit; they were the true masters of the market. They were violently opposed to any undertakings that threatened to undermine their activities—conspiring, if necessary, against the kings of São Salvador — and defended their monopoly against European competitors. During the early years of the seventeenth century they aroused the people of the coastal region against these rivals and even gave a prize for every Dutchman killed or captured.[107] In this general conflict of desires and interests, during this series of attempts to seize the wealth and power, the progress of an original civilization, which 'towns' and villages of the Kongo gave evidence of for a time, was obscured.

CHAPTER 5

The Fragile Towns

The towns and even more so the villages of the Kongo were vulnerable—built less to belong to the land than to allow the people a certain mobility. The seats of the provinces changed their locations, notably in the case of Mbanza Mbata and Mbanza Mpangu. Toward the end of the seventeenth century, in the wake of the wars among pretenders to the throne, the capital itself was abandoned; it resumed a modest existence among its ruins in the early 1700s, with the restoration of Pedro IV. As for the villages, designated by the general term *divata*, their instability appears to have been extreme. Everything conspired to make this so: agricultural methods, the struggles of factions, the beliefs which required that the place where the chief had just died be abandoned. The precariousness of the habitations allowed and encouraged this constant shifting of human groups, which led Pigafetta to declare that 'these people build . . . like shepherds'.

It is difficult to reconstruct a clear picture of the population of the kingdom of the Kongo in the sixteenth and seventeenth centuries, and still more so to form a sure estimate of its size. The chroniclers describe the country as 'very populous'. The figure of 'two and one half million inhabitants', suggested by Father de Busseto in 1676, seems likely when compared with the excessive statistical findings of Father Cherubino da Savona, who counted (*sic*) five million subjects around 1760. *The História do Reino do Congo* provides what seems an accurate description of the distribution of the towns:

The villages . . . are ordinarily very small. They are located a certain distance from the public roads, for fear travellers will consume what they have, particularly servants of the king who, wherever they go, consider themselves the owners of everything. This remoteness from the public road discourages enemy incursions, for in this country wars are frequent. There are well-populated towns, but they are few. The houses or huts are at a distance from one another, as they are in the mountains here.[1]

This presentation rightly distinguishes between those aggregates called *vata* (hamlet, village) and those that received the general name of *(m)banza* (seat, capital). Pigafetta explains that the second term 'signifies in a general way court, residence of the governor or king'.

The House

Most of the villages were situated not only off the roads, but also in defensive positions, for fear of wild animals and surprise attacks. Cavazzi observed as much;[2] live hedges (often formed by the *mungyengye* tree), enclosures with narrow entrances, walls surrounding the principal habitations, formed a complex pattern which rendered approach difficult. A casual remark by Father de Lucques shows this: 'The distance to their huts, where they sleep, is great, because they make so many walls with palm branches that you think you are in a maze.'[3] The towns themselves followed the same principles; they sometimes gave an impression of confused structure. The French priests expressed this in a lively fashion in describing their first visit (1766) to the capital of the kingdom of Loango:

The missionaries went through . . .the town of Loango which is said to have a circumference of one league and to be so thickly populated, according to the Negroes, that its inhabitants cannot be numbered. What is certain is that one of the missionaries, who was a bit short-sighted, could have traversed the whole town without seeing a single house although it were broad daylight, if by ill fortune he had forgotten his spectacles. This is because the houses are low, widely spaced, and surrounded by trees and grass eight or nine feet tall, with which vegetation all the roads are also supplied in such profusion that there is only a very narrow path left in the middle. They finally left the town after having circled it many times. . . . [4]

Father Proyart adds his own commentary which, though certainly exaggerated, is revealing: 'A large town is a real maze from which a stranger would never emerge if he did not take care to bring a guide.'

The techniques of architecture have undergone very little change until recently. The plan of the houses was generally rectangular;* and they were small and low with a single narrow opening permitting access and the entrance of light, when they belonged to common people. Vegetable materials were used in their construction; the author of the *História* observes simply, 'They [the Bakongo] live in huts which are [sometimes] large and which they construct easily from stakes and grass.' A wattling of wood bound together with vines rested on stakes driven into the ground; a woven covering of palm or a matting of straw covered this framework. Laurent de Lucques describes in various passages of his accounts the procedures used in the province of Soyo. He must be quoted, for once again his ethnographic testimony is more satisfactory than that of the other chroniclers:

The houses, with respect to their dimensions, may be compared to the tiny cells of monks. Their height is such that when you stand up your head reaches the roof, so to speak. The doors are very low. In the homes of the nobles they are somewhat higher. The houses receive no other light than that which comes in through the door. There are no windows. . . . These houses are made of tightly interlaced palm branches, which present from either side the same effect and the same harmony. The impression is of twigs arranged together and very well fitted: this web forms the walls. It is covered with straw. The construction requires very little time. . . . Inside their houses, they have almost nothing. Thus when they must move, they can do so easily.[5]

De Lucques's language is accurate: the Kongo habitation was more reminiscent of the arts of weaving and basket-making—techniques these people had mastered with great skill—than of the art of building. As he made his way toward the province of

* Although Cavazzi does mention (*Descrizione Storica*, Book I, No. 275) a type of habitation with a circular plan.

Mbanza, de Lucques noticed a difference in the design of the houses: '[They] have palisades made of very stout stakes and straw closely woven with sticks, forming a very solid construction. They are obliged to build in this way because there are no palm trees and also so that these huts will offer adequate protection against lions.'[6]

Finally, our author states that the best 'way of building' in these regions is to use branches and earth.[7] He seems to be recording the appearance of mud over wattling, which Cavazzi confirms when he mentions the use of a wall finishing composed of straw mixed with mud.[8] This borrowed technique, which was just beginning to be known, is the one that prevails in the modern age.

The roofs, which rested upon light framework, were of thatch. In the region of Soyo, the inhabitants used a dry grass called *soyo* which seems to have given its name to the province; it was a species of graminaceous plant which abounded in the vicinity of the seat of the ancient chiefs.[9] According to the author of the *História*, the walls of the house were sometimes decorated, inside and out, with painted mats which gave them a 'fine appearance'. But only aristocratic houses must have featured this embellishment. It was these houses that had the maze-like enclosures, as a naïve picture illustrating Merolla's account shows—and were the first to adopt modifications designed to reinforce the owner's prestige. In connection with these houses, Cavazzi notes the appearance of windows in the regions of Mbamba and Soyo.[10] And Father de Lucques mentions the existence of 'palaces' in this same province:

In the first days of my visit I was invited by the prince to go and see a habitation which he was having built. . . . This palace was made entirely of boards, with several rooms to the story which were separated from one another. One encounters very few homes or palaces of this kind in all of this principality. Only the prince and one other person possess them. They are covered with straw like the other houses.'[11]

This was a dwelling indicating a superior social status and entirely new in conception, since it used boards and had a second story in imitation of Portuguese 'colonial' constructions.

Aristocratic houses were likewise open to 'rich' furniture, which rendered the poverty of the traditional domestic equipment all the more evident by contrast. As for the latter, the *História* indicates: 'The furniture consists . . . one or two mats for sleeping, a pair of gourds for palm wine, a vessel for cooking, and an earthen pot locally made and decorated with designs.'[12]

The missionaries of Loango were amazed and distressed by such discomfort: 'The furniture consisted of four pieces of wood joined to form a square and placed on the ground; on this were placed two thick mats and two very small pillows; and this was table, chairs, and bed.'[13]

The inventory given in each of these accounts is incomplete, however: if furniture was sparse, instruments and vessels used to store property or prepare meals were present and diversified in the form of basketwork, pottery, and dried gourds. The introduction of objects manufactured in Europe and the local reproduction of some of these affected only a small number of 'noble' homes, but it did modernize them in an obvious way: Cavazzi has mentioned the presence of chests and trunks, tables, seats and armchairs (sometimes upholstered in velvet), tapestries, and rugs.[14] The early chroniclers often exaggerated these changes; they accentuated the impression of wealth by multiplying the objects indicating luxury, whether rare fabrics or expensive crockery. The truth is more humble. A document from the Vatican Archives provides the needed corrective when it says of the sovereign: 'The furniture in the house of the king is not much more impressive than that of the other Negroes.'[15]

The Kongo habitation was born of technical knowledge and symbolic necessity. The optimum use of the vegetable materials available has just been mentioned. We must also mention the use, under certain circumstances, of a method of prefabrication: the component elements of the house were prepared separately and transported to the site, with the result that construction was then completed with extreme rapidity. An observation made in Loango indirectly alluded to this method: 'They brought [to Prinze Zinga] the two sides, the two gables, and the roof of a hut which they immediately put together so that he might spend the night in it.'[16]

The role of symbolism is not evident in connection with ordinary houses, but it becomes apparent when one considers the method of construction of 'princely' habitations. In this case, the symbols belong primarily to the two related domains of the sacred and the political. As soon as the decision to build was made, all the necessary materials—palm branches, stakes, etc.— were collected with the cooperation of all. Certain specialized authorities were responsible for the ritual procedures; one, a 'noble' and blacksmith, purified the site and protected it from all harmful influence by first manipulating his bellows and then sprinkling the ground with water from his forge. In Soyo, when the house of the 'count' was being built, three principal chiefs, 'mani Vungo, mani Quime, and mani Pangala', participated in the preparation of the site, in the presence of all the chiefs of the villages under his authority. Laurent de Lucques's careful description helps us to understand the meaning of their actions. It was the mani 'who, according to custom, took part in all the superstitious practices'; together they laid the sacred foundations of the house where the possessor of power would reside, of this habitation which was in a certain sense a symbolic replica of the universe of the people of Soyo; they were renewing this universe by ritually creating the foundations of the new 'palace' of local government. Here is the initial ceremony: 'When they arrive at the site of the house to be constructed, they begin by digging a hole. In it they place certain superstitious objects, while the chiefs, with prophetic looks, accompany this gesture with certain words.'[17] The properly political symbolism is also revealed on this occasion. Of the three notables present, one, 'the mani Vungo', represented the central power. He proclaimed the supremacy of the sovereign and the loyalty required of the 'governor' of Soyo. And this in spite of the extensive and traditional autonomy of this province:

The count [the chief of Soyo], who has been sitting on his seat, rises and goes and plants a stake in the hole [containing the sacred objects]. Just then the mani Vungo comes and takes the stake away. He does this because at one time the count was appointed by the king of the Congo. The king was the possessor of this land. The removal of the stake signifies the sovereign rule of the king of the Congo over this land. To acknowledge this rule the count offers one hundred hoes. After this present has been made, the stake is returned to its place.[18]

While publicly designated as a subject of the sovereign of São Salvador, the chief of Soyo was at the same time shown to all as owner of the most important house in the province. The *mani* Quime and Pangala were two of his four electors and 'two of his principal chiefs'; they participated in the secret war ritual which the 'count' performed once a year (at the time of the ceremony of tribute and homage) in the presence of the 'countess'; and the *mani* Pangala was obliged to request the daily 'benediction' of his superior in order to avoid misfortune and sterility. These notables symbolically built the habitation of the chief of Soyo, just as in time of succession they ensured by their choice the continuity of the government of the province. They laid the sacred foundations of power, and they helped to keep this power strong and fertile, but they remained subordinate. Their 'houses' could not be built in competition with that of the *mani* Soyo : 'While the count is having his house built, none of the three *manis* who are assisting in its construction can have a house built for himself, for this could bring about the death of the count; if they did not observe this prohibition, he would punish them severely.'[19] This primacy was demonstrated not only before the town 'principals', but also before the village chiefs, all of whom gathered on this occasion.

The homes of dignitaries who held political offices always had a structure that was both material and symbolic. The labyrinthine enclosure—the *lumbu*—afforded military protection and traced the boundary beyond which numerous prohibitions were in force, the most private place being the one where the chief and his principal wife spent the night. In Soyo, 'nobody, with the exception of a slave whose job was to keep up the fire, could enter the house where the count and countess slept'; anyone who ventured there 'would be severely punished', for it would cause the sterility of the noble couple and a decline in fecundity and fertility throughout the province.[20] From fragmentary descriptions of the enclosure and houses of the *mani* Soyo we can discover the general plan of the whole. From the periphery, where the guards were, one moved toward the masculine and political pole of the chieftainry : the two 'palaces'—one, of traditional type, was built at the time of the seizure of power, while the other, of modern conception, was primarily designed for the reception of foreigners—the shelters containing the drums, the huts that housed the services and provided the necessities of daily life. The feminine pole, which was also a religious center, consisted of the 'palace' of the 'countess' and the neighbouring cottages—the ones belonging to her companions and attendants and the one that ensured her privacy during menstrual periods. The first lady of Soyo was confined to a narrow domain and the company of her slaves. It was here that certain rituals determining general prosperity were performed and the communal meal required every year during the month of December was taken; here the chief of Soyo went at the time of the annual celebration in his honor to receive ritually the bow and arrows that guaranteed his vigor and invincibility. This section of the chief's residence was also the most sacred and the most private: the 'countess' communicated with the outside world only on rare occasions and then under the protection of a strict etiquette.

The Towns

There is a correlation between the development of the political organization of the Kongo and the birth of a primitive form of urban civilization. How is one to evaluate the extent of this urban civilization? In the early seventeenth century, on the occasion of the nomination of the second bishop of the Kongo, various witnesses reported on the state of the diocese. Summarizing the information furnished by one of these witnesses, Cuvelier and Jadin remark: 'The diocese . . . includes the towns of Bata, Pango, Sundi, Pemba, Sonho, Bamba, Motemo, and others which the witness does not remember, and small localities numbering around 10,000.'[21]

He was referring primarily to the capitals of provinces and to a few secondary centers whose names have been forgotten; as for his estimate of the total number of villages and hamlets, it seems to have been characterized by arbitrariness and exaggeration, in view of the desire to favorably impress the Roman authorities. The same statistical difficulties exist in the case of the capital of the kingdom, Mbanza Kongo or São Salvador. They are explained by the absence of even a crude census, by uncertainty as to the opportunity of including in estimates numerous slaves working for prominent citizens on the plantations along the River Luezi, and by demographic variations affecting the town as a result of the political and economic circumstances. Pigafetta gives the higher figure: 'over one hundred thousand persons' occupying the plateau on which the capital stood.[22] At about the same period (late sixteenth century) Carmelite missionaries estimated that São Salvador numbered at least 30,000 inhabitants. Around 1604 the dean of the cathedral of this town counted 'about two thousand homes', which implied a population on the same order as the preceding estimate. Later—during the second half of the seventeenth century—Cavazzi estimated that the capital might contain sixty to seventy thousand persons *in time of peace*. The disparities in estimates are wide, then: twenty thousand and fifty thousand seem to define the zone of plausibility in the series of known estimates.

This information is sufficient to convince one not to disregard the urban aspects of Kongo society. Was the situation similar outside of São Salvador in the small provincial towns? And especially in the case of the capital of the most important of the provinces, Soyo? In his *Viaggio al Congo*, Monari stated that Mbanza Soyo measured five leagues in circumference. The town was both large and sprawling: it was a town in terms of population, an overgrown village in terms of the material structures that still remain. The author of the *Pratique missionnaire* brings out this fact: 'There is by no means a united population as in Europe, but on the contrary scattered houses. . . . In my mission in Sonho [Soyo], which was situated on a large plain, I could see from my quarters only the habitation of the prince and four or five other houses.'[23]

Various chroniclers confirm this observation, but the agreement ceases as soon as it is a question of determining the population of the capital: thirty thousand according to some, four hundred homes or five to six thousand persons according to others. Size alone is not enough to classify Mbanza Soyo as a town. More significant are the essential functions that were performed there: political, under the authority of the chief of the province, the *mani* Soyo; economic, as a result of the business done in the nearby port of Mpinda; religious and cultural, according to the trader Pieter van den Broecke who, around 1610, counted 'five or six churches' and 'eight or ten schools'. Although this estimate seems approximate and optimistic, the chronicles do agree in recognizing the existence of several churches and the presence of several hundred pupils being instructed in the Portuguese language.[24] The foreign influence, that of merchants and clergymen, tended to favor urbanization, but Mbanza Soyo continued to grow in the manner of a gigantic village, a phenomenon that is seen today in the African quarters of modern colonial towns.

This aspect of 'an overgrown village', to quote Father Proyart, was further accentuated in the provincial capitals of the interior, which were less open to European influences. The concentration of population was fundamentally determined by the presence of a chief of high rank and by the bustle of a major market. The *mbanza* (political center) existed as a function of the *mani* (holder of power), and their two destinies were linked. They rose or fell together; when mobility showed both the vulnerability of power and the fragility of these towns constructed of earth, wood, and palm branches. One thing remains certain: from very ancient times the Bakongo have shown an aptitude for organizing and administering large human collectivities. In his *Giornate* dating from the end of the seventeenth century, Marcellino d'Atri revealed the existence of populated centers which were not the seats of provinces but merely the residences of vassal *mani*; for example, Ngombela, on the frontiers of Nsundi, a town sprawled 'over a length of five or six Italian miles', whose 'natural setting was very pleasant and finer than any other place in the Congo'.[25]

It was at Mbana Kongo (São Salvador) that urban civilization had progressed most visibly. What was the state of the capital at the time when the first Portuguese caravan entered it? Cuvelier, after recalling that the royal city was already 'very large', gives a brief description of it:

The streets were not laid out in straight lines . . . ; there were no avenues bordered with palms or decorative trees. Narrow paths ran in all directions through the tall grass. The habitations of the important dignitaries were close to the king's enclosure. Distributed according to individual taste or whim, they sometimes occupied considerable space. The houses were of unadorned straw, except for their interiors, where there were mats with designs. . . . The dwellings of notables were distinguished from those of ordinary people by a little more room and a greater number of painted mats. They were surrounded by walls made of perennial trees. . . . To the north the mountain was crowned by a dark forest, a kind of sacred wood in which the sound of the axe was never heard. . . . It was in this wood that former kings were buried. The founder of the kingdom, Ntinu Wene, was buried there. To the south lay a large square which was known as *mbasi* or *mbasi a nkanu*, court of justice, because under the great wild fig tree . . . which shaded one corner of this square, the kings were accustomed to dispense justice. It provided a large open space where the people assembled to receive the benediction of the king, or to attend dances and triumphal reviews of the troops.

Not far from the public square was the residence or enclosure of the king, which the local inhabitants called the *lumbu*. This enclosure had a circumference of over one thousand meters and was made of stakes tied together with vines. . . . At the different gates of entry, *mavitu*, the king's guard and a few trumpeters, were stationed. Inside the enclosure there was a large yard; then there was another palisade which enclosed the dwelling of the king, which was approached through a maze. This dwelling was only distinguished from the others by being more spacious. Within the royal enclosure the queen had her dwelling, which was surrounded by the huts of her attendants, who accompanied her when she left the enclosure.[26]

The complex arrangement of the royal enclosure is alluded to in most of the accounts, notably, in a letter (1563) from a Jesuit missionary who mentions 'ten or twelve conciergeries [which] all have their porters, with keys'.[27] This description is a reconstruction from incomplete data, a kind of mechanical portrait, but it gives an over-all impression which is certainly accurate. The structure of the town was dictated by the royal ancestors and the royal couple: sacred wood where the dead kings lay; place where the sovereign dispensed justice, received homage, and displayed his military power; palace organized around a masculine pole (the king's quarters) and a feminine pole (the queen's quarters). The houses, finally, were arranged according to affinities created by clanic affiliations and according to the hierarchical principle which was so powerful in the society of the Kongo: the distance from the royal *lumbu* expressed, as clearly as the size of the habitations, the degree of importance

of the occupant. The appearance of disorder is therefore misleading, although the large distances between houses and the
presence of numerous enclosures preserved the aspect of village-
town at Mbanza Kongo. The fragility of the structures and even
more the absence of a *traditional* monumental architecture distinguished the capital sharply from ancient towns of Eastern
Africa, especially those in the country of Benin.[28] Here urban
civilization remained more potential than real: the intervention
of Portuguese counsellors and masons would not suffice to give
Mbanza Kongo the brilliance and permanence of those magical
cities.

Toward the end of the sixteenth century Pigafetta attempted
a description based on information furnished him by the slave
trader Duarte Lopes. In the process he suggested the changes
that had occurred, the most important of which was the establishment of a separate foreign quarter for the Europeans:

The town is . . . open to the south. It was Dom Afonso, the
first Christian king, who surrounded it with walls. He reserved
for the Portuguese a place also surrounded by walls. He also had
his palace and the royal houses enclosed, leaving between these
two enclosures a large open space where the main church was
built; a square was left in front of it. The doors of aristocratic
homes and of the houses of the Portuguese face walls of the
church. At the entrance to the square a few great lords of the
court have their homes. Behind the church, the square ends in a
narrow street provided with a gate. When you walk through
this gate, you find a great many houses to the east. Outside the
walls which surround the royal residences and the Portuguese
town there are numerous buildings belonging to various lords,
each of whom occupies whatever location pleases him, so he can
live near the court. It is impossible to determine the area of this
town outside the two enclosures, since all the countryside is
filled with rural houses and palaces. Each lord with his group of
habitations encloses a little village. The circumference of the
Portuguese town measures about a mile, and that of the royal
quarter as much. The walls are very thick. At night the gates
are not closed or even guarded.

In an appended commentary, Pigafetta states that the people

knew how to build 'wooden buildings roofed with straw and divided into convenient rooms which were all on the ground floor, for they do not build houses with stories.'[29]

This description of the capital city, despite its apparent precision, does not draw a perfectly accurate picture. According to the author of the *História*, King Afonso surrounded the Portuguese quarter with a strong wall made of stones and lime, but the city as a whole does not seem to have been enclosed with walls. In his account published in 1668, Dapper is positive on this point: 'São Salvador has no ramparts; there are walls only on the southern side.' As for the royal quarter, it was enclosed, according to the ancient custom, by a barricade of stakes and straw; only the section facing the Portuguese homes was constructed of durable materials. Opposite the main church — the Church of the Holy Saviour, built between 1517 and 1526—two closed 'towns' were symmetrically arranged. The topography anticipated that of the colonial towns of the twentieth century. It revealed a racial division: 'In the capital, São Salvador, there are over one hundred Portuguese merchants and over one thousand other natives of Portugal [figures undoubtedly excessive] who have their homes in a separate part of the city from the Blacks.'[30]

The royal enclosure formed the second of these units of private access, but here traditional principles of arrangement and construction reigned supreme: the palace itself, despite the efforts of Dom Afonso, 'was not made of stones and lime'; it was only 'larger than the other habitations'.[31] Thus two types of town coexisted. One—that resulting from foreign efforts—was better constructed and conceived to endure. This was the domain of the Europeans; of commerce; of the imported religion, with its six or seven churches and—at the end of the sixteenth century—its episcopal seat—and the domain of modern learning, which at one time reached one thousand students, 'sons of nobles of the kingdom'. The other town retained the structures of the overgrown village. It remained fragile and its ruins, with the exception of the royal tombs, would be totally obliterated by war and time. It appears to have been a complex system of which the royal enclosure was the center: immediately adjacent to the palace, the habitations of notables of the first rank; on the margins, the domains constructed by the various 'lords' surrounded by their attendants and protégés. These last clusters were so many satellites following an order that forced minor powers toward the periphery.

In less than two centuries, the capital of the Kongo would have lived her glorious moments and received the blows— invasions, defeat at the hands of the Portuguese, conflicts result- ing from rivalries for the throne—that destroyed her. When Father de Lucques arrived for the first time in 1706, he saw only the vestiges of an 'unfortunate town'. A precarious town, clustered about a palace made of 'stakes and straw', was attempt- ing to rebuild itself a short distance from the old ruins. The ruined churches, near which the tombs of the kings were located, the crumbled missionary dwellings were overrun with dense underbrush. Of the cathedral, only the walls remained standing in the shelter of the sturdy rampart erected under the reign of Afonso I. And Laurent de Lucques concludes his retrospective and edifying reflections (for 'this other Jerusalem was destroyed because of the sins' of its inhabitants) by drawing a rough sketch of the dead city:

The enclosure, whose circumference was very large, could very well have served as a fortress. The wall of the enclosure had been joined to the cathedral by some arcades under which the council met. Here the king had been crowned. The place was very suit- able for such an event, for it dominated the whole square, which was very large. One could also see the ruins of other churches and of buildings which, for this country, must have been quite remarkable.[32]

The attempts to restore the kingdom which were made under Pedro IV at the turn of the eighteenth century would succeed neither in re-establishing the lost power nor in restoring to the fallen capital its former splendor. Despair was so total at this time that the young Kongo aristocrat Dona Beatriz, mystic and prophetess, a kind of African Joan of Arc, exhorted her com- patriots to reconstruct São Salvador and founded a national religion to strengthen the failing royalty.

CHAPTER 6

The Fabric of Daily Life

In the Kongo a way of life managed to survive where towns fell in ruins and powers collapsed. This way of life made it possible to make a new start without being disloyal to tradition, without forgetting a style of existence which remained a precious possession inherited from the ancestors. The setting and the institutions might change; the Mukongo slowly altered the habits that governed his daily life. Innovations did not worry him, as long as they did not disturb the ancient fabric of his days.

Time
Besides the natural rhythms that governed collective activities—the course of seasons and days—and individual lives—birth and death—the Mukongo lived within a time which was not so free as certain chroniclers have supposed. The author of the *História*, for example, did not hesitate to declare that the men 'sat on the ground with their legs crossed all day long'.

The week, more than any other unit of the native calendar, imposed its rhythm on all undertakings. It was four days long, as Laurent de Lucques has remarked: 'The holiday is called *sonna* by these people. After this day comes the others: the first day, which they call *gandu*, the second, *chenge*, and the third, *conzo*.'[1]

We should read these names as *nsona, nkandu, nkenge,* and *konzo*. Karl Laman's dictionary defines *nsona* as a holiday devoted to certain religious rites, including that of the ancestors. Even the early documents referred to this day as the one on which one abstained from work and devoted oneself to the 'demons', to use the common missionary expression. These pas-

sages generally referred to our seven-day week, no doubt because
it was rapidly forced upon the people of the Kongo, although
we have no way of knowing how the adjustment of the two
systems was made. An uncertainty of this kind makes it difficult
to identify times of the week marked by a special significance :
for example, days favorable to enterprises of power (Tuesday),
or unfavorable to fruitful marriages (Friday), or dangerous for
pregnant women, who would give birth to a monster if they
went to work in the fields (Saturday). The Christian week was
designated by the word that signified 'Sunday, holy day',
lumingu, from the Portuguese *domingo*; except for Saturday,
which was called *nsabado* (from the Portuguese *sábado*); the
other days were referred to in an ordinal manner as the second
(*kiezole*), the third (kietatu), and so on. This system of nomen-
clature, which had an abstract quality except in the case of the
two days that had religious and magical implications, must have
been used rarely except in dealings with foreigners.[2] Although
equivalents for the above terms have never been clearly established, the Kongo week retained its full usefulness; it regulated
the traditional cults, which continued to exist alongside the
'religion of Sunday'; it governed the economic week, for each of
its four names referred to one of the regular markets which were
held every four or eight days.

The month corresponded to the lunar period and received the
same name as the planet: *ngonda*. The return of the moon and
its light were an occasion for joyous demonstrations; fears were
dispelled, for it was believed that pernicious and aggressive
spirits might be reborn under cover of the *ngonda mpimpa*, the
'darkened moon'. This was a time for joy and dancing. Laurent
de Lucques concluded from this that the Bakongo practiced a
veritable star worship :

It is the custom among these populations to worship the new
moon, like the Turks. This gives rise to many superstitions. They
call the moon in their tongue *engonde*. When the new moon
makes its appearance, they hold a great celebration and express
their joy in their habitual manner. They say, 'Zunga Moniaco
Engonde' [*zunga* (come), *monika* (to appear), and *ngonda*
(moon)], which means, 'Let us welcome our moon which returns
to us again'. It is generally believed among them that the moon

dies and then is born again, although in these regions they are only deprived of the moon for one day, since it is always visible. When it appears again (according to our view), it provides only a thin beam of light. Many worship it as God, as experience has shown me. . . . Such are their follies. There are many other superstitions relating to the moon, but because they are practiced at night, we cannot know them all.[3]

Pigafetta, in discussing the provinces of Soyo and Loango, mentions these same beliefs: 'The inhabitants are pagans. . . . They worship whatever they please, regarding as the most important gods the sun, male element, and the moon, female element.'[4]

But in both cases the interpretation is false. The Bakongo did not develop a lunar cult any more than they associated the sun (*ntangu*) with the supreme being (*Nzambi mpungu*). The latter was conceived as creator of the sky and stars, without this relationship affecting a religious practice that was fundamentally oriented toward the ancestors and certain specialized spirits. In fact, Pigafetta's remark can be understood only in terms of the dualistic system of thought that prevailed among the people of the Kongo.[5] Sun and moon symbolized two groups of antagonistic elements: day and night, light and darkness, world of men and world of spirits, male and female, order and disorder. The magical practices associated with the 'darkened moon' referred to this method of classifying and interpreting the universe. Everyday life, commonplace and peaceful, went on by the light of day; a proverb stated, *Tudianga ye ntangu, ka tudianga ye ngonda*—'We live and eat by the sun, we do not eat by the moon'.[6]

The natural facts were accorded such importance only by virtue of their role as landmarks with which to measure the flow of time. The movement of the stars—regular, cyclical, intangible —gave the Bakongo a way of understanding this time which governed every human life. The moon governed the rhythm of the months. The sun regulated the succession of the days, the sequence of the seasons, the flight of the years; it counted the years for men: *ntangu mvu*. This statement becomes more meaningful if one knows that the word *ntangu* signified at the same time sun, time, exact moment, hour, and instrument for measuring time.[7] More than by the lunar god invented by certain early observers of their society, the Bakongo were fascinated by their own representation of the god Chronos.

In the Kongo, the year (mvu) also seems to have had a dualistic structure. The 'utilitarian' period lasted around nine months. It corresponded to the interval separating two long dry seasons. These dry seasons coincided with the period of most intense social activity, from June to September; this was the time for visits and voyages, the period most favorable to ritual demonstrations and initiations. The useful year—itself called mvu in the northern Kongo—began with the first rains which drew the women to the plantations. It included two main harvests, in January and in May, although certain products like beans ('which yielded in great abundance') could be harvested over a period of several months. It was marked, in November or December, by the performance of the rites of fertility and prosperity which opened the season of most extensive agricultural labor.[8] The part of the year that might be described as 'ceremonial' presented at least two culminating points: the solemn ceremony and feast honoring the ancestors, which was attended by 'blood' relatives, allies, dependents, and friends; and the demonstrations accompanying the payment of the tribute and the rendering of the homage of the village chiefs to the mani of the province or district, demonstrations which glorified the power and the hierarchy by a feast of notables at which each received bounty according to his rank. Hence the requirements of technology, economic activities governed by the regular return of the markets, religious obligations, and political duties formed the fabric of the months and the years. It was upon this fabric that everyday life worked the design of humble and recurrent tasks.

Diet

The humble worker who shouldered the cares of daily life was the Kongo woman. It was her duty to produce offspring, provide the goods necessary for common consumption, and manage her home. All the early authors agree in contrasting her lot with the 'idleness' of the man. In the words of the author of the História, 'the women constitute the wealth of the country'; they provided everyone with food.

This responsibility was not without difficulties. Certain oral traditions—for example, those of the people of the province of Mpangu—attributed the first migrations to a lack of cultivable land, an insufficiency of food resulting from excessive demographic pressure. In 1774, missionaries living in the neighboring kingdom of Kakongo mentioned the presence of a 'colony' of four thousand Basolongo, a tribe that had left the province of Soyo 'several years before' because it was overpopulated.[9] Indeed, it appears that the balance of food had often been precarious, in spite of a statement in a document of 1595 declaring that the kingdom was 'opulent' and 'provided in abundance the principal products necessary for the sustenance of its inhabitants'. The História, however, referred to the lack of storage and to a dangerous improvidence: 'They [the villagers] do not bother to keep anything for the morrow. When they have food they eat it all in one day and fast afterward.' The statement is excessive, but it reveals a real problem; the role played in the diet by noncultivated products, especially in the period between harvests, confirms the impression.

This insecurity persisted in spite of the agricultural skill of the Bakongo: the range of their crops was extensive and their 'gastronomy' adapted itself to radical changes, for example, the transition from the cereals to manioc and the banana. The staple food was a paste to which Laurent de Lucques attributed the name of infundi (but the word fundi means mouthful) and whose preparation he has described: 'With the flour from this grain [which is similar to corn], they make a porridge called infundi, which is prepared in an earthern pot with boiling water. This porridge takes the place of bread.' Eleusine coracana (luko), whose flour produced 'a white bread agreeable to the taste', according to Pigafetta, and sorghum were essential ingredients in this mixture. A description dating from the end of the sixteenth century recalls, with some element of fantasy in its botany, this dominance of the cereals, which were ground by means of 'hand mills': 'Millet, which takes the place of wheat with them, is very abundant. It is found in various colors: white, black, red, and blue. The flour, however, is perfectly white.'[10]

During the seventeenth and eighteenth centuries manioc gradually replaced these basic foods. Cavazzi notes that the manioc root, ground to a powder, provided food for aristocrats and common people alike.[11] Father de Lucques prepared an inventory of the culinary uses of this plant, which could be used as flour, dried in the oven and eaten 'like bread', or cooked in the manner of biscuits; regarding the latter, he said that these titbits, which were called 'bites', had a 'very good taste'.[12] The missionaries of Loango and Kakongo, in their turn, mentioned manioc as the 'most ordinary food' : '[After peeling and soaking the manioc] these people then roast it over the coals or in a copper basin, or else they steam it by placing it in a pot, at the bottom of which there is a little water, and arranging it in such a way that it does not touch the water.'[13]

The description is accurate and corresponds to a practice still followed today. Dishes based on manioc, in the form of flour or of a paste which is cooked after fermentation and kneading, have formed the foundation of the Kongo diet for over two centuries.

In addition to these substitutes for bread there were legumes, sauces, and rather rarely 'a bit of fish, chicken, or meat' — a luxury of 'people of high rank'. The principal leguminous plants were *wandu*, a grain which resembled peas, and *nkasa*, a product of the bean variety (green bean or kidney bean); Cavazzi mentions these two varieties and de Lucques cites 'beans and other kinds of legumes' as the principal elements of the Kongo meal. These 'other kinds' seem to have been yams, pumpkins, and various tubers gathered in their wild state. Corn and rice were included in the diet only in a secondary way. The banana was widely used, especially the variety referred to today as the bread banana, which 'was roasted over the fire in the manner of apples'.

The whole of African culinary art lay in the making of sauces to enhance dishes which tended to be plain. The inventory of spices reveals their variety; but the chief ones here were the various kinds of peppers (especially *Capsicum frutescens*, the hot pepper, onions, cucumber seeds, and more rarely the rhizomes of *Curcuma longa*, or West Indian saffron. In the Kongo, it was by her preparation of *mwamba*, a sauce made from the oil of the palm, that one judged the talent of a cook. Laurent de Lucques distinguished dishes cooked in the oil derived from the fruit of the palm tree by the general term *maoma*. A more recent author gives the following recipe, which has not varied over the centuries :

To do his cooking the Mukongo takes fresh palm nuts, which he selects very ripe. These nuts are boiled in water for almost an hour and then allowed to cool. Then the nuts are kneaded with the hands; the fibers of the fruit are broken, the oleaginous substance runs out, and the mixing continues until the kernels are emptied of pulp. The kernels are set aside, leaving a magma of pulp and fibers which is thinned in the amount of water necessary to the preparation of the dish. When this has been mixed well, the pulp is removed by hand and placed in the bottom of a small basket so as to form a filter. This filter strains out the last remnants of fiber, producing a yellowish liquid which is boiled. Boiling causes oil to form and when water is added this forms an emulsion. As soon as the emulsion is formed, the foods—meat or fish—are added and cooking is continued until the dish is ready. All dishes prepared in this way are called *moambe*. The *moambe* . . . are almost 'impossible' to the European palate: excessive amounts of a pepper called *pili-pili* are used, producing in the mouth an intense burning sensation.'[14]

The Kongo diet was a 'hot' diet—a sixteenth-century chronicler noted the 'lack of taste for sweets' and the infrequent use of sugar cane—which required strong spices and abundant use of salt. At this time salt was a rare product, obtainable only at certain markets, the object of profitable transactions and of greed; de Lucques mentions salt robberies and writes that injured merchants consulted sorcerers in order to establish the identity of the culprits and then expeditiously administered justice. In the coastal regions, salt was obtained from sea water, either by natural evaporation from 'holes' dug near the shore (province of Mbamba), or by induced evaporation by boiling the water in very large earthern vessels (kingdom of Kakongo). In the interior, in the absence of salt of marine origin, housewives used cinders obtained by burning either the male inflorescences of the oil-producing palm or the pith of the palm tree; these cinders were either used as they were, sometimes mixed with ground peppers, or subjected to 'washing' over an earthenware colander.

Fruits occurred in the Kongo diet, although their relative importance has grown since the time of the kingdom, especially during the modern era. Oranges, lemons, and wild bananas were eaten. But certain other fruits enjoyed the preference of the villagers, or were reserved for uses exceeding mere satisfaction of appetite. This was true of the *nsafu*, a fruit produced by a tall and beautiful tree of the same family as the balsam. It had a turpentine flavor—Cavazzi identified it—and was eaten after brief cooking; cooked and wrapped in banana leaves, it was a favorite travelling provision. It was also true of the cola nut, *nkasu* (or *nkaazu*), which was sought after by virtue of its tonic and even aphrodisiac effects, its role as a pacifier, and its therapeutic uses. Pigafetta's informant, and numerous later travellers as well, have remarked how highly the fruit of the cola tree was valued in the Kongo. It was usually chewed slowly, but was sometimes consumed grated or powdered for medical purposes. The 'true' cola was the leading stimulant used by the Bakongo. The *mundyondyo* roots of the shrub *Alchornea floribunda*, which were regarded as a powerful aphrodisiac, were sometimes substituted for cola. After being soaked in palm wine, these roots also helped to inflame the passions and induce visions in time of war or initiatory rituals—which may explain some of the miraculous interventions witnessed on fields of battle in the Kongo.[15] Later Indian hemp, significantly identified as 'Congo tobacco', was used as a narcotic; unlike the preceding one, this plant named *dyamba*, whose use required a veritable ceremony, generally produced torpor and agreeable sensations. The first increased the forces by tenfold, the second favored reverie and enjoyment.

In the matter of drink, the people of the Kongo consumed water and palm wine, or *malafu*. Pigafetta sang the praises of the latter, which was nourishing and diuretic, and explained that it was obtained 'by boring a hole in the top of the palm tree' at the base of the immature inflorescence. After the sap, which had a slightly milky appearance, had been collected in this manner, it underwent a brief period of fermentation. This drink was so highly regarded that de Lucques declared, 'They [the inhabitants of Soyo] do nothing but drink'. In reality social necessity signified more than the pursuit of alcoholic stimulation; *malafu* was required on many occasions: in the context of civility and commerce, at festivals and marriages, during rituals and ceremonies honoring the ancestors. Palm wine might be called the life blood of Kongo society and civilization. In his ninth *Relation*, Father de Lucques mentions a drink called *ovallo* which Antonio Zucchelli also recalls; describing it as 'a kind of wine made from corn and other ingredients, which was very light and resembled our orgeat'.[16] But this corn beer seems to have been used regionally in the province of Mbamba, near Angola. Later, new fermented drinks such as 'sugar cane wine' and 'pineapple wine' were invented—after spirits introduced by traders had made alcoholism one of the least disputed European imports.

Appetite, necessity, and therapeutic ideas had dietary consequences which disconcerted foreign observers. Cavazzi has mentioned the consumption of caterpillars, insects, savannah rats, snakes, etc.;[17] craving for meat, but also refinements of taste, explain this custom. The mediocre flour derived from the kernel of the palm nut, which Pigafetta mentions, was used by villagers only 'in time of famine', as the compiler of the História remarks. Geophagy—the soil of termites' nests being the only dirt consumed—was a way of outwitting hunger; but under certain circumstances it was prescribed for pregnant women; it also answered the needs of gourmets who wished to 'drive away the taste of fat' after too heavy a meal.

Laurent de Lucques does not present a flattering picture of 'the everyday life' of the 'Ethiopians of Soyo'. He criticizes both their gastronomy and their 'table manners':

In the evening they go to their houses. Here they lie on the ground like animals and stuff themselves with food. They eat only one meal, the evening one. During the day they make do with a few peanuts or a handful of manioc, and smoke tobacco. After they have eaten, they lie by the fire. Overcome with drowsiness, they fall asleep.[18]

The description lacks sympathy and accuracy. It is true that the main meal was the evening meal, but it conformed to rules which the Capuchin missionary chose to ignore. The men and boys of a single large family ate together, served by the women, and expressed their solidarity by consuming common food and drinking water from the same enormous gourd. The women, the girls, and the young boys ate around the edges of the room. For all, the meal was characterized by codified gestures: holding pellets of solid food with the first three fingers of the right hand, drinking the sauce with the aid of a scoop made of a piece of banana leaf or of *matete.*

The role of convention and etiquette was greater in the case of aristocratic families, where it sometimes followed a veritable protocol. The *História* presents a crude picture of the ritual that governed the king's meal:

When he eats, a large caldron of the type we have spoken of, filled with boiled or roasted meat, is set in front of him. He eats with his fingers, and makes distribution to his servants, giving each one his share, which they receive with great clappings of their hands to show their gratitude. They would consider it a great disfavor if he did not give them this share.'[19]

Eating was in reality less primitive; officials of the palace, servants, tasters verifying the purity of food and drink, and other dignitaries were present, and the royal furniture was embellished by European contributions: tables, armchairs, mats, and crockery. The meal of the sovereign, taken with solemnity and in a solitary fashion, has always had a semiritual quality. The *História* indirectly reveals the requirement of precedences in describing the position of the *mani* Mbata, the second power in the kingdom: 'He sometimes eats at the king's table, but lower than him and standing up, a privilege which is granted to nobody, not even sons of the king.'[20] In fact, recent descriptions (late seventeenth and eighteenth century) show that in some sense the meals of distinguished persons followed two 'models'. The first, 'westernized' model was used especially for the reception of foreigners, as Father de Lucques reveals after his first 'collation' with the 'prince of Soyo', when he observes: 'He entertained us . . . according to the customs of the Whites.' The second model was faithful to the ancient practices and expressed the permanence of tradition. De Lucques suggests this when he describes a meal offered by the *mani* Soyo at the time of the annual festival celebrating his power:

On another day, the feast given by the count took place. He served food to everyone, so that it was necessary to kill a large number of oxen and other animals. . . . There were only a few mats laid on the ground, and some wooden vessels into which

the food that had been prepared was placed. . . . After the benediction the count sat down on a mat and began to make distribution in the following manner. To each *mani* he sent a dish containing meat with a proportionate quantity of *infundi*. . . . The
mani, surrounded by their subjects, were placed in the square
where the count was, in order. When they had received the dish,
they proceeded to divide it up among their people, who only
received a quantity equal to two nuts.[21]

On this occasion the meal became less a means of distributing
food than a symbolic act demonstrating relationships of power
and dependence.

Dress

The Bakongo, who were highly skilled as weavers, very early
accorded great importance to the art of dressing. The costume
varied according to social status and circumstances; it expressed
wealth and power, or their absence; it also indicated the wearer's
occupation. On this subject the *História* offers only the briefest
notations, but they do reveal that dress was indicative of social
class:

They [the people of the Kongo] are clad from the waist
down. . . . The men wear the skins of wild animals in the manner
of an apron. Chiefs are distinguished by fabrics and skins of better
quality. Over their shoulders or over the skin they wear a net, a
small garment which falls just below the knee and protects them
from the cold. Those who can, trim their clothing with velvet or
fringe. The women do not wear the skins of animals like the
men. They wrap their heads in scraps of cloth. Their heads are
shaved.[22]

Pigafetta is more specific, if not consistently accurate in his
descriptions. Of the 'common people and the poor', he says that
they wore a piece of rough cloth secured at the waist and covering the lower part of the body, the upper part remaining bare.
Dapper mentions the same type of loincloth, a kind of 'long
robe' that covered the men 'from waist to feet'; Laurent de
Lucques refers to the palm-cloth garment with which the
Bakongo 'girded their loins' as the *(n)tanga*; and Father Proyart

describes the traditional garment in the kingdoms of Loango and Kakongo as a piece of cloth used to 'drape the loins' and resembling a 'kilt of the type worn by our bakers and brewers'.[23] These observations, made from the sixteenth to the eighteenth century, clearly reveal in different terms the permanence of the male national costume. Variety was not excluded, however: by the material used and the workmanship, the loincloth indicated the wearer's social rank. In Loango wide use was made of 'a cloth made from grass two feet long and woven in the manner of our fabrics'. According to Dapper, four kinds of loincloth woven from palm fibers were distinguished:

The finest ones are figured, and although they are only two and one half spans wide, it takes the most skilful weaver fifteen or sixteen days to make one of them. Only the king or those who have his authorization can wear these garments. . . . The other two kinds are for the common people, and they are crude and plain.[24]

In speaking of the Kongo, Dapper also mentions a cloth made for men of humble rank which 'took the place of clothing' for them, was likewise 'crude and plain', and was made from the fibers of the *matombe* tree; Laman identifies the *matombe* in his dictionary as a 'type of bamboo'.

On the subject of feminine dress, Pigafetta states:

The women cover the lower part of their bodies with three strips of cloth, the first long and falling to the heels, the second shorter, and the third still shorter . . . each being draped about the body and opening in the front. They cover their breasts with a bodice which falls to the waist. These garments are made of the same palm cloth. . . . The women of middle rank also dress in this manner but use coarser materials. As for slaves and women of the common people, they cover only the lower part of the body, the rest remaining bare.[25]

A century later, Laurent de Lucques described a similar feminine costume, with the difference that the three strips of cloth were replaced by a single loincloth secured at the waist: 'In addition to the *tanga*, the women wear another piece of cloth with which they cover the breasts and yet another with which they cover the shoulders like a mantle. Hence their appearance is not immodest, as some persons imagine.'[26]

And the Jesuit Bras Correa also points out that the dress of the 'Mocicongo' 'was always very decent in comparison with that of other barbarian peoples'. Several accounts confirm the wearing of a strip of cloth wrapped around the chest, but the most common style of dress seems to have consisted of the loincloth alone, leaving the breasts free.

The early chroniclers naturally devoted more attention to the costume of 'men of high rank' than they did to the very simplified attire of villagers. Pigafetta meticulously reconstructs the clothing of the king and his 'courtiers' as tradition had established it before the introduction of 'Portuguese customs':

[They] wore fabrics made of palm . . . ; they covered the lower part of the body, securing the cloth with a belt woven of the same material and finely worked; in front, as decoration, they hung apron-style pretty and delicate skins, such as the skins of small tigers,* civets, sables, martens, and the like, with the heads left intact. For greater ostentation, they flung about the naked flesh of their shoulders a kind of round surplice called in their language *incutto*, which fell below the knee and was woven like a net of fine palm fibers: the links were bordered with fringed tufts, making a very graceful effect.[27]

The description is inaccurate however: the term *incutto* (*nkutu*) referred to the little holy sac filled with protective objects with which vested chiefs armed themselves when they travelled. Indeed, de Lucques mentions this use of it. The cape described by Pigafetta as a surplice was called *zamba*; made with consummate skill by a process similar to crocheting, it was reserved for leading dignitaries. The bust of Antonio Manuel, the ill-fated Kongo ambassador who died in Rome, suggests the fineness of this honorific garment; Fransesco Caporale, who sculpted the bust which is preserved in the basilica Santa Maria Maggiore, has faithfully reproduced this 'ethnographic' detail.

Laurent de Lucques's observations at the turn of the seven-

---

* He must mean panthers.

teenth century reveal an alteration of the aristocratic costume. Skins used as decoration and to indicate social importance are no longer mentioned; superior rank was indicated by the wearing of a large draped garment caught at the shoulders and partly concealing the loincloth, 'one end of which was allowed to trail on the ground'. The mantle, identical to 'those of Europe', was now used; but the notables still wore over it 'a garment fashioned from palm-leaf fiber which they called *sacco*', which was a modern version of the ancient *zamba*.

In the matter of dress, the privileges and symbols of pre-eminence were maintained with extreme care, as the above indicates. Dapper provides further proof when he considers the kinds of fabrics—those that were finest and 'figured'—and the kinds of garments of which the sovereigns or great notables had the exclusive use. The art of weaving and dressmaking was intimately associated with royalty for reasons which were both mystical, since costume was identified with personality, and economical, since cloth was the basis of taxation and played the role of currency. Proyart mentions a significant prohibition with regard to the kings of Kakongo. During one period, they were able to keep only that merchandise from the European countries which excluded fabrics. The possession, the touch, the very sight of imported fabrics was forbidden them; the person of the sovereign and the first national industry were thus jointly protected.

This protection did not last; it even seems that the kings of the Kongo managed to avoid it. The traders very soon noticed that the natives of the kingdom preferred clothing, caps, and red cloth to 'hardware'. During the seventeenth century, with the growth of the Negro slave trade, the importing of fabrics increased and the 'piece' became a measure of exchange. Competition multiplied the types of fabric offered: printed linens and cottons, striped linens, solid-colored cottons, crude flannels, Dutch chasselas, and striped, checked, and solid-colored fabrics of all kinds.[28] The seduction of the exotic succeeded in causing the slow decline of local weaving.

Dress — at least when it was necessary to appear in the presence of foreigners—was modelled upon European fashions. Pigafetta stresses this development, which he links with the adoption of the Christian faith:

[The nobles of the court] wore mantles, capes, overcoats of scarlet and silk, each according to his means; they began to wear hats and caps, sandals of velvet and leather, Portuguese boots, and broadswords at their sides. . . . The women also dressed in the Portuguese style, except that they did not wear mantles; but they covered their heads with veils and over this wore caps of black velvet trimmed with jewels, and gold chains around their necks.[29]

Later, at Soyo, Father de Lucques observed two forms of aristocratic dress. The first, faithful to tradition, used the 'local cloths' —those velvets or brocades 'that were every bit as good as silk'— and was the exclusive prerogative of the *mani Soyo* and those 'principals' enjoying his authorization. The second, which was required for audiences granted to foreigners, was characterized primarily by a mantle made of silk. According to the circumstances, the costume expressed the permanence of the traditional order or the acceptance of a tempered modernism. There should also be mentioned the taste for certain imported costumes expressing the *sacred* character of power; but the wearing of these remained the privilege of a restricted élite, very close to the sovereign. There was, for example, the costume of the knight of the order of Christ, which the kings of the Kongo assumed the right to grant during the seventeenth century.[30] And again, the special dress of certain missionaries: the old queen Dona Anna, for the visit which Father de Lucques paid her, wore the habit of the Capuchins, which led the latter to observe ironically, 'She is as hairy as a man, so that if she did not shave, she would have a long beard like the Capuchins'.

This anecdote suggests the importance every Mukongo attached to his personal appearance, to the image of himself he presented to others. He had a taste for the emblems and adornments of social pre-eminence. The notables wore arm bands, *dyenge a mfumu*, made of copper and decorated with motifs based primarily on a masculine symbolism; the kings themselves wore them in the seventeenth and eighteenth centuries; and descendants of old aristocratic families still exhibit them today in order to enjoy a consideration which their present condition no longer inspires. Young girls of quality were allowed to use the *nkwangu* as their first finery: it was a very plain little bracelet or anklet which was nevertheless regarded as a mark of elegance. Women of high rank loaded themselves down with heavy rings displaying their dignity. Their neck bands (*dyenge dia nsingu*), made of copper and decorated with rich stylized designs, weighed several pounds. Their ankle bands (*dyenge dia kulu*) were also heavy pieces, whether solid or hollow, often weighing over seven pounds; linear motifs traced with a pointed instrument symbolized their rank and wealth. Most of the chroniclers were impressed by these cumbersome adornments, which were at once a mark of aristocratic status, an ornament, and a 'travelling fortune'. Lighter jewels satisfied feminine coquetry in a less selective fashion: nose rings of the type known as 'creole style', rings, buckles, and earrings.[31] The Portuguese influence, by widening the conception of luxury, modified the tastes of the upper class: the women coveted 'jewels' and gold chains or, more modestly, pearl necklaces and belts; the men wore broadswords, which were known as 'knives of respectability'.

Concern for appearance also required a treatment of the human body, a utilization of the resources of cosmetics. Palm oil was rubbed into the skin to make it soft and shining after the bath. To this, juice from the sugar cane was sometimes added to accentuate the dark and gleaming appearance of the body. But the principal cosmetic ingredient was *tukula* powder, which was prepared from the red wood of a tree of the species *Pterocarpus*. It had multiple uses: for beauty care, in medical preparations, in dyeing. Pigafetta notes that *tukula* entered into the composition of certain remedies and, after being reduced to a powder and mixed with palm oil, was used to 'anoint' the entire body. A contemporary of his, Father Garcia Simões, likewise mentions the various uses suggested by 'gallantry' and medicine.[32] *Tukula* appeared in the course of the initiation undergone by the young people; specifically, while they were serving their complete apprenticeship—including their introduction to aesthetic rules and conventions—and arriving at the fullness of masculinity and femininity. To be fully a man or fully a woman was, in a certain sense, to be beautiful. Pigafetta alludes to a fragrant powder of 'gray sandalwood' which was also used in cosmetics and unguents; Cavazzi and Da Silva Correa, a historian of

Angola who lived in the eighteenth century, confirmed the practice, but this variety of 'sandalwood' has eluded identification.

Little is known about the art and fashions of feminine coiffure. A certain diversity has always prevailed[33]—not just the practice of shaving the head mentioned by the compiler of the *História*— as the use of flat combs of wicker or carved wood suggests. The sharpening of the teeth—those that had been sharpened to a point were sometimes referred to as 'laughing teeth'—corresponded more to an aesthetic requirement than to an initiatory obligation or the need for a mark of identity. The concern for elegance was dominant: it was said that teeth 'broad as those of a goat' were not beautiful. Tattooing (*nsamba*) had more complex functions. It took the place of identity cards; each region, each village even, had a type of tattooing peculiar to itself, which was recognized by its location (forehead, cheek, shoulders, back, chest), and by the arrangement of its motifs. *Nsamba* also had a therapeutic and protective role; the engraving of the skin with a reed needle and dyes was accompanied by the imposition of personal prohibitions. But tattooing also represented a quest for elegance which seems, in the case of women, to have been associated with a refinement of erotic technique.

Laurent de Lucques describes a practice observed in the case of little girls of five or six which presents the *nsamba* as a test of future fecundity:

The little girl is made to lie on the ground and then this man [the specialist] begins to carve a rose or some other object with the point of a knife. . . . If the little girl endures these incisions without crying out, they say that she will be good for childbearing; but if she cannot endure them and cries, they abandon the operation and say that this girl will be good for nothing. And some, when they wish to marry, first ascertain whether the girl bears a perfect design on her belly.[34]

Here tattooing becomes a guarantee of fecundity, a factor in the covenant between men and women.

Love
The *História*, that testimony of an age and mirror of the indignation of missionaries, says of the Bakongo that their sins 'are

those of sensuality or of lust with several women'. At the beginning of the seventeenth century Bishop Manuel Baptista
observed bitterly that few people 'regard the vices of the senses
as sins'. Polygamy was then considered an undeniable proof of
sexual promiscuity, and one chronicler even tried to attribute
this aberration to the abuse of spicy foods.

The facts, although varied, do not confirm the impression of
license. Kongo society was marked by a dualistic conception
which, in the final analysis, was based on a system of relationships between masculine and feminine symbols. This suggests
that relations between the sexes could scarcely be free, since they
were the model for a whole group of real and symbolic structures. The evidence furnished by everyday life bears this out.

From infancy, boys and girls were separated not only by their
occupations and the different educations they received, but also
because they gathered in very separate places: the boys spent
the night in the house of the men (*nzo kiyakala*) and the girls in
the house of the women (*nzo kinkento*). When they were older
their mutual relations were dominated by reserve and modesty,
or *nsoni*. The initiation they underwent to render them fully
adult and full-fledged members of the clan expressed less a
separation of the sexes than a desire for adjustment. The women
took some part in this total education, which led some early
observers to regard the initiatory schools as centers tolerating
'shameful practices', notably in the apprenticeship in dancing
which, according to Laurent de Lucques, 'had to do with idols'
and 'was always obscene'. In reality, initiation recognized and
confirmed the state of sexual maturity, but it did not thereby
grant unlimited freedom. It taught self-control and traced boundaries that were not to be crossed. A young Congolese sociologist
recalled this when he wrote that on this occasion one learned
'when and how to give in or to refuse . . . where the limits of
normal flirtation and horseplay lay.'[35]

Nor were the dances of the Bakongo, to the beat of the drums
(*ngoma*), a pretext for mass release, in spite of appearances. In
certain dances men and women were divided into two facing
rows. The partners alternately stamped in place and rushed
toward one another to simulate the act of copulation. This sug-
gestive choreography was not merely a technique for provoking
sexuality. It attested to the condition of a society in which all

efficacity of human action was associated with the great natural forces and with demonstrations of fecundity. In such a context the prototype of all effective action is the sexual act. The early chroniclers confused representation and fact, symbolic behavior and license. And a certain missionary went so far as to write that 'the pen of a devout person refuses to put such things on paper'.

The code of conventions and the hierarchy of punishments clearly indicate that relations between the sexes were precisely defined. Children were soon familiar with the 'mysteries of generation', as van Wing puts it; but their adolescence was not therefore abandoned to the freedom of desire. Encounters between young people of different sexes were subject to control which did not always exclude experiment, but which punished promiscuity by means of physical sanctions and placing in slavery. Sexual attempts made on women returning from work, or at the bath, entailed the same risks; and sometimes a greater risk if the attempt was classified as adultery or rape. Moreover, the vocabulary proper to sexual matters appears to have been complex: direct or allusive, reserved for young people or for adults, proper or obscene. Dignity and deportment did not tolerate errors; punishments existed to ensure their respect.

To the people of the Kongo the solitary vice was not a vice, but homosexuality was severely chastised. The molesting of a young girl belonged less to the realm of infractions invoking the punishment of the ancestors and strong moral condemnation than to the order of injustice; it was a wrong done to the girl's family and reparation had to be made to compensate the injury suffered. Adultery disturbed both social relations and relations with the gods. It was said to cause a specific malady called *kesa*. It always entailed punishments which became more severe when the social status of the wronged party was higher. The two culprits were sometimes condemned to death, in which case they were burned alive after being transformed into torches by being wrapped in dry banana leaves. Or their lives were spared, but they lost their condition of free men and were sold as slaves. Adultery often caused wars between villages, for the ordinary procedures—payment of a fine and ritual purification—seldom operated in an immediate way.[36] For all these reasons 'adultery was very rare', as a missionary working in the Kongo toward the

DAILY LIFE IN THE KINGDOM OF THE KONGO

middle of the seventeenth century observed.[37] More criminal still was incest. It was the very essence of crime, which brought the most terrifying calamities on the whole collectivity: droughts and famines, sudden and terrible maladies, sterility of women and of the earth. It was the instrument of the return to chaos, and everyone sought to avoid such a catastrophe.

The amorous amusements of unmarried men safely avoided these fearful boundaries. They were free to try their chances with the girls, to anticipate marriage during the long engagement period, or to profit by the complaisance of certain notables who were the possessors of numerous slave women. They seldom had the opportunity of addressing themselves to women of easy virtue except in the few towns, where the foreign presence had caused the appearance of 'a licentious life', to quote the História. And with the latter, the spread of syphilis had begun. Pigafetta makes mention of this 'French malady' (called chitangas, according to him), which was 'treated by means of a sandalwood ointment'.[38] The European influence did not limit itself to this deplorable effect; it also modified the forms of feminine modesty and coquetry, as an early observation made in the kingdom of Loango suggests: 'In Loango, the purebred African woman covers her breasts and fears the curiosity of masculine gazes; if she meets a European, she raises her loincloth and strikes, not without coquetry, the pose of the Venus de Medici.'[39]

It is more difficult to imagine the evolution of the amorous sentiment. The relationship leading to marriage made considerable allowance for love, although considerations of familial strategy and incest taboos (which excluded union between persons regarded as of 'one blood') limited the choices. The market was generally the occasion for the first encounter: here young people observed one another, began courting, and exchanged small gifts, after making certain their relatives were agreeable. Affection continued to exist after marriage, but it was restrained: if conjugal jealousy was deemed necessary, it rarely gave rise to passionate outbursts. Emotional scenes were less often the result of disappointed love than of some breach of the mutual obligations binding the spouses. Indeed, nkundi—the term designating the favorite wife of the polygamous notable—described a bosom friend as well.[40] The relationship of the couple was based as much on respect for a kind of tacit agreement as on mutual inclination. The moment distrust developed, divorce threatened. The first wave of missionaries were scandalized by this kind of union which, out of ignorance and prejudice, they compared to a precarious concubinage. Hence, de Lucques writes:

These Blacks have the custom, before entering into marriage [in the Christian sense], of buying the woman, taking her to their home, and living with her for several years in concubinage. . . . They give as the reason for this that before marrying they wish to discover the inclinations of this woman. . . . When a difference arises between them, they part without the slightest difficulty. In these parts no one cares about loss of reputation or dishonor.[41]

The interpretation is false and tendentious. In reality this was a true marriage—with its contingent and regular period of probation—in accordance with the custom of the Kongo, if not with Christian conventions. It was a marriage which appears always to have been an important matter, especially since the polygamy of 'nobles and dignitaries' monopolized a great number of women. The chronicles confirm this over the centuries.

Free or slave, woman was a rare and coveted possession; the *História* notes: 'women have more value than men'. All women did not arrive at marriage by the same process. One woman— the slave—was purchased; another was exchanged for a matrimonial compensation, by means of negotiation and a complex etiquette. In spite of his disapproval, Laurent de Lucques describes the practices observed on such occasions in the province of Soyo with some accuracy:

It is the general custom in these African countries that a man who desires to marry a young girl first goes to see her father [error: her maternal uncle] and discusses above all the price to be paid, for the husband buys his wife. When the price has been agreed on, the young man immediately becomes the young girl's master, but before taking possession of her, they drink *malaffo* [*malafu*, palm wine] together. . . . Before living [with her husband], the woman who has been bought goes to spend a specified period of time in a small hut (*kikumbi*). After she has entered this hut, she follows certain prescriptions, for example, to wash her head a certain number of times every day and to rub her body with *tucula* [red wood powder]. . . . In these huts, the fire is always kept lit. . . . [The young girl] cannot leave for any reason other than the one mentioned above [she must go and receive the benediction of her maternal uncle a specified number of times]. Here she eats, here she does everything. And she must be careful not to throw anything out of doors. . . . While the wife is living in the little hut, the husband goes to live on an island in the Zaïre [Congo] River until she has completed the pre-scribed time. He is required to send her a needle, a roasted chicken, some *tucula*, a certain number of sugar canes, and other things. Her brother is required to send her some *tucula* in a piece of cloth which she wraps about her loins in the superstitious belief that this loincloth will give her strength and many children. . . . When the period for staying [in the hut] is over, they prepare a superstitious meal in which the fiancée and her relatives take part. Of the remaining *tucula* she gives some to her father and mother, who rub their bodies with it, and she uses some to rub the body of her husband, unless she takes it to a place where two roads intersect and leaves it there, for a super-stitious reason.[42]

This brief description reveals the symbolic order that underlay marriage in the Kongo. At the beginning of the process, the consumption of palm wine expressed the giving of consent; at the end, the common meal represented the conclusion of the union established between the two partners and their respective families. The seclusion of the two young people echoed, on an individual level, the collective seclusion that operated at the time of the *initiations*; it was a test; it helped to reinforce the femininity of the wife and the masculinity of the husband; it provided a transition toward a new social status—adulthood—achieved through the marriage and the progeny that would result from it. But the practice was also significant in another sense. It revealed the role of the young wife's brother, the 'option' he assumed with regard to future children, who would be legally and sentimentally related to him. It was he who trans-mitted the fertility belt. This symbolic action finally expressed the fertile alliance of two families, two lineages which shared the same anointing with *tukula* or were signified by the meeting of two roads. A procedure so charged with meaning cannot have been associated with a frivolous conception of marriage. It sanctified it; if divorce was a possible solution to discord, it nevertheless remained a serious matter.

Certain unions did not conform to the foregoing practices. For instance, in the case of the marriages of women with the rank of slaves; a feast sufficed to publically demonstrate the bond established. On the other hand, the upper aristocracy was subject to obligations or enjoyed privileges which revealed its independence from the common rules. The king of the Kongo, to give his power a religious basis, had to marry a woman of the 'house' of the province of Mbata, as a statement (1595) recalls : 'The king has the custom of taking as a wife only a daughter of the duke of Batta, who according to tradition has the privilege of confirming him in the royal power.'[43]

In the kingdom of Loango, the 'princesses' chose their husbands themselves and renounced them at will; they could impose monogamy on them and had the power to 'have them put to death when they gave them any cause for jealousy'. The missionary J. J. Descourvières, who reports this fact, adds, 'The men cannot refuse these alliances, which are honorable but inconvenient for them'.[44] This reversal of roles, which gave the woman of royal family an authority and freedom which the common man did not possess with regard to his wives, had already been remarked by Olfert Dapper. He interpreted it by asserting that the 'mother' and 'sisters' of the sovereign could sleep with as many men as they wished.[45] This solution made it possible to avoid the risk of incest within a restricted aristocracy, but did not affect the status of 'princesses' whom an ordinary marriage would subject to the rule of a husband of inferior rank. In the province of Soyo—and undoubtedly elsewhere—the rank of *mani*, or holder of power, was accompanied by special matrimonial privileges. Pieter van den Broecke describes them as follows :

The count [the *mani* Soyo] has the custom, despite his age, of taking into his home some beautiful young girl and, when she has a child, giving her with this child to one of the principal nobles. The latter count themselves very honored, and the gift ordinarily brings them other advantages.[46]

A century later, Laurent de Lucques described this practice in connection with one of the foremost chiefs of the same province:

When he takes possession of his territory . . . he is presented with a young girl whose choice he has approved. He keeps her in his home until she is pregnant. Then she regains her freedom; and the man who is able to enter into marriage with her is considered very fortunate. When she is married, he is presented with another young girl, and so on . . . as long as he remains in power.[47]

This last observation, which implies that the child born of the *mani* belonged to him, recalls similar customs observed in other regions of the Negro African world, where the same functions were found: in this way the chief increased the number of young women at his disposal, increased his progeny, and, by receiving and conferring coveted women, multiplied alliances which reinforced his power. If the Kongo noble knew how to reserve the element of affection and show it to his favorite wife, he was not unaware that matrimonial policy was in all times and places an instrument of politics.

Etiquette

Kongo civilization may be seen as a system of proprieties and conventions. The latter were numerous: there were a great many occasions when a ritual or a protocol had to be observed. An apprenticeship in the prescribed forms of behavior started with the first years of life, which is common; but this apprenticeship appears to have been harsh, which is less so. The child learned to honor his parents and to fear the 'malediction' which, in the case of a serious breach, would exclude him from the familial group and cause him to be pursued by an evil fate throughout his life. The young Mukongo discovered early that he was in the position of a 'subject' (*nleke*) with respect to an elder or 'ancient one' (*mbuta*). He owed the latter not only demonstrations of deference but also obligations of service and labor. These primary submissions prepared him to revere and dread his political superiors.

Relations between equals were least hampered by the rigors of formalism. But in the case of the 'principals', protocol was never absent, and the rules of courtesy expressed the subtle distinctions within the hierarchy. Observations made in the late nineteenth century show the persistence and complexity of these rules, despite the blows endured by Kongo society:

In a gathering of chiefs, this is how the salutations proceed : The most important of the dignitaries grasps his own right wrist in his left hand, places the index finger of his right hand on the ground, carries it to his temples three times, opens the hand, presses the tips of the fingers to the ground, and then with closed fists beats the hands together rhythmically. This last gesture is repeated by every person present.[48]

The same document describes methods of salutation which recall those reported by the early chronicles: hand-clappings accompanied by knee-bendings. This agrees with an observation made by Laurent de Lucques: 'When they meet some person of quality on the road, they fall to their knees and greet him by clapping their hands, and then go on their way; if they are equals, they simply go on their way.'[49]

The rubbing of dirt into the temples was required behavior for a dignitary who held an office in the presence of the high-ranking *mani* on whom he depended: 'Falling to his knees, he claps his hands several times, throws himself on the ground, and smears himself with earth and dust.'[50] The conventions regulating feminine decorum were just as rigid: the woman, kneeling or with bent knees, clapped her hands in greeting and then 'she carried those hands one at a time to either temple and finally pressed them to the center of her forehead'.[51] Only aristocratic women in possession of power commanded formal consideration and were obliged to maintain attitudes indicating their 'nobility'. Zucchelli mentions one of these postures which necessitated keeping a finger in one nostril during a public conversation, 'as a sign of nobility and high birth'.[52]

The man of the Kongo lived in a world of symbols, prescriptions, and prohibitions all indicative of a religious order. Language revealed social rank and the respective positions of those who used it. Only a few 'nobles' could speak in the presence of the king; only a slave communicated directly with a 'foreigner', persons born in the clan making use of an 'interpreter', only minor chiefs conversed with a visitor on the day of his arrival. The entourage and equipment accurately indicated the rank of the man (or woman) who was its center and beneficiary. Thus, toward the end of the seventeenth century, the chief of the province of Soyo rivaled the weakened kings of the Kongo in splendor; he tried to overwhelm them by his pomp as much as by his ambition and intrigue. Laurent de Lucques describes the ritual for audiences granted by the 'prince' when he reports the reception of a French ambassador in 1702. After mentioning the tributes rendered by 'many soldiers', and describing the noise of musketry, drums, and 'other barbarous instruments', he notes:

At last we entered the audience chamber, where the prince was seated. His throne was decorated with a Dutch tapestry and a red damask cushion trimmed with gold braid. The prince wore a mantle, according to the custom of the country, but it was of very fine multicolored silk. He was surrounded by the four electors of the principality, the captain general and other officers of the militia, as well as by numerous fidalghi [fidalgos] and lords of his court. The electors wore mantles of various colours.[53]

The 'princess' herself could not appear unless she was accompanied by slave women of her house and persons belonging to her retinue.

The movements of high-ranking dignitaries required the same honorific manifestations, together with certain ritual precautions imposed by a conception of power and authority as sacred. On such occasions 'the custom was to repair and clear the roads' and to cover with mats places where the dignitaries might have to make contact with the ground by descending from their 'wooden horses' or litters. The idea was to keep wild nature at a distance, even at a short distance, although it was a serious threat to the civilized order, and to protect the powerful from the injurious contact of the earth. They never went without an escort and musicians announced their approach. As soon as the king decided to leave the confines of his palace, his 'servants plied bells, trumpets, and drums with a noise that was heard from afar'; when it was the queen who left, 'her ladies accompanied her, playing castanets with their fingers'.[54] Public appearances of the queen were exceptional, however, and owing to her rank and her religious functions, the rules were all the stricter for those who found themselves on her path.

The king was at the center of a whole system of rules, prohibitions, and obligations which isolated him, protected him mystically, and made him the object of demonstrations of respect and fear. An etiquette, which was modified in imitation of European practices, and a strict protocol expressed this at all times. Pigafetta mentions the prostration by which one greeted the sovereign and expressed total obedience to him. Father de Lucques describes a group of notables—'councillors and princes of the court'—'lying on the ground before their king like dead men, all covered with dust'. But it was during meals that the royal person best appeared in its state of sacred isolation. Pigafetta reports that the *mani* Kongo 'always ate alone' and Dapper confirms this observation. In Loango, according to Dapper, nobody ('neither man nor beast') could watch the sovereign consume his meal, 'under pain of death'; when the king was about to drink, a servant struck two iron staffs together so that all present might fling themselves face down on the ground during the necessary time.[55] The homage rendered to the holder of the supreme power seems, therefore, to have been addressed to a man who was half deified: it combined fear and trembling with the conventions of protocol.

CHAPTER 7

Master and Slave

The early chroniclers or observers of daily life in the Kongo were disconcerted by manners and customs they regarded as 'savage' or 'pagan'; they were even more bewildered by certain aspects of the social and political organization. This is not surprising. Their 'sociology' was very often poor and faulty, if only because of their frequent ignorance of the Kikongo language. A brief review of their observations shows this to be true. Polygamy was of paramount interest, for it symbolized the fundamental incompatibility between the imported Christianity and the indigenous civilization. The *História do Reino do Congo* mentions it, pointing out the dominant role of the principal wife (the *mobãda*, a term adopted by colonial Brazil to designate the favorite slave girl), and suggesting that the number of wives varied according to the man's rank. It also alludes to the 'dowry', that is, the matrimonial compensation which permitted the legal acquisition of a wife.[1] Later observations, collected in the eighteenth century, confirm and complete these remarks; they show the intensity of competition for wives and the consequences of a practice that condemned the 'poor' to prolonged celibacy. The basic social relationships, those created by lineage, kinship, and alliance, appear in general to have been poorly observed or poorly interpreted; however, the existence of clans and their distinctive features, the role of relations between brothers and the preeminence accorded to the elder brother, the extent of the family group, and preferential marriages (considered scandalous) between certain categories of 'relatives' were all recognized facts. Similarly—and for obvious economic reasons, since the Negro slave trade permitted the most profitable foreign transactions—

180

domestic slavery, and especially commercial slavery, was the subject of observation or comment in most of the descriptions. The
most complete testimony concerns the organization of political
life in the Kongo: the 'foreigners' always had to act through
the intermediary of the chiefs or notables; moreover, they did
not fail to conspire in order to guide local affairs in accordance
with their own interests.

Blood, Uncles, and Nephews

An old proverb states that the Mukongo who has left his clan is
like 'a locust who has lost his wings'; he has crossed the boundaries beyond which security, solidarity, and affection are no
longer guaranteed him in all circumstances. The clan, or *kanda*,
which consisted of the descendants of a common line, 'whether
they lived underneath [the dead] or above [the living] the
ground', established a kind of generalized kinship which was
justified by community of blood. Only women of free status
carried this blood, which conferred membership in the clan. The
system was, therefore, strongly matrilinear: the mother and son
were of the same clan; but the father remained a stranger in the
clanic sense, even if he did provide access to paternal kinship, or
kitata. It was the maternal uncle (*ngawa nkazi*) who was the
closest male blood relative; he transmitted his privileges, his gifts,
and his property to his nephew. The French missionaries of
Kakongo noted this fundamental aspect of social relations: 'The
children do not inherit from their fathers, but only from their
mothers and their maternal relatives. The father's property
passes to the children of his uterine sisters.'[2] This method of
transmission operated not only in the case of material wealth,
but also in the case of social status and position: the 'rank of
prince . . . is passed on to posterity only by women, so that to
be a prince or princess one must have been born of a princess'.[3]

The blood community, which one shared through the mother
and whose social implications one discovered through the uncle,
was expressed with varying degrees of intensity: maximal and
generative of respect in the case of the mother and uncle, just as
vigorous but freer in the case of real or 'classificatory' brothers,
progressively milder as the degree of kinship became slighter.
The clanic 'fraternity' and unity were forcefully asserted. Everything that might threaten them was seen as the gravest of

dangers, and sorcery was all the more feared in that it seemed sometimes to operate within the community.

Beginning with a limited number of original clans whose historical origin was associated with the origin of the kingdom itself, a double process of fragmentation and emigration operated over the centuries. Growth of population and internal tensions and rivalries determined the first; political considerations motivated by the expansion and reinforcement of the central power, economic exigencies leading to the quest for new territory, determined the second. Clanic traditions, sole sources of usable information, reflected this double movement. Van Wing offers a kind of 'model' to explain this mechanism, which affected the organization of the clans:

The traditions may be reduced to the following. There was in the Kongo a woman who was our primeval mother (*ngudi u kisina*). She gave birth (*buta*) to a certain number of girls, usually three, which is to say that in the course of time, three or more of her direct female descendants founded lines. Let us call the original mother Ma Mpolo, and her daughters Ma Lengi, Ma Mpemba and Ma Nkengi, respectively. The latter are referred to as *ngudi zi kanda*, clan mothers. Their descendants bear the names of their respective mothers and constitute lineages or branches of the clan. . . . The lineage, like its foundress, is called *ngudi*.[4]

By analyzing the formation of the province of Mpangu as an example, van Wing shows how, by a constant dynamism, tribes, clans, and lineages were formed. Every account dealing with these facts and their legendary interpretation goes back to the original couple, the Lord Kongo and the primeval Mother, and refers to the site of foundation of the kingdom, Mbanza Kongo. It was to the lack of cultivable land that the first wave of emigration was attributed: the people of Mpangu received the order to move in a northeasterly direction. The Mpangu clan led this movement of expansion, which justified the fact, noted by Pigafetta, that the chief who governed the province resulting from this conquest belonged 'to the nobility of the most ancient family of the Kongo'. The Mpangu clan did not move by itself, but in the company of affiliated clans. Such an association, more exten-

sive than the clan, was called a *luvila*. During the period of
migration and occupation of the region open to Kongo civilization, the principal group divided and scattered: 'Upon the
original line there formed a dozen other clans which all recognized the authority of the great chief, as did the other chiefs of
related clans who accompanied it on the expedition.'[5]

Hence, around a central clan which played the role of guide
during the migrations, a group of associated clans and secondary
clans born of the first clan formed in a relationship of dependence. This body formed the nucleus of the Mpangu. Later, with
the growth of population, the lineages (*ngudi*) multiplied within
the clans. They aspired to a certain autonomy, and the most
dynamic among them formed new clans which enlarged the
zone of the Kongo population.

This review brings out two fundamental facts. It shows that
migration for conquest and colonization was the basis of the
provincial powers; nevertheless, the chief of the clan ruled,
retaining his status of notable of the first rank in Mbanza Congo.
It also reveals the slow process of formation and aggregation of
social groups resulting from the blood community and their
hierarchy, which might be represented as follows:

Group	Geographic Unit	Kikongo Term
Tribe	Province	Luvila
Group of related clans	———	Luvila
Clan	Clanic territory	Kanda
Lineage	Village or section of village	Ngudi

The clan was the best differentiated and most powerful social
unit. It bore three names: the first was esoteric (known only by
the initiated), the second honorific, the third historic, recalling
the founder and stating a specific motto. It was often associated
with an animal or vegetable symbol — Cuvelier mentions the
nkima (a small light-faced monkey), emblem of the royal clan,
the *dyevo* (prairie dog), associated with the Manianga, a variety
of kite and of snake distinguishing two of the Nzinga and
Mboma clans[6]—but the only function of these emblems was to
classify the clans by associating them with groups of animals or
plants. The proliferation from twelve original clans necessitated
this systematic classification. In addition to distinctive marks and

symbols, the clans seem to have had specializations which resulted in a certain division of labor, as Father van Wing reports: 'In the Kongo, from the beginning, each clan had its trade . . . as extraordinary as this may seem'; and again, Father de Lucques observes around 1700 that artisans were all honored in the kingdom.

The clan, which was represented and administered by a chief chosen from the lineage 'closest' to the founder, regulated most social relationships. It defined incestuous sexual relations, for the blood community forbade relations between a man and woman who bore the same clanic name. It conferred the status of free man, for the slave was always situated outside the clans; this explains the protestations when the Negro slave trade, aggravated by competing greeds, went so far as to seize 'brothers in the clan' and put them up for sale. The blood community involved specific rights and obligations. It guaranteed access to the clanic territory of which the ancestors, founders of the first settlements, remained the 'owners'. It created the conditions for a powerful security and solidarity. But these advantages had their corresponding obligations: respect for the rules and taboos peculiar to the clan, military assistance, participation in funerals. Indeed, the clan and even more so the lineage have been and still are today the social units governing the Mukongo's daily existence.

Within the lineage it is relations of kinship, in the strict sense of the word, that determine attitudes and behavior. Modern ethnographic studies of Kongo society have revealed four principal groups (or classes) of uterine kinship: mothers, maternal uncles, uterine nephews, and brothers and sisters (including maternal cousins of both sexes). This system of maternal authority was misunderstood by the early witnesses and chroniclers. One writer mentions it and expresses his amazement. Certain texts put sons and maternal nephews of notables on the same level; this confusion is explained by the fact that a single name (*mwana*) designated both, while a son born of a slave woman 'belonged' to the father and remained with him and his nephews for life. A remark made by Laurent de Lucques suggests, however, that the avuncular relationship was a very privileged one at the time of his stay in Soyo; he points out the ritual role of the nephew toward the widow of his maternal

uncle, and his matrimonial prerogative over her.[7] The French
missionaries of Loango and Kakongo were able to observe and
describe accurately the method of matrilinear descendance.
Cuvelier mentions the peculiar bond linking uncle and nephew,
the community of residence, the association in the area of power
and prestige; but he does not identify his sources. And Father
Girolamo da Montesarchio notes clearly the transmission of land
rights and the line of descent operating from maternal uncle to
nephew.[8] This evidence, although incomplete, leaves little doubt:
maternal right predominated in the Kongo, even if there were
regions outside the central provinces where paternal right prevailed.

Kimpangi—genuine fraternity—constituted another group of
familial relationships that had multiple implications. It existed
between uterine brothers and also between maternal cousins.
It created deep affection and strong physical and spiritual
solidarity; it ensured the cohesion of villages or sections of
villages. It had an exemplary value, so that two chiefs who were
friends but not related by blood could become more closely connected by becoming symbolic *mpangi*: they mingled their blood
by making an incision in the arm. Although fraternity could be
characterized as a warm relationship, it did not exclude the expression of a certain inequality, which worked to the advantage
of the elder, *mbuta* or *yaya*. The younger brother, or *nleke*,
found himself in a position of inferiority with regard to the
elder; he 'submitted in everything and everywhere'. The word
by which he was designated (and which the early missionaries
used to apply to slaves of the church) also meant subject,
subordinate, servant. This broadening of the original meaning
makes it easier to understand the obligations of deference and
service under which the younger brother found himself. Primo-
geniture was a source of privileges in another sense: it was
transmitted to all 'descendants of the oldest daughter of the
founding grandmother',[9] who formed an elder lineage whose
members had pre-eminence over members of the so-called
younger lineages. Inequality was therefore rooted in the very
heart of the relationships governed by kinship.

Within the familial group, relations between mother and
children were all the more affectionate in that clan membership
reinforced their sentiments. In the Kongo, as in the majority of

African societies, progeny, as numerous as possible, were keenly desired. The mother was at that place in the society where the most intense emotions converged and she enjoyed a regard that was rarely threatened. She was woman in her fullness, woman as idealized by the ancient sculptures representing 'motherhood'. And the existence of the barren woman was a veritable tragedy; incompleteness and divorce threatened her. She did not know which 'idol' to turn to. Laurent de Lucques explains:

There are several idols which attract married people desirous of having children. They perform ceremonies and utter vows. If afterward they have a child, they keep their promises punctually. If a daughter is born to them, they call her *Divida*, which means debt. He who wishes to marry her must give her ten hoes. This is the explanation of her name . . . which involves this obligation for the future husband. If he does not fulfill it, they say that he will never have children.[10]

The obsession with sterility could lead to desperate measures, to the extreme resources of magic. The risk of being condemned to death seems in this case to have been preferred to the consequences of the social limbo which was the lot of the infertile woman. Again it is Laurent de Lucques who enlightens us when he relates 'a curious thing [that] happened during [his] visit':

I have never heard the like. The concubine of one of the principal notables put to death a child of about three to carry out some superstition which she thought would procure her children (sterility is marked with infamy), or to simulate miscarriage. She took the hands and bowels of the child and put them behind her. Then she pretended to be in labor. The hands and bowels appeared, and the infanticide was discovered. She was turned over to the executioner. . . . [11]

It would be difficult to find a more tragic illustration of the craving for motherhood. An uncommon fertility, as in the mother of twins, for example, seems to have been disturbing, however. It required treatment; otherwise its very excess threatened to turn into an opposite excess. Such a woman was regarded as 'related' to all mothers who had given birth to twins;

together they formed a kind of sect, a 'fertility clique', with its
secret rituals, its laws, and its medicine. Individually they were
no less honored: 'They were given the first vegetables that
ripened in the fields to eat.'[12] First fruits, like themselves, were
in a privileged relation with the forces of generation; and these,
in turn, were the key to the metaphysic of the Kongo.

The conjugal family was polygamous, provided the husband
was of 'good birth' and maintained his rank. The *História* states
that 'the nobles and the principals' monopolized the wives—
'some of them had a hundred'—whereas the common people had
trouble marrying at all. Among these numerous wives—all of
whom, save the head wife, the missionaries regarded as concubines — there were many slaves: these were *nkuni bakento*,
'planters of women'. One of these could become the confidante,
the favourite (*nkundi*), although her social status always placed
her in a state of inferiority. This provoked jealousy and conflict
with the other wives, especially with the *mobāda*, who had
authority over the harem. Reasons for quarrels were not lacking
within the group of co-wives; for that matter, they were constantly competing in their pursuit of the master's favors. Relations between husband and wife, however, seem to have been of
an authoritarian and contractual nature. This has been observed
in Kakongo and Loango: the wives 'are almost slaves to their
husbands, they never eat with them, they ordinarily speak to
them and serve them on their knees';[13] and the same observers
have remarked the strict separation of rights that operated
within the household: 'Ordinarily each wife has her own house,
fields, gardens and slaves, over whom the husband has no control.'[14] Domestic quarrels sometimes threatened these unions,
causing Laurent de Lucques to remark, 'The wife is easily
repudiated'.

The early missionaries, who were judges and critics of
domestic practices in the Kongo, condemned behavior that was
incompatible with Christianity without the ability or even the
desire to understand it. They denounced marriages 'which disregarded blood ties'[15]: wives inherited from maternal uncles,
wives chosen by preference—daughters of the uncles, sisters of
former wives — without realizing that such 'blood ties' were
foreign to the clan, that legal union resulted primarily from the
operation of social exigencies and not from the cravings of the

senses. They persecuted 'concubines' in order to establish monogamy, but to their astonishment they encountered a united front
of both men—as furious as if they had just 'had their guts torn
out'—and women 'who, feeling rejected, burned with rage and
fury'.[16]

The Uncleless Child

The Mukongo of slave rank had legally neither uncle nor
maternal nephew. He was outside the clanic community; he
depended on a master, and his position with respect to any free
man was always one of inferiority. The descendants of a slave
woman were 'children of the house' (bana ba nzo), whereas those
of a free woman were 'people of the clan' (bisi kanda). The
absence of clanic identity continued until the slave had purchased
his freedom (kimfumu) with the aid of his original family. This
was often impossible owing to either geographical distance or
genealogical distance, a long family history of slavery making
liberation very improbable. Moreover, modern studies have
shown a massive predominance of villagers of slave status in
certain regions; this was the result of gradual accumulation by
an aristocracy which originally possessed only the advantage of
freedom.

The methods of enslavement were few. The most common was
based on simple transaction: buying and selling, as is suggested
by the term muntu a nzimbu (man acquired with money), which
designated a slave obtained in this manner and dragged to the
house of his master by a kind of wooden halter. Pigafetta mentions this type of trade among others, and particularly the 'commerce in men' that existed between the country of the Anzika
(Bateke) and the Kongo.[17] The História points out, 'Powerful
men have a large number of slaves whom they have captured in
war or bought'.[18] Today, in the region corresponding to the
former province of Mpangu, the memory of past transactions is
still preserved: sale to the caravans of the Bambata, to distant
chieftainries, to neighboring tribes. Father van Wing states, 'It
was formerly a custom among the Bampangu to sell subjects who
were given to vice, thieves, disputatious persons, murderers, and
incorrigible adulterers as slaves'.[19] Similarly, in Loango, 'theft
and adultery were punished with slavery'.[20] Placing in servitude,
which was accompanied by a kind of ostracism, an exclusion

from the clanic community, occurred only in very definite circumstances, as a punishment for 'some crime'. In periods of adversity, however, during the great famines by which Kongo history is marked, men, children, and above all women (who had higher commercial value) were sold in great numbers. After the invasion of the Yaka, who drove King Alvaro I out of his capital in 1569 and forced him to withdraw to the Isle of the Horses, the country suffered total economic disaster; the ravages of the war, the exodus which disorganized the villages, and the constant insecurity caused a lack of food. Pigafetta reports the consequences of this situation, which intensified the struggle for mere survival:

The populations, which were reduced to wandering in these regions, starved to death. . . . A small quantity of food came to cost as much as one slave, that is, at least ten écus. Driven by necessity, father sold son, brother sold brother, so desperately did each try to procure food for himself, by no matter what villainy. . . . The sellers said that they were slaves, and those who were sold as such confirmed it, in order to be delivered from the torment of hunger.[21]

The principal beneficiaries of these sinister transactions were, however, the merchants and colonists of São Tomé, who sent 'boats loaded with foodstuffs' and acquired men and women cheaply in exchange for food.

War and raiding were ways of compensating for the inadequacies of a commerce which, in normal times, was subject to very strict rules. The missionaries of Loango and Kakongo clearly defined these limitations: 'Fathers and mothers never sell their children; the law of the land forbids sale to the Europeans of Negroes born in the same kingdom, even if they were born slaves. . . . '[22]

Capture pure and simple raised fewer problems; any prisoner became a slave, ngwayi, with the same status as a bought slave. The insecurity of travelling, as soon as the Mukongo moved outside the regions in which his clan brothers and allies lived, resulted primarily from this search for 'strangers' to be sold into servitude. Moreover, Cuvelier has shown that wars had the quality of 'manhunts' even in the time of the wise Afonso I.

Conflicts waged on precarious frontiers or in regions turned rebellious were motivated as much by the capture of defeated warriors as by the control of land or even by booty. 'Captives were sold as slaves; the sturdiest of the young men captured in Anzika country supplied the royal guard of Mbanza Congo.'[23] From the seventeenth century on, when slave trade became the main impulse of the economic life of the Kongo, petty wars for the purpose of acquiring manpower increased and accelerated the decline of power.

Other processes helped in a secondary way to bring about the state of servitude; men were sold in payment of blood money, as security to guarantee a loan (a child — *muntu a mfuka* or human security—was then given), or as compensation to cancel a debt. As a motive for war, a medium for long-range trading, an instrument of law and justice, or a factor in power and prestige, slavery constituted one of the foundations of society. It was already well established by the time the Portuguese arrived at the end of the fifteenth century; King João I offered slaves to the first navigators.[24] Hence slave trade formed a backdrop for the familiar scene which associated 'the child of the house' with the daily activities and preoccupations of the master.

As long as greed did not disturb its functioning, domestic slavery excluded violence and the abuse of power. Father van Wing writes, 'The condition of the slaves hardly differed from that of the free men'. Jean Cuvelier likewise observes that 'the institution of slavery, as it existed in the Kongo, appeared tolerable'. Early accounts implicitly confirm these judgments. The *História* points out a certain equality in the material conditions of existence: 'There are no poor people among them [the people of the Kongo], because they are all poor.' Father Proyart stresses the affection felt for domestic slaves of old lineage, who were regarded almost as members of the free families that possessed them.[25] Behavior varied, however, according to whether it was a question of old slaves associated with the master's family, who were treated with respect and were sometimes confidants or representatives of the chief, or recently acquired slaves, who were treated according to the owner's interest and traded if an advantageous offer appeared. Indeed, the vocabularly distinguishes between the two groups; *bana nkulu*, children of the past, and *bana mpa*, new children.

What was the law and what were the facts? The slave was a piece of property, transmitted by inheritance, which the master could in principle dispose of as he would. His labor and his services operated to the profit of his *mfumu*, and the latter granted him only the use of the durable goods left to his disposition. On the other hand, the owner had to treat him properly (public opinion and fear contributed to this) and arrange for his marriage, and that of all the 'children of the house'; for the men, it was sometimes difficult to find a wife, who could be a woman of free status; for the slave women, the true capital of the lineage, it was easy to find a husband, a maternal nephew or dependent of the master. This balance of mutual obligations sufficiently justified the institution in the minds of the native authorities. The correspondence of King Afonso I reveals the clear conscience of a sovereign who was nevertheless a reformer. As Cuvelier says:

He has the conviction . . . that one man may be the property of another and may be forced to submit to this state by birth, poverty, punishment for a crime, or the laws of war. He has never doubted that a slave, like any other property, may be passed on by the habitual methods of transmission: sale, trade, gift, inheritance.[26]

To be sure, tolerance was more conditional on the part of the slaves, who were capable of resistance. Dissatisfied slaves tried to escape tyranny by secession (founding a separate hamlet and paying rent, demonstrating their subordination from a distance), or flight (placing themselves under the protection of a new authority who set them free). In extreme cases rebellion, the killing of the master, and exodus seemed the only recourse. Cuvelier mentions a true rebellion in the reign of Afonso I which was originally caused by the sale of an important convoy of commercial slaves to the Negro slave traders. The rebels 'engaged in plunder in the vicinity [of Mbanza Kongo], in stealing at the markets; they destroyed the enclosure of the king and set fire to the houses'.[27] The paternalism of the notables was thus disturbed, but the institution of slavery survived the shock without injury.

The *História* helps to explain this permanence. Its compiler

suggests a form of division of labor established in the Kongo:
'There are no men who work the land, nor men who work by
the day, nor anyone who is willing to be the servant of another
for a salary. Only the slaves labor and serve. . . . Through these
slaves, [powerful men] trade by sending them to the markets.'[28]

Slaves were used for agricultural labor, construction jobs, or
drudgery; it might be said that they formed the bulk of the male
working class. The Portuguese colonization reinforced this structure of subordination by combining it with exploitation pure
and simple. A colony settled on the frontier of Angola and used
servile manpower, sometimes on a large scale. Thus in the early
seventeenth century a certain Gaspar Alvares, anxious to prepare an edifying death, gave his possessions to the Jesuits: he
left 'one hundred plantations or *arimos* [small farms] in the
Kongo and Angola, and thousands of slaves'.[29] The bishops and
missionaries all used slaves who were said to belong to the
Church for their service, their plantations, and their transportation on tours of evangelization.[30] Following their example, relations between the master and the 'child of the house' began to
change.

Without slavery commercial transactions on a large scale
could not have been established. This is obvious in the case of
the trade based on traffic in men. But the remark must be understood in another sense. Portage and the human caravan were the
sole method of transport used in the Kongo: convoys of 'servants' (to use Pigafetta's term) furrowed the kingdom with
columns heading toward the commercial zones of the north and
east. This was a supplementary economic justification. However,
other reasons which were not of a secondary order came into
play. In a society in which man was the most precious capital—
because the number of dependents was more important than the
volume of wealth possessed—women of slave status produced
offspring who remained in the clan and augmented its vigor
accordingly. Moreover, the prestige of the aristocrat required a
large retinue. His entourage or escort indicated the rank he
occupied; a proverbial statement expressed the idea: 'The chief
must not lack men'. The same was true of women of rank, members of the royal family endowed with fiefs, or head wives of
important notables; slaves were at their service and at the service
of the formalities which maintained their authority by exalting

their 'nobility'.[31] Under certain circumstances the slave enabled the master to avoid the rigor of the laws and to save face, or his life: he was given in compensation when a man was required to atone for a 'crime' involving the responsibility of his *mfumu*; he served as a substitute in the ordeal by poison; he became the scapegoat in grave circumstances threatening the cohesion of the clanic community.

The Royalty and Its Guardians

The king symbolized the Kongo, although his actual power declined outside the limits of the central region. His person and the land were one, mystically united and interdependent in the system of forces governing life and prosperity. And he had to demonstrate his vigor by triumphing over his rivals, by capturing the royalty; a very well-known proverb expressed this requirement. A weakening of the king was thought to cause a weakening of the people and the kingdom. 'During a serious illness, only the electors were permitted to visit him; nobody was informed of the progress of the disease, to avoid prematurely raising the question of succession. Even his death was concealed.'[32] More than political strategy, it was the conception of royalty that seems to have been involved here.

This implicit theory becomes clear only after several apparent digressions. The first leads to Soyo, which had become almost independent after 1636,[33] and was governed by a *mani* who was then a replica of the king of São Salvador. In his accounts, Laurent de Lucques describes in detail the 'superstitions' associated with the death of the 'count' and his succession. In Mbanza Soyo, as in the capital of the kingdom, the illness of the *mani* was concealed from the people; his palace was off limits except to the four electors, so that 'the people might not know his condition, whether he was still living or whether he was dead'. But uncertainty sometimes caused panic and disturbance, as it did in 1715, so deep was the conviction that the lives of the people and the 'health' of the country depended upon the vitality of the chief.[34] At the time of the (belated) burial service the convoy did not take the roads habitually travelled by the dead man, for if they did 'the new count would die that same year and not a single drop of rain would fall'. This prohibition can be understood only if one recalls the existence of numerous rituals surrounding the *mani* and his head wife, the function of which was to ensure a long reign and maintain prosperity. In Soyo, too, the power was taken by force. The electors considered the acceptable candidacies and tried to agree on the choice of one of the pretenders. But the election was ordinarily 'in favor of him who has the most power and who is supported by a greater number of people'. A decisive and symbolic test concluded the process of nomination : 'A seat is placed among the electors. The pretender who succeeds in *sitting in it first* is declared prince. His government lasts as long as he is alive.' There could be no clearer expression of the fact that the power devolves upon that one of the legitimate candidates recognized by the four electors who conquers the throne.

After a preliminary public ceremony involving the offering of homage, the enthronement of the new *mani* required the performance of symbolic rites already discussed in a previous chapter.[35] They evoked primitive techniques (among them the arts of metal, which were aristocratic), they glorified female and fertility symbols, they employed procedures of reinforcement and protection against hostile undertakings. In the center of this complex symbolism was the couple formed by the *mani* and his principal wife. This couple regulated the solidarity of the sexes, the fertile and fertilizing union, order and prosperity. It was in a certain sense the original couple, the one on which the destiny of all unions depended. At a certain point in the ceremony of enthronement the 'princes' withdrew to their 'houses'. After mentioning this fact, Laurent de Lucques adds, 'There is no reason to describe what takes place. [Afterward] they are convinced that they will have many children and will be victorious in battle.' The new reign opened with a ritualized coupling, and the sexual life of the sovereign couple was subject to prohibitions which protected it from a sterility which would contaminate the land and the people. Moreover, the periodic agrarian rites invoking rain and fertility were performed under the direction of the *mani* and his wife. The natural order and the political order were interdependent, and the 'princess' participated in the power in a ritual manner to prevent this power from being exclusively male and therefore sterile.

According to Father de Lucques, the power was also symbolized by two wooden drums kept in the palace enclosure. At the time

194

of his election, the 'count' must lean upon the larger of these drums, 'and the countess on the smaller . . . [The 'count' and 'countess'] remain there for a time, as if they were praying. Then they begin to dance all around, while the onlookers sing and shout joyously.' That there was a mystical relationship between the drum and the person of the *mani* seems unquestionable: an accident to the instrument threatened, by contagion, the very existence of the chief. The voice of authority, whether it was a question of a call to work or a call to war, was identified with the beating of drums; whether the pair of instruments associated with the sovereign couple was actually used is not specified, however. This symbolism suggests, in impoverished and softened form, that of kingdoms of eastern Africa where the sacred drum effectively constituted the royalty. It reveals the characteristics of royal power: its coercive aspects, its ritual force, and its martial vigor.[36]

Opposite Soyo, the kingdom of Loango obliges us to extend the inventory of political ideas peculiar to the Kongo. Here the sovereign did not assume his duties until after a long interregnum. 'The deceased king was believed to reign as long as he was not buried'; and this final ceremony was sometimes delayed for several years, for the techniques of embalming made it possible to preserve the dead body. At the period when the French missionaries were settling in Loango (1770), the apparent vacancy of power lasted 'for four years'. During this uncertain period the government of the country was taken over by the most powerful of the aristocrats, who therefore received the title of *ma-booma*, 'lord of fear'.[37] Even so, the principal men of the kingdom competed for the power. There ensued 'conflicts resembling civil wars between the princes'. Order was restored in a permanent manner only with the triumph of one of the pretenders to the throne: then the fiction of the power exercised by the dead sovereign was abandoned and the reign of terror ceased. The conquest of royalty is obvious. The competitive ordeal lasted until such time as the victory of one faction became incontestable. The new king had to hold supreme authority and guarantee strong enforcement of an order which was both social and cosmic; the vigor of the sovereign and the prosperity of the land were interdependent. In Loango, too, the power was necessarily feminized. The queen mother, called *ma-kunda*, who must

195

be the oldest female uterine relative of the sovereign, was the actual monarch.[38] The ritualized union of the king and his wife does not seem to have been prescribed in order to maintain the fecundity and force of the kingdom; but it may be appropriate to regard the practice reported by Dapper as a substitute which permitted the (true) mother and 'sisters' of the king to have great freedom in the choice of their sexual partners.[39] Finally, the exceptional and unique nature of the personality acquired at the moment of accession to the throne was indicated by the requirements of protocol. The sovereign could not be seen taking his meals by any animate being, under pain of death for the culprit.[40] His subjects 'showed him extraordinary signs of subjection, when they were in his presence'.[41] He held an absolute sway—'all regarded themselves as his slaves'—and the land, the people, and their property theoretically belonged to him. He symbolized a sanctified order, because the threat of a return of chaos always hung over the familiar universe and the society.

Before returning to the problems of royalty in the Kongo, it may be useful to consider the foregoing facts derived from historic documentation in the light of the findings of modern ethnology. As the central power deteriorated, the authority of local chiefs increased proportionately. Indeed, at the time of the last colonization in the nineteenth century, the remaining political power belonged exclusively to the 'crowned chiefs' (mfumu mpu). These chiefs, who were the guardians of symbols which had the quality of regalia (headgear, bracelets, double bell, etc.), were closely associated with the clanic order. They belonged to the most vital part of the clan, the lineage considered eldest. They enjoyed such a privileged relation to the ancestors that their personalities were affected by it. A material sign revealed the possession of this exceptional quality without which their power would not be effective, for it would lack the complicity of the sacred. The crowned chief had religious and judiciary functions, and he never at any time acted as a military leader. He was on the side of fertility and of peace, not on the side of violence and death. He established a bond between the community of the living and the ancestors who regulated the destiny of men and the fullness of the harvest. His person was sacred and he was subject to prohibitions which protected it as such. His health and the prosperity of the land were interdependent :

if he were declining and ill, in olden times he had to accept a 'ritual execution' which had the sense of a preventive action 'against the risk of sterility'.[42] His power, which was primarily directed toward fertility, was nevertheless feminized. A chief woman (*mfumu-ankento*) who was invested at the same time he was, but with no sexual relation existing between them, was associated with him. She dispensed peace and serenity. She practiced her ministry over the women. She acted in all cases in which sterility threatened individuals or the collectivity. Such, crudely drawn, was the modern portrait of political power in the case of a single large clan or a group of related clans. Similarities to the forms described in connection with Loango and Soyo are seen, but differences are also apparent: the *mfumu mpu* was not above the clans, and he did not take office by force. He represented only one of the aspects of power, which was ambivalent in Kongo society, as it is in any society.

The traditional image of royalty was distorted when, after the sixteenth century, the king of the Kongo presented himself as a Christian sovereign, so that the indigenous ideas, symbols, and rituals took on numerous foreign elements. The ceremony of coronation provided in a sense a double consecration. Nevertheless it lends itself to reconstruction and analysis of the system of political ideas concerning the supreme power. A report of 1624 describes in detail and from direct observation the presentation of the royal insignia. It is a precious document, the work of a canon who was very familiar with the country and the Kikongo language, and tempts one to look for meanings under the symbolism.[43]

Before turning to this account, it is well to remember the complex procedure that led to the nomination of the 'pretender to the kingdom' or *mani mwivi* (the word *mwivi* referred to someone who takes by force, or ravishes). Among the candidates for succession, one had to prevail—which did not happen without violent confrontations — and be recognized by the college of electors. Indeed, the strength of his faction implied the recognition of these authorities, and his victory, thus accepted, transformed a power taken by force into a legitimate power, sanctified by the rituals of enthronement. When the Portuguese sovereign João III proposed the creation of a dynasty and a hereditary monarchy to King Afonso I in 1529,[44] he was merely betraying his ignorance of the political system of the Kongo and his own political intentions. A power that had to demonstrate its vigor and win the acceptance of authorities who were necessary to its efficient exercise could not be transmitted automatically. It required several pretenders. Who were these? According to Cuvelier they had to belong to the royal family: 'sons, nephews, brothers, uncles, to the exclusion of women'.[45] This list, based on the information of the early chroniclers, raises a problem.

Father van Wing observes that the matrilinear system made it obligatory to find a successor among the uterine relatives of the deceased (brother, nephew, or maternal uncle), and he adds, 'When the documents mention sons, either they mean sons in the broad sense—members of the royal clan—or else they are referring to an exceptional and excessive case'.[46] Scholarship appears to be incomplete. A son born of a slave women belonged to the royal lineage; such was the condition of Mpazu a Nimi, the king known as Alvaro II, who reigned from 1587 to 1614. The reference may also be to sons kept outside the lineage of the mother because she was a woman who had been given to the sovereign and had lost her rights. Alvaro III (1615–1622), described as 'a bastard son', seems to confirm this possibility. Finally, it should be recalled that an attempt was made to introduce direct masculine succession: Ravenstein points this out, although he contends that succession normally occurred according to the matrilinear principle.[47]

An examination of the sequence of kings from the first Christianized sovereign (1491) until the disastrous battle of Ambouila (1665) confirms the uncertainty. The group reveals an almost equal distribution of sons (?), descendants related to the deceased sovereign by special bonds, brothers and one maternal uncle, and relatives whose relationship is unclear. Above all it reveals the appearance of a *second* royal clan with Alvaro VI (1636). The first—Ki-Mpanzu—had provided all the kings until then; more than twelve of them were buried in São Salvador in the church of Saint James. The usurping clan was the clan of Ki-Malaza, which prevailed 'by massacring and exiling many Chimpazu [Ki-Mpanzu]'. The first beneficiary of this dynastic revolution tried to found a new legitimacy and to 'stabilize himself in the royalty'. 'He asked the Sovereign Pontiff for the crown, which was granted him with a paternal benevolence.'[48]

On this occasion Christianity became a temporary substitute for the traditional religious support. It was an inadequate substitute, for the struggle between the two houses, which contributed to the defeat of Ambouila, continued for a long time, despite alternate attempts to entrust the power to each one.

In spite of these vicissitudes, the ritual of coronation presents a remarkable stability. Behind the Christian style of investiture, which represented a modernist façade and a supplementary consecration, the essential investiture survived. Two notables 'dominated this occasion': the *mani* Vunda and the *mani* Mbata. It was their responsibility to recall the high deeds of the dead king and announce the vacancy of the throne, to enumerate the qualities required of any pretender, to name the successor and conduct him solemnly to the royal throne (*kyandu*), to direct the ceremony and present the insignia of which they were the guardians. The normal functioning of the royalty depended upon their intervention. The *mani* Vunda was 'the most highly regarded personage in all the kingdom'. According to Father Cherubino da Savona, he was called 'Lord of the earth and grandfather of the king'.[49]

This appellation and the privileges to which it referred hark back to the origins of the kingdom, as if each new reign was obliged to recall symbolically the beginnings of the Kongo. The *mani* Vunda belonged to the Nsaku clan, who were the oldest occupants of the region including the royal province and the province of Mbata; therefore this clan received the title of eldest and regarded the kings of the Kongo as its grandsons (*ntekolo*). Ntinu Wene, the founder, was able to consolidate his conquest and perpetuate his influence only by accepting the cooperation and alliance of these first masters of the land. The cooperation was primarily ritual. The *mani* Vunda—intermediary between the living and the ancestors, master of rain and fertility; preserver of the hunting rites—was responsible for it. The alliance was both matrimonial and political. It associated the royal clan reigning in Mbanza Kongo with the lineage pre-eminent in Mbata, that of the Nsaku Lau. The latter had the right to govern the province formed by their land without the king having the power to intervene; their chief occupied second rank in the hierarchy of the kingdom, and as Pigafetta notes, if the royal lineage were to die out, succession would be transmitted to him.

A certain obligation consolidated this association by creating bonds of kinship: the Kongo sovereign had to marry a daughter of the Nsaku Lau lineage and confer on her the status of queen. This woman, called *ne mbanda* (an expression suggesting both a choice and authority exercised over a territory), received a tax levied in her country of origin (according to Dapper) and became the mistress of a fief. She was the feminine counterpart of the king; she offered him the vigor of her lineage and the mystical power of her ancestors; she was a guarantee of order and fertility. Hence the functions of the *mani* Vunda and the *mani* Mbata, during the ceremony of enthronement and afterward in court, received their justification from the history of the early times.[50]

The coronation of the sovereign took place in the presence of the dignitaries and 'all the nobles', arranged according to their rank and displaying the symbols of their office. They stood in the great public square known as *mbasi a Kongo*, or royal square. Opposite them was the king's enclosure, a palisade made of stakes and vines in the early sixteenth century, then a little wall of stones and lime reinforced 'at every corner' according to descriptions dating from the 1620s. Beyond this sacred boundary lay a large open space in which there stood the royal platform used during great demonstrations, or later, a kind of stationary throne room 'made of well-constructed arcades'. Beyond that the buildings of the palace could be seen. So much for the physical setting. Let us examine the ceremony that took place in 1622, when Pedro II Afonso took office.[51]

The throne, 'of crimson velvet, all fringed with silk and gold', was protected from the ground by a magnificent imported rug. It was flanked by young 'nobles' bearing the royal insignia which were concealed by 'veils'. One of them had charge of a large flag bearing the arms of the Kongo which the Portuguese sovereign Manual had sent King Afonso I together with the coat of arms and seal.[52] Behind the throne stood the bearers of the *nkumbi*, or traditional coat of arms of the royal clan; the motifs, formed by 'feathers of parrots and other birds', were appliquéd upon 'curtains of braided straw' hanging from poles 'seven or eight spans high'. In addition to the place containing the royal seat, two other places were sanctified. The first bore the altar stone and crucifix which made it possible to give the sovereign of the Kongo the title of Christian king. The second, which was even more sacred, bore the great drum (*ngoma*), known as both *simbu* and *busto*, which represented the royalty in its coercive and violent aspect. This drum embodied absolute power. It rested on a piece of ornate cloth, protected from the earth as the king himself had to be. It was 'all trimmed with leopard skins and an ounce's tail', with silken and gold embroidery to which teeth had been fastened. 'These were the teeth of those who had died in rebellious wars against the king.' Recipient of the royal power, 'this *engoma* was shown in public only when the king went to war, when he died, or when he was crowned'. Death and enthronement of the sovereign, and national war: these were the only circumstances permitting public presentation of this dreaded symbol. On these occasions, the royalty was celebrating its vigor and permanence.

Near the drum, during the coronation, three men each held 'two iron implements the size of small well-made carbines'.

They strike them together, producing a sound similar to the one the blacksmith makes when he brings the hammer down on the anvil. They call this *zimie* [*zima*, to strike]; it is the oldest royal symbol, and only the king and the duke of Batta may use it. There is also a man with his nose completely covered who blows into a bellows. . . . They call this symbol *sambo ansure* [from *sambu*, invocation, worship], and only the king may use it.[53]

There can be no doubt that this was an act of veneration referring to the shades of the first kings, symbolized by the drum (*ngoma*), and especially of the founder, the warrior creator of an empire and 'blacksmith of the Kongo'. At each decisive moment in the life of the kingdom reinforcement was sought in a symbolic return to the origins, in an act of communion in which the notables and the people were associated.

The ritual that began the enthronement supports this interpretation. 'All kinds of musical instruments' contributed to it—those that were among the attributes of power (drums, bells, ivory trumpets), and those of a more commonplace nature. After an initial appearance of the *mani* Vunda, who extolled the reign of the dead sovereign, all the musicians began to play.

They produce a sound so melancholy that its like has never been heard. They repeat this music twelve times. This ceremony recalls the twelve generations of the Kongo from which the first kings were born. All mourn likewise the death of the king.[54]

The general meaning of this phase of the ritual is clear, but one point must be clarified: the 'twelve generations' mentioned correspond to the twelve primordial clans regarded as the foundation of the empire of the Kongo.

It was after 'this moving ceremony' that the two directors of the enthronement solemnly announced the vacancy of the throne and reviewed the qualities required of the pretender. 'Immediately the musical instruments played, but in a very different manner; this time it was a sound of celebration which delighted everyone.' It was the *mani* Vunda and the *mani* Mbata who had the honor of announcing the name of the chosen candidate; 'they named him first to the people, who replied with great joy that he was the one they wanted; next they took the king-elect by the hand and led him to the royal throne'. The coronation, that is, the Christian part of the ceremony, was performed immediately. It was brief: 'Placing his hands upon the book of the Holy Gospels, the king swore on the altar to faithfully perform the duties of a Christian king', then a priest blessed him together with certain of the symbols of his responsibility.

The traditional ceremony — essential, slow, and majestic — then took place. It had three phases: the presentation of the regalia, the homage and the return to the palace, and the oath of fidelity. The first of the insignia was the headdress, or *mpu* (a term which in the western region also meant power and supreme authority). J. F. Lafitau, in a description of a diplomatic reception, states that this 'crown' was 'a small cap of palm leaves in the shape of a mitre'.[55] Bishop Manuel Baptista was outraged by the fact that the king and the nobles wore 'on their heads a kind of bonnet called *impua* which, according to their custom, they failed to remove either in church or in the presence of the very Holy Sacrament of the Eucharist'.[56] Indeed, no holder of power could appear in public without this headdress, which was the most important symbol of his rank. After receiving this emblem, the new king had to put around his neck the *simba* (from *simba*, to hold firmly or seize), which was 'a very well made iron chain with many pendants, also of iron'. Regarding the latter, 'the king placed them on his back, as a woman holds her child'; 'thus he was not king, but father, and he had to take care of his vassals as he did his sons; he had to worry about them always'. The *simba* symbolically expressed the extent and nature of the royal power. The sovereign was regarded in a certain sense as the father of his people, while his function as unifier of Kongo lands and dependencies was clearly evoked.

The insignia that followed, according to the order of the ritual, reveal the ambivalence of a power doubly sanctified: by the royal ancestors, and by Rome. The king received a 'very ancient' emblem which only the *mani* Vunda and the *mani* Mbata, 'his grandfathers', could possess beside himself. It was a 'shoulder belt' (in fact, a special form of the tax collector's sack) which was worn over the right shoulder and fell 'below the left arm'. The sovereignty of the king was thus affirmed. Then the two directors of the enthronement ritual placed around the neck of their sovereign 'a brocade purse bound in silk', containing a papal bull called *sanctissimo sacramento* from the reign of Diogo (sixteenth century). This document was associated with the regalia and was to become the object of keen competition during the period of the rival kings. Among the major emblems was 'a bracelet of iron completely covered with gold' which was placed on the right arm of the sovereign. The comments that accompanied its presentation specified that this *lunga* 'represented the whole kingdom' and stressed the necessity of 'leaving it whole'. The bracelet of iron 'was the kingdom of iron'; its Kikongo name signifies literally, 'Kongo of iron',[57] an indirect reference to the first sovereign, forger of the state and civilizing hero. The new king then received a bow which he held in his right hand, a lance, the flag bearing the coat of arms of the Kongo, and some other insignia not identified by the chroniclers. 'Which being done, there followed a long music and shouts of joy'.

The ritual of homage was performed immediately: 'The dukes, marquises, and grandees of the kingdom and the most important *fidalgos* (nobles) went to kiss the hand of the king'; 'all clapped their hands and uttered cries of joy'. Then they formed a procession behind the sovereign and accompanied him to the palace. 'Along the road there were *sembos* [*simbu*], a kind of very large drum; the king had to touch them with his hand

and strike them a few times [to make a noise]. After this, he gave the drummer a gift.'[58] The relationship between royalty and drums was once again demonstrated, at the very moment when the new king was about to take possession of the royal enclosure.

The oath of fidelity was sworn two Kongo weeks (eight days) later. 'The great dignitaries and the principal *fidalgos* who drew income from the territories of the kingdom' swore obedience and loyal service. They recited their genealogy, for it justified their rank, and declared that none of their ancestors had rebelled against the central power. 'If, by chance, a man nevertheless felt associated with a crime of this nature, he gave many excuses' and denounced this error. 'They finished all their speeches by saying that nothing would prevent them from serving the king, their lord', and they enumerated his titles.

The ritual of enthronement, with its very elaborate symbolism, accentuated certain aspects of power. It recalled its origins, its foundations in a mythical history, and it sanctified it. It expressed its political and military aspect. The king was the holder of the supreme power, the guardian of Kongo unity, the central point of a hierarchical system which was vulnerable. The great annual demonstrations, in which the royalty was exalted and the presentation of the taxes was made, helped to assure the preservation of this system; they provided the material resources; they symbolically expressed submission to the king, who was 'absolute lord'. He triumphed at the time of the succession because of the power of his party; his position of force had to be constantly defended; his place was at the head of the armies in certain grave circumstances. In his person it was power and order as such that were honored and, in a sense, deified.

This glorification of order implied a respect for the rules—the law—on which it was founded. The character of the strong king was associated with the character of the righteous king. Force was an exceptional method; conciliation was the method commonly used. According to Dapper, each region had a royal judge who acted in the name of the sovereign and remembered that the latter had the prerogative to render justice in the last analysis.[59]

What is certain is that the king sometimes sent commissioners into troubled regions to settle disputes between chiefs. Royal

justice was administered primarily in cases involving the great
vassals, and by appeal in cases involving the other chiefs. . . . It
was their authority as dispensers of justice that remained intact
longest in the hands of the kings. After their political power had
waned they continued to be judges.[60]

The sacred character of the power imposed certain partners on
the sovereign. Identification with the land required an agreement with the ancestors who were the guardians of the land and
guaranteed the intervention of the fertilizing forces. The power
resulting from conquest and coercion had to be associated with
the power resulting from divine favor. In the case of the king of
the Kongo, the constant intervention of the *mani* Vunda and
the ritual functions performed by the queen provided this vital
association. It was through their agency that influence over men
became influence over the cosmos, connivance with the ancestors
and the powers of the beyond. In Loango, according to Father
Proyart, 'the people are convinced that the power of the king is
not limited to the earth and that he has enough influence to
make the rain fall from the sky'; but 'he relies for this purpose'
on a specialized notable of very high rank.[61] In the Kongo, the
provincial powers recognized the same necessity—the case of
Soyo is significant—and the holders of chieftainries depended to
some extent on the cooperation of the *nsongi* (from *songa*, to be
similar) or the *kitomi*,[62] specialists in the agricultural rituals.
Political structures and organizations raise as many problems
as the interpretation of ideas concerning power. The establishment of a state did not reduce the authority of the elders acting
within clans and lineages. Dapper states that the king of the
Kongo was attended by a council of twelve notables, the *ne
mbanda-mbanda*, who would seem to have represented the
twelve original clans; while the *mani* Vunda vigorously demonstrated the existence of this archaic power on behalf of a privileged clan recognized as the oldest, that of the Nsaku. This
coexistence of two organizations—one of the state, the other of
the clan—appears on all levels, from the capital down to the
seats of districts. Corresponding to and in a sense opposing the
hierarchy emanating from the sovereigns was the hierarchy
emanating from the ancestors. The first was the hierarchy of the
mani: a term that applied, according to the *História*, 'to all

those who had some authority', a generic term defined as an office received from or recognized by the king. The captain of the armies was a *mani*, as was the governor of a province or the chief of a vassal country. The notion implied any authority delegated by the first *mani*, the *mani* Kongo; it had an essentially political meaning.* The second of the hierarchies was that of the *mbuta* (elders) and the *mfumu* (chiefs) born into the clans or lineages and associated with the clanic territory. Their power did not result from delegation, but from the ancestors and from their genealogical position; it was defended by tradition and the preservation of the landed domain; it was religious as much as political. The mottoes proudly exalted this old order and its luminaries. They upheld clanic law beside the law of the king.

Indeed, the kingdom of the Kongo is the product of a complex and precarious combination of relations based on power (direct domination or vassalage) and relations based on clanic affinities and alliances. In the sixteenth century the Kongo included six provinces and certain outlying territories which were connected by relations of vassalage—for example, Loango to the north and Ndongo (Angola) to the south, which were straining at their bonds during this period. The situation of the provinces varied. In Mbata, the king had virtually no voice when it came to the appointment of the governor; the power *belonged* to the Nsaku Lau lineage. In Soyo, the lineage of the first Christian chief had acquired 'ownership' of the local government. In Nsundi, the sovereign established one of his potential successors, thus indicating his preference; a proverb stated moreover that the chief of Nsundi was 'like the hummingbird, who hovers near the opening from which the palm wine trickles'. Finally, the province of Mpemba was 'the center of the state of the Kongo'; here, according to Pigafetta, were 'the seat and the capital of the other principalities'. The king lived here and a number of the nobles who attended him had 'their possessions and their estates' here. In all cases, however, the sovereign intervened in the appointment of provincial governors, either to make the choice or to confirm it. The supremacy of his power had to be demonstrated in all circumstances. Within the provinces, different solutions governed the distribution of authority. Certain districts had the

* The *mani* Vunda was a *mani* insofar as his religious function was at the service of the royalty. He was at the juncture of the two types of hierarchy.

quality of precarious fiefs (contributing merely income) and were allotted to members of the royal family, including former queens and 'princesses'; in others, the choice of chiefs depended on the *mani* of the province. In addition there were enclaves or marginal territories similar to protectorates which had retained a kind of autonomy, where the royal family merely recognized or confirmed the authorities chosen according to local custom. Historical vicissitudes, relationships of power, and empiricism diversified the solutions. The Kongo has lacked the material and cultural means by which the great unifying enterprise might have been brought to completion. Strained communications, overlapping territorial claims, local armies instead of a national army, inadequate administrative staffs, religions that remained particularist owing to the failure of Christianization, ill-restrained antagonisms: these are weaknesses which explain the precariousness of the empire. The kings tried to remedy this situation by laying, with the help of relatives, allies, and immediate dependants, a single foundation on which their power might rest; under all reigns, this foundation remained fragile.

The titles — dukes, counts, marquises — suggested by King Manuel of Portugal and used by the early chroniclers have spun a web of illusion. They give the impression that, like European kingdoms, the Kongo was a strongly centralized state, whereas it was a diffuse state. The king, the provincial chiefs, and the governors of the vassal territories all found themselves in an identical situation with respect to the officials to whom they delegated a part of their power. The same procedure operated from various centers of political life. Several accounts describe the prescribed ritual. For example, Laurent de Lucques's on Soyo (1705):

When the count wants to confer some rank or office upon someone, the drums and other instruments announce the news the evening before. This signal is always given for public ceremonies. The next morning . . . he who is to be chosen is led in. He presents himself to the prince and begins by genuflecting three times and clapping his hands three times. Then the count tells him, 'You shall be *mani* of a certain village', that is, governor of a certain town or territory. These governors have authority over many villages; these head *mani* have the right to appoint other *mani* in the subject villages, and they profit a great deal depending on the extent of their territory, for those whom they appoint chiefs are obliged to give them so many chickens, pigs, or other products of the region, according to their means. After the appointment of the *mani*, the people applaud and thank the prince by shouting and playing instruments. Meanwhile the *mani*, on his knees before the prince, claps his hands several times, throws himself on the ground, and smears himself with dirt and dust, and the onlookers also throw dirt on his back. . . . Then he returns home surrounded by his people, who loudly express their joy. . . . After the proclamation of his election there is another ceremony, the presentation of the cap. . . . Meanwhile he must procure a gift to give to the prince; otherwise he cannot take possession of the government. When all is ready, he presents himself to the prince with the gift. . . . The count places the cap on his head. This cap is of linen, which among these people resembles silk. It is very well made. When he has received it, the new chief goes outside, giving demonstrations of joy.[63]

This ceremony, which is described very accurately here, was observed on all levels where a delegation of power took place. The political organization of the Kongo had a repetitive quality: the *mani* were 'replicas' of the king, the small capitals replicas of São Salvador.

Only the sovereign, by virtue of his position, intervened as a unifying force. From him all territorial authority proceeded, toward him the tribute converged. He inspired devotion and useful collaboration by conferring honorific titles which were transmitted by inheritance. He delegated vital functions to faithful and powerful notables; hence the governor of the province of Mbamba, that 'shield' of the kingdom, was captain general of the royal army, 'lord of authority', *ne tuma*. The king gave the bureaucracy a certain effectiveness. He was assisted by a council and a group of specialized dignitaries. He had at his disposal an execut've staff, a staff of directors of the public treasury, and one of collectors of duties and taxes; although he never had an opportunity to establish a bureaucracy that would consolidate his government. He possessed a judicial administration consisting of a chief justice in the capital and district judges whose duty it was to publish the law in the market places, to punish infractions, and to settle disputes.

It was the state and the Kongo itself that were glorified in the person of the sovereign. The royal isolation, pomp, and ceremony were the instruments of this religion of power. The king and above all the queen appeared to their subjects only under exceptional circumstances. A strict protocol imposed its restrictions and a 'minister of the palace' (*ne lumbu*, chief of the enclosure) saw that this protocol was respected while also overseeing the management of the household. Numerous dignitaries made up the private council and household of the king. Within the former, a dignitary who enjoyed the confidence of the sovereign, later known as *mfila ntu* ('he who guides the head'), influenced the management of public affairs. As for the king's domestic staff, it assumed traditional duties (table service, beverages, farmyards, etc.) and duties created in imitation of the customs of the court in Lisbon (chamberlain, high officer of the crown); both functions made it possible to have powerful men near the king and to grant flattering privileges to certain clans.

The palace, confined within its enclosure, with the royal couple as its double nucleus, formed a world which was a microcosm of the kingdom as a whole, symbolically reconstructed and revealed: 'The Kongo of the king', was all of the Kongo in miniature.

Part III

THE MAKING
OF MEN

CHAPTER 8

Education

The newborn child was a mere 'caterpillar'; the uninitiated
adolescent awaited the metamorphosis which would transform
him into a man and a citizen. Education in the Kongo was a
slow process which was accompanied by changes of status or
induced alterations of the personality. From early infancy to the
age of five or six, boys and girls were subject to the dominant
influence of the mother. They lived in her intimacy; from her
they learned the fundamental restrictions; to her they owed
their apprenticeship in the language, their knowledge of family
history, their discovery of the legendary or fabulous world celebrated in its songs; they also learned to imitate her gestures, to
recognize foods in their natural state, to observe the boundaries
that delimited places and actions that were prohibited.

Next came a period of separation: the girls went to sleep in
the 'house of the women', the boys in the 'house of the men'.
The dividing line between the sexes destroyed the integrity of
the family unit formed by the mother and her young children.
The boy very quickly discovered the superiority and advantages
of the masculine condition. He lived as much as possible in the
company of his father. He served his apprenticeship as a man,
practicing the making of implements for hunting and fishing,
the handling of agricultural equipment, being initiated in the
recognition of plants and their use, helping with the clearing of
the fields. Gradually he organized his relationship with nature:
the search for fishing spots and the laying of nets, hunting, and
the setting of traps were so many 'lessons in things' which he
studied with passion. Finally, the father inculcated in his son
the code of the conventions, the meaning of prohibitions and

symbols concerning them both. This traditional pedagogy, which has been described by a Mukongo sociologist, must have persisted down through the centuries:

In this education, the child's spirit of observation is tempered, controlled, and developed by question and answer, and often even by tricks, paradoxes, and concrete examples as well. The father, in a nonchalant manner, will invite the child to solve a certain problem which looks easy but whose solution will require the father's experience. Depending upon his success, the child will receive a pleasant or unpleasant nickname, and will be chosen in preference to his peers to carry out certain missions or to accompany adults on their travels.[1]

The girl pursued her education at her mother's side. She had to prepare herself to become skilful in domestic tasks and the work of the fields; she had gradually to learn the role of the wife; she had to give very early proof of those talents which would attract the attention of young men. Marriage and motherhood—glorified by certain works of Kongo sculptors—were the conditions of her entrance into society, her accession to social fulfilment. Boys and girls also received the diffuse education which the entire clan tried to give them: the elders (ba-mbuta), the maternal uncles, and the elder brothers, who imposed their authority effectively. Kikongo proverbs recognized these determining influences: 'Like mother, like daughter'; 'Like elder, like younger.'

As the apprenticeship proceeded, the child enjoyed greater autonomy and increased responsibilities. The girl participated fully in household tasks and agricultural activities which were, for the most part, in the hands of the women; she began to take care of her younger brothers or sisters; she began to perform the duties that assisted and enhanced solidarity with respect to her relatives; she took part in the ceremonies accompanying marriages and funerals. The same mechanism of participation in familial and public affairs operated in the case of the boy. He took part in masculine labors—clearing of fields, construction or repair of houses, maintenance of agricultural equipment; he took his place in the network of clanic solidarity; he participated discreetly in discussions and celebrations concerning the collec-

tivity; he used his initiative and proved himself capable of contributing to the needs of the group. In this way the child formed
his personality and 'awakened' to social life; he was less and less
a *nleke* (from *leka,* to sleep) and was slowly becoming a *mbuta*
(from *buta,* to beget, fertilize).

This transition from a passive condition to an active condition
in which all his forces served the community as a whole was the
period that most profoundly affected the course of the child's life.
It implied physical maturity, the capacity to beget offspring and
to produce goods or services. But these natural qualities were not
enough; they remained savage as long as the formative social
process had not operated. This was the goal of initiation: it
transformed mere puberty into social fullness; it symbolically
killed adolescents in order to bring about their rebirth, which,
from the clanic point of view, was the only birth that counted.

Birth Through Death

The rites of nubility and initiation varied according to the region
of the Kongo and according to sex, although certain initiatory
'schools' sought a mixed enrollment. The early chroniclers
pointed out the large number of circumcised males and wondered
about the origins of this practice. Pigafetta emphasizes the universality of this custom: 'These tribes practice circumcision in
the manner of the Jews.'[2] Father Bernardo de Gallo, in a report
dating from 1710, makes the same observation while describing
the collective demonstrations that accompanied the reappearance
of the circumcised males: 'Others practice the circumcision of
children or young boys and celebrate it publicly, and certain
Whites allow this. The latter belong, perhaps, to the race of
traitors [Jews].'[3] Separated by over a century, the observations
are unchanged. Circumcision sanctified virility and women required it of their future husbands. It might be the occasion for a
terminal ceremony—the boys who had become completely male
then wore long sarongs and ornaments—but this was not a
common rule. It was indeed a necessary condition for initiation,
but it was not to be confused with the latter.

The girls were subjected to a retreat and a series of tests which
rendered them marriageable. In his description of the Kongo,
Dapper considers the rite known as *sikumbi,* which confirmed
nubility or accompanied betrothal: actually the word *kumbi*

designated a virgin, a ritual of preparation for marriage and motherhood, and a fiancée enhanced by red coloring. Father de Gallo confirms the popularity of this 'superstition': 'It is called *ncumbi*, it consists of a certain ceremony followed by a celebration which takes place when the woman arrives at marriageable age.'[4] And Laurent de Lucques describes the retreat that was imposed on girls of the region of Soyo before they could contract their first union. Without this preparation, which was a variant of the initiatory procedure, husband and wife could not obtain the right to cohabit;[5] it was obligatory and was followed by a kind of trial marriage which the missionaries interpreted as an abandonment 'to the power of the devil'.

In certain parts of the Kongo the *kumbi* has retained its character of feminine initiation into the modern era. Ethnographic documents help to illuminate an institution which has survived the passing of centuries. As soon as they reached puberty the young girls had to go into seclusion in the *nzo kumbi* hut. For the occasion they had their bodies entirely covered with a red dye made of *tukula* powder and palm oil, and wore all their finery: metal bracelets and ankle bands, necklaces and belts of pearls or glass beads. This period of partial isolation, which might last a year or more and was characterized by the enforcement of new prohibitions, allowed ample opportunity for the dance. It provided an occasion to exhibit the future wives and attract fiancés and candidates for marriage; an occasion, too, to receive gifts, which were presented to the mother in exchange for the right to certain precisely defined intimacies. A second retreat preceded the marriage ceremony and concluded with a procession leading the fiancée to a river, where the girls took a bath which cleansed the future wife of her layer of *tukula*.

These practices did not exclude an initiation which was more complex, more charged with significance, richer in revealed knowledge. It varied from one province to the next—so much so that it has been possible to distinguish four clearly differentiated schools—and did not always have a compulsory quality. The best known of these initiatory methods was the *kimpasi*, which was widely practiced in the eastern part of the kingdom of the Kongo. The term—from *ki*, indication of place, and *mpasi*, suffering—designated the site of the ordeals and the ordeals themselves. It described the setting of a real seclusion outside the villages which provided a harsh apprenticeship and ended with the second birth of those who were subjected to it.

This initiation, which might bring together several hundred young people in a single 'class', was mixed. It occurred every time the community felt the need to ensure its reinforcement, to restore the foundations of the society by subjecting a new generation to the rigors of tradition and of the sacred. It served an order which resisted change and very early it provided a way to counteract disintegrating influences acting from without: the first missionaries regarded it as one of the greatest obstacles to their activities. Early observers of Kongo life could not have been unaware of the *kimpasi*, or *kipaxi*, as it was sometimes called. Cavazzi reports some of its external characteristics and alludes to obscene rites—songs and dances with sexual symbolism—without trying to understand the meaning or function of the institution.[6] His testimony, which has been translated into French by Father J. B. Labat, nevertheless deserves to be quoted at length:

The *nquiti* [*nkita*, the initiate after his symbolic resurrection] form a sect of the most infamous variety. For the sites of their gatherings they choose the most remote spots, the deepest valleys. The infamous ministers of this sect hold their heads up and do not bother to hide. Their houses can be recognized by the large number of tree trunks planted in a semicircle in front of them. These trunks, which are crudely carved, represent their idols, and are painted with as little art as they are carved.

It is in front of these disgraceful images that they execute by night their shameless dances, sing their abominable songs, and perform actions even more horrible. But all this is shrouded in a secrecy as inviolable as the confession among the Catholics. Absolutely no one is permitted to set foot within these confines unless he is initiated in these mysteries; and so the people will have more respect for it, they have even given this enclosure the pretentious name of 'Wall of the king of the Congo' [*kongo* is one of the words that designates the initiation and the place where it occurs].

As soon as the candidate appears, accompanied by his sponsors, they throw in front of him a cord prepared according to magical rites. He is ordered to walk back and forth several times over this enchanted cord. He must do as he is told; soon, by the virtue of the hemp which he has been made to consume, he falls to the ground unconscious. The *nquiti* pick him up and carry him into the *chimpasso* [*kimpasi*, place of ordeals]. When he has recovered consciousness, they make him promise to be a faithful disciple of their sect as long as he lives.

Father Jerome de Montesarchio, after being secretly introduced into one of these gatherings in order to discover their practices and mysteries, heard damnable blasphemies uttered by these ministers and by apostates of our Holy Religion.

They call those who, although born of a black father, remain very white, with blond curly hair, *ndundu* [albinos]. These *ndundu* hold second rank among the *nquiti*. The ministers use the hair of these miserable creatures for their sorcery.

Those who are born with crooked feet and who are called for this reason *ndembola* [ndembo, another name for the initiation in the province of Mpemba], hold a very high rank among the *nquiti*, as do pygmies or dwarfs, who are called *mbaka* or *ngudi ambaka*.

There is a minister, a famous magician, who boasts that he can raise the dead. He calls himself *nganga matombola* [*tombula*, to raise, restore, or teach].[7]

The full meaning of this description is clear only when it is compared with modern ethnological findings concerning the *kimpasi*, and the institution is seen in all its amazing formal permanence. The site of the initiation was a secluded spot near a river—to provide water for ablutions—and a natural palm grove. The place of ordeals properly speaking consisted of an enclosure with two doors made of palm branches planted in the ground, and a few huts. Statues hastily carved into the wood acted as guardians of the sacred hearth by inspiring fear and 'binding' inauspicious spirits; while sculptured figurines immobilized the forces which the initiates would learn to manipulate in order to protect themselves from the dangers of sorcery and master their beneficial influences.

The local directors of the *kimpasi*, men and women, directed the rites, provided instruction, and saw that the domestic regulations which were imposed on initiates from the first morning

218

were respected. The most distinguished of these persons was the *ngudi nganga,* or 'eminent possessor of wisdom'; Cavazzi calls him a 'minister and famous magician'. His assistants performed definite functions of surveillance, stewardship, and sanitary discipline. At the head of the women was the *ma ndundu,* the venerable albino, an extraordinary and dreaded personage, a creature from the other world, who was regarded as 'the most influential agent';[8] she occupied second rank according to Cavazzi. She was attended by several women, including the 'possessor of forces', the 'mother of pleasure', and 'the mother of consolation'. As for the *mbaka,* Negrillos, the little men, they took part on several occasions, notably at the time of the oath sworn by the initiates; they represented the earliest occupants of the land, creatures from the time of the beginnings, and were believed to be 'sons of the spirits'; Dapper mentions the role they played at the court of São Salvador as well as at that of Loango.

The symbolism and the ritual drama that characterized the *kimpasi* referred to the earliest times: the emergence from the original chaos, the appearance of men and the fruitful union achieved by the primordial couple, the birth of the Kongo. At times when the community found itself weakened or threatened, this symbolism and ritual ensured its safety by re-creating for the cream of its youth* the beginnings of the collective enterprise which achieved its order, its civilization, and its history. The community recovered its vigor by dramatizing its origins. It accomplished its own rebirth by giving birth, in accordance with its norms, to the young people molded by the initiation. This was its fundamental intention. The very harshness of the restrictions endured and the punishments prescribed—including the death penalty—revealed the importance of the stake.

The initiatory procedure had three phases. The candidates, supported by their sponsors, died *ritually.* They were struck by the *'nkita* death', stripped of their clothing, lined up like corpses, bound by the oath, and transported to the shelter which was reserved for them. They were turned over to the *ma ndundu,* who had to lead them to their second birth as she would carry a child in her womb. They grew like embryos; they 'learned' feeding, corporal discipline, the prescribed words and phrases, the

* Disreputable persons were excluded from the initiation.

rules; they were totally dependent upon their 'mother'. The second phase began with the resurrection of the initiates: the master revived the 'corpses' by massage and mouth-to-mouth resuscitation. Each of the newly born in the *kimpasi* participated in a special dance, recited the oath of loyalty, and chose an initiatory name. Then a banquet and festivities lasting all night celebrated the happy event. The neophytes joyously began their lives as '*nkita* children'; now they would have to 'grow and ripen'. They received a civic and religious instruction; they danced and deepened their understanding of the techniques governing sexuality; they became adults who were responsible to the collectivity. The *nkita* achieved self-control as well as the ability to influence natural and supernatural forces. The third phase of the initiation corresponded to the emergence of the initiates and the enthusiastic welcome which the villages gave to the new generation; after months or years of trials, this was the moment for 'feasts of celebration and gifts of congratulation'. Once again the masters of the *kimpasi* had produced exemplary men and women, 'full-fledged representatives of social values'.[9] Initiation was one of the procedures designed to ensure the preservation of society, an instrument of protection and conservatism.

The sovereigns of the Kongo did not disregard this powerful institution. One—António I—alluded to it in the list of his honorific titles. He claimed the title of Master of the Initiates at a time when the kingdom, defeated, disunited, and a prey to competing forces, was undergoing a very serious crisis. The *kimpasi* played a political role[10] and it must have contributed to the struggle against the 'Portuguese party' — that is, the modernists. It covered a wide geographical area in the seventeenth century. The Capuchin missionaries discovered it around 1645, even in remote provinces. Cavazzi describes it, incidentally revealing the existence of its southern counterpart, the *ndembo*. Dapper does not mention it, but he does provide information on the *kimbo* (*nkimba*), which was the initiatory instruction practiced in the Mayombe and in Loango.[11] This was the third of the great schools which were active in the kingdom of the Kongo over at least three centuries, the one that played the role of spreading ultimate wisdom and transmitting techniques for the preservation of social harmony.

Knowledge as Power

Initiation was generally the necessary condition for apprenticeship in the specialized profession of 'diviners and magicians', as
the early writers called them. Laurent de Lucques, among other
observers of life in the Kongo, made a careful study of this
category of specialists, who were regarded as hostile to the spread
of Christianity. He acknowledges their usefulness: 'There are
here a great number of people, men as well as women, called
fetishers. . . . They are not in league with the devil and are not
given to the destruction of their fellows, but do them
good. . . . '[12] and mentions the instruction received and the skill
acquired: 'These fetishers, men as well as women, in all the
villages and places have their schools, which produce very skillful doctors.'[13] Bernardo de Gallo, less knowledgeable and more
intransigent, indiscriminately denounced the 'fetishism and
idolatry' that was revealed 'especially during illnesses'.[14]

These practices were the province of the *nganga*, 'which
means priest, doctor, surgeon, priestess'.[15] In fact, the term
evoked the notions of competence, skill, ingenuity, and experience; it implied a type of knowledge and a mastery of the techniques for applying it. It was therefore a concept that had to be
made more specific. The *nganga*, who formed actual associations
or confraternities, were qualified in a very precise way. Distinctive titles, based on the names of the *nkisi* (magical forces
or powers) used, indicated areas of specialization. Cavazzi
enumerates more than twenty of these;[16] but the diversity is
much greater due to numerous local variants.

Most of the interventions had a therapeutic nature .They were
based on experience and a knowledge of natural remedies which
were transmitted all the more discreetly in that they were a
source of income; secrecy was a way of protecting the 'profession'. They were often accompanied by a ritual designed to
influence the forces known to be responsible for the illness. They
combined magical or mystical treatment with mechanical and
chemical treatment. Pigafetta mentions medicaments 'derived
from herbs, trees and their bark, oils, water, stones'; and alludes
to the use of bleeding, cupping vessels applied 'by means of
certain small horns', and vegetable saps ensuring the healing of
wounds.[17] Father de Lucques mentions a primitive form of
auscultation: 'The fetisher . . . makes the sick person lie down

on the ground completely naked. He palpates him to examine him thoroughly.'[18] Once the diagnosis had been established, the patient received the first attentions: rest, medication made 'of roots and other ingredients, finely ground', and massaging of the body 'with drugs'. These were merely adjuvants to a cure whose first requirement was that the illness—a force contrary to the forces of life—be expelled: 'the administration of medicines was accompanied by dances, music, and invocations'.[19] This curative method has meaning only if it is seen in relation to certain metaphysical and physical conceptions regarding the human being. Four elements made up the human being and ensured its existence by virtue of their association: the body (*nitu*), the blood (*menga*), which was the vital fluid and carried the soul (*mo-oyo*), and the double, which was both the shadow of the body and the principle of perception. Death alone could dissociate these components, but illness disturbed their relationship. The curative treatment acted on each of them in order to re-establish this relationship; one may say without exaggeration that this treatment was always a species of psychosomatic medicine.

Each disease identified was thus subjected to a double therapy, both parts of which depended on a single specialist surrounded by disciples who were often his former patients; for the cure bound the sick person and his 'doctor', either by bringing them together on the occasion of ritual practices in connection with the saving *nkisi*, or by necessitating the initiation into the secrets of the art of a young boy belonging to the 'house' of the former patient.[20] These schools were numerous, as were the magician-practitioners: for a very small region, Cuvelier mentions 'fetishers' treating hemoptysis, back ailments, convulsions, nervous maladies, and madness.[21] Laurent de Lucques and Monari mention women who helped people become 'stronger in the head', others who promoted pregnancy. Another chronicler mentions 'fetishers' who operated against 'the malady of the stone'. The complete list of specialties would be very long; as long as the list of real or imaginary maladies.

The role of the diviner was to guide a sick person whose illness did not yield to the usual remedies to the appropriate specialist. He was the *nganga* who practiced the science of the hidden on a higher level. With his hands, the *nganga amooko* sought to determine whether the malady was of natural origin or resulted from a trick of sorcery. The *nganga manga* identified sorcerers who acted against the life and health of others. A general term, *nganga ngombo*, covered various experts who determined the causes of deaths, illnesses, pains, and disorders. The register of causes was brief: ancestral wrath, intervention of 'fetishes' (*mikisi*), influence of sorcery or *ki-ndoki*. The primary function of the diviner was to discover the type of power responsible for the trouble.

Their duties were not limited to this therapeutic role. They took part in public and private affairs. They acted as prudent and powerful counsellors to the 'principal men'; they decided the most opportune moment for military operations; they denounced real or imagined conspiracies. It was from their wisdom that the art of omens arose: the songs of birds, objects found, obstacles encountered during the march, and numerous other signs provided information about joys or misfortunes to come.[22] The diviners helped in the discovery of thieves; Laurent de Lucques reports this practice in connection with the stealing of salt and adds, 'How many innocent persons are put to death at a single word from these accursed necromancers!'[23] The administering of ordeals intended to demonstrate the guilt of 'sorcerers' (*ba-ndoki*) must be considered in this connection; its purpose was to eliminate stealers of vital forces, eaters of souls. Trial by poison was the most formidable. It used, in paste or liquid form, a powder made from the wood of 'a certain tree called *ngassa* (*nkasa*), which is red and so bitter and noxious that the birds cannot endure even its shadow'.[24] Bernardo de Gallo has described a ceremony performed by a 'minister' called *ngola ankasa*, who is active and dreaded even today:

This *ingolangassa* first eats or drinks the *ngassa* himself . . . perhaps in a weak dose. Then he summons each of those who must take it, saying more or less these words, according to the occasion: 'If you are guilty of disturbing the peace or are a traitor, if you have committed such and such a crime, if you have stolen such and such a thing, if you have robbed and killed such and such a man, or if you have cast some spell or other, die from this *ingassa*. If you are innocent, vomit it forth and be free of all evil.' If a man who eats or drinks the *ingassa* dies, he is

223

considered guilty, and his body is denied burial and is often
burned. If the crime is serious, they rob and capture his family.
If, on the contrary, he vomits the *ingassa*, he goes free and is
judged innocent. . . . The king has also used this cruel superstition to discover treason and to bind his vassals to loyalty.[26]

An institution of this kind not only guaranteed the elimina-
tion of culprits, suspects, or troublemakers; it also contributed,
by means of a tragic ritual, to the reinforcement of the social
order. The execution of the 'sorcerer' temporarily restored a kind
of ideal society.

The diviner influenced the course of individual lives. He was
the counsellor, the giver of confidence, the protector who
defended people from insidious threats. He suggested which
mikisi (or fetishes, as the early chroniclers called them) ought to
be honored or propitiated. He helped to discover personal taboos.
He indicated which specialists should be consulted in case of
illness. In numerous circumstances affecting the ordinary course
of days, he imposed his knowledge of 'hidden things'. A trip
could not be undertaken without the assurance of its happy
conclusion. It was the *nganga ngombo* who foresaw its outcome:

When he has heard his question [the question of the client],
the diviner makes him sit on the ground. He sits down himself
and takes his client's hands. He pulls them and rubs them very
hard, meanwhile spitting, panting, shaking his head, and roaring
like a demon. He does this three times, and performs other rites.
Then he tells him what will happen.[26]

In all emergencies or on all occasions when the future was
unknown, the Mukongo wanted a guarantee of security or good
fortune; for this he went to the diviner.

Certain professions fell between the knowledge of the *nganga*
and the skill of the artisan: the technique of forging, for
example, which was full of prestige in the Kongo. The blacksmith was a *nganga lufu*. He had to undergo an initiation, honor
particular powers, and respect numerous prohibitions. His principal implements—the hammer and forge—evoked the era of
mythology and of the first ancestors; they fell into the domain of
the sacred and of magical operations; they figured among the

symbols that protected authority. Furthermore, the water of the forge and the air of the bellows were used therapeutically; they were believed to 'preserve health for a long time'.[27] Noble calling and symbolic activity as well as material creation, metalwork was in intimate communication with those powers operating on forces, men, and things. This explains why, as has been mentioned several times, the sovereign was called the 'forger of the Kongo'.

More commonplace techniques also required an apprenticeship, a knowledge of the methods and rules of the profession, and the symbols and practices it included. This was true of weavers and tappers of palm wine. Young men who wished to devote themselves to one of these activities applied for instruction to a skilled elder 'and paid for their schooling'.[28] In the Kongo, except for the great initiations, all knowledge was communicated by means of the numerous 'schools' which each master, *nganga*, or artisan emeritus organized around himself.

This principle applied to the transmission of court etiquette and the art of politics. Boys belonging to noble families were sent to the *mbanza* (capital towns), where they lived near the king or 'governor'; here they learned suitable manners and military art, and were introduced to public affairs through the numerous services they rendered. After the Catholic missions were established, they also attracted the young men by offering an apprenticeship in 'the customs of the Whites'. They became, without being completely aware of the fact, centers of modernism. Laurent de Lucques mentions a 'prince' of Soyo who 'had been in the mission serving the fathers from very early boyhood'. And he adds, 'It is the custom here that the leading *fidalghi* [*fidalgos*] send their young sons to serve the missionaries'.[29] These boys of high lineage collaborated as interpreters and assistants in the religious services. In this way they acquired a certain knowledge of the outside world, a *savoir-faire* indispensable to relations with foreigners. The assistance provided by the Church made it possible to adapt the aristocratic education to new conditions. This was one reason for the attraction remarked by the early observers:

Some of them [the Blacks] are *maestri*, masters. Their job is to act as interpreters during confessions. Others are called *ajutanti*, auxiliaries, who, along with the *maestri*, sing at masses and other services. This title is in great esteem among them. As a rule, all are chosen from the leading *fidalghi* [*fidalgos*] of this principality.[30]

Western civilization was imposed on the people of the Kongo because of its relative material power, the effectiveness of its technology, and the allure of its manufactured goods. From the sixteenth century on, discovery of the 'European secret' was a constant preoccupation. It was sought on the level of revealed knowledge — Christianity — and recorded knowledge — book learning. The *História* expresses this with pious optimism: 'Almost all . . . are learning to read in order to be able to recite the divine office [and] they sell everything they have to buy a manuscript or a book and if they manage to obtain one, they carry it with them always.'[31] 'Almost all' is obviously excessive; but the attraction of the new knowledge, the presumed source of new powers, was incontestable in Mbanza Kongo and Soyo. King Afonso I asked the Portuguese sovereign to send missionaries, doctors and surgeons, pharmacists, and artisans capable of teaching, and set the example for application to study. The Jesuits tried to run a college in the capital from 1625 to 1675. The merchant Pieter van den Broecke mentions the presence in Mbanza Soyo, in the early seventeenth century, of 'eight or ten schools of the Portuguese type'.[32] The inventory is doubtless inaccurate, but the influence of modern education cannot be disregarded: secretaries wrote in Portuguese, ambassadors from Soyo to Brazil understood Latin and held forth in that language, and half-breed or Negro clerks formed the rudimentary administration used by Portuguese, priests, and Kongo authorities in dealings with outsiders. Political vicissitudes and intensified mercantilism ended, however, by nipping this potential élite in the bud. Again and again the Kongo missed its opportunity to enter the modern age: the freedom of action and the necessary assistance were lacking.

CHAPTER 9

Language and the Arts

The tyranny of words claimed the Mukongo from the first days of his existence. He became a *mwana*, a human child, only when he received a name, in about the second or third month. Until then he was, in a sense, on the frontiers of life (for death hung over him) and of the community. He was nothing but 'a stomach that works' (*nsedia*): a little male (*mwana-bakala*) or a little female (*mwana-nkento*). The family did not recognize the young child or grant him his final portion of existence (a personal name) or status until they were persuaded that he might live. The clan welcomed him by naming him. It assigned him a first name known as the 'birth' name, which recalled a circumstance, sign, or ritual occurrence that accompanied his entrance into the world. *Makiadi* meant he who appeared on a day of 'sorrow'; *Mabwaka*, he who was born with a 'red' skin; *Masamba*, he who 'cleared the way' for other boys; *Nsona*, she who owed her existence to the fertilizing intervention of *Nsona Mpungu*. A second, more official name superseded these evocative appellations. This name perpetuated the memory of an ancestor, whose name was 'distinterred' in this way because of the veneration of which he was the object, or of a relative to whom the infant bore a certain resemblance. The spread of Christianity tended to substitute saints' names for these mementos of the dead. It operated through necessity at the time of baptisms, and then by contamination: the commercial caravans helped to disseminate a veritable vogue which was more indicative of a taste for prestigious names than of belief in the imported faith. Cavazzi derides this practice and the abuse of titles which multiplied the *ndo* (Dom) and *ndona* (Dona).[1] The new names were rapidly

'Kongolized' and adapted to the phonetic exigencies of the Kikongo language: João became Nzuau; Afonso became Fusu (or Funsu); Bernardo, Mbelenadu; Pedro, Mpetelo; Cristina, Kiditina; Inès, Fineza. Certain names received an indigenous justification: they were explained by means of analogies. Domanuele (Dom Manuel) connoted intelligence and sometimes qualified a 'well-behaved' child. Ndonderi (Dom André) suggested vivacity or God-given force, and was applied to a boisterous child. This usage of foreign names has continued from the sixteenth century to the present, and has led to the formation of veritable 'fraternities' of homonyms.[2]

Titles and nicknames often completed the Mukongo's identity. These were added when the personality changed—notably, by means of initiation — or when it asserted itself by attracting attention,[3] and they reveal a conception of human existence which saw the individual as a slow and continual creation. The rites of puberty, arrival at the *kimpasi*, membership in a specialized cult: these were so many occasions on which new names were required to express changes in the personality. These names generally had an allusive meaning based on popular sayings or revealed knowledge. They might also have double meanings involving plays on words or associations of ideas; for example, the name *Lutete* associated the boy who received it with the leaf of the pumpkin (*lutete*), and predicted his skill in settling (*teeta*) differences. In the case of chiefs, ceremonial names used by the elders of the clans evoked their pre-eminent position. Some of these appellations very soon showed the mark of Portuguese colonization. A notable of the province of Mpangu was honored by the name of Ndolumingu, which should be translated Dom Sunday: *ndo* (dom) and *Lumingu*, from the Portuguese *domingo*. Native power donned the trappings of foreign power, preened itself in imported terms and titles. Pigafetta notes in passing the role of these denominations which were born of the instruction and influence of the Portuguese.

Language as Power
From birth to death the Mukongo was subject to the influence of words; he believed them to be the source of good and evil. They contributed to the formation of his personality. They connected him with his lineage and they were the main testimony

to a revered past. They formed messages destined for the ancestors, but they also composed the formulas from which the magic of aggression derived its effectiveness. They expressed the sentiments of affection, but they were also the instrument of the dreadful malediction which banished the unworthy child from the family hearth. In the form of mottoes, they expressed the glory of the chief, his will, and his authority. Every clan chief liked to hear them and find in them the proof of his greatness; like the chief of the Nsaku clan: 'The clan of Mfulana Nsaku / it is as boundless as the sea. / One can travel across it on foot / one cannot encompass it with the eye / We, the Mfulana Nsaku / are mighty warriors.'[4]

The Tales, proverbs, and songs explained the significance of the names and mottoes. Hence they were associated with a literature which did not exist on the margins of life, as a mere division or a luxury of a few, but was part of the rhythm of daily existence. This literature was primarily conceived to glorify the king and, through him, the power of the kingdom. For this reason it was presented by the voices of heralds, to a solemn-sounding accompaniment, during the magnificent ceremonies that reinforced the power and its alliances:

Our king is the greatest king on earth. His kingdom is the largest and most beautiful in the world. He treats his subjects well. It is only the most deserving on whom he confers honors and dignities. When he gives a feast for the principal men of the capital and the chiefs who come to visit him from everywhere, he regales them magnificently with the best millet bread, much meat, and *mwamba* in abundance. He pours palm wine in profusion. All his servants proclaim his goodness. He does not give them more work than they can do. The father (?) of the king was a brave man who won many and great battles. His mother was a very good woman who was honored by all the women in the country. . . . [5]

Coexistent with this literature created to serve the religion of power were the revealed texts, formulas, prayers, and songs which established communication with the gods and the ancestors. The initiation at the *kimpasi* was an occasion for a true festival of 'letters' and learning. The early documents allude to it, and modern documents present passages which still reveal this richness of expression. Mystical and esoteric elements predominate: 'Lord Mata [word] of Nzambi [supreme being] is a son of Nzambi. / He repeats: strike the leopard, strike the leopard. / And Nzambi from the lake, create the earth, create the sky.'

The love song describing the joy of physical union, and allusions revealing a bold eroticism—an object of horror to the missionaries—were present as well:

I went to the *kimpasi*. / I was offered three hundred pearls / with which I bought three peanuts [three women] / and ate them. / A man and a girl were lying down. . . . / He waved to me. / Here was the ecstasy . . . / of the torrent that flows from the mountain onto the plain. / The river Lukanga has overflowed, / the girl has gone away. / O beloved woman / O thou, dearest / O well-beloved / O adored one![6]

Cavazzi has referred shamefacedly to these 'abominable songs'. He associates them with 'actions even more horrible', overlooking the role played by demonstrations and symbols of fertility in the system of collective representations of the Bakongo.

Because it altered the operation of beneficial forces, because it was the negation of earthly life, death was also an occasion for a veritable mobilization of words. In addition to the anguished cries of those who found themselves cruelly sundered, it required statements and songs to accompany the slow progress of the deceased toward the land of 'lasting life'. Every burial ceremony of an eminent man provoked a literary creativity which added new *mbembo*—funeral songs which were improvised, but preserved because of their excellence—to the treasury of Kongo literature. The theme of abandonment dominates these, as it continues to dominate modern works mourning the death of revered chief or 'saviours' who have founded the religions of salvation:

Ah! father, where you are bound / go there gently, ah! father. / Are you not the seed, the eldest of our clan? / And the rest of us, your children, you leave us thus! / To whom do you leave us? / Oh! father, it is all over for us.[7]

In addition to these works which might be called totally committed, since they help to influence men and the forces that rule their destinies, there is a literature whose purpose is to explain, instruct, and amuse. It is extensive, as an inventory made some thirty years ago shows.[8] Classification of works into well-defined types is difficult. Some refer to clanic history and to remote events, others present aspects of religious thought or illustrate moral prescriptions, while still others, such as proverbs with indirect morals and riddles, train the intelligence or arouse curiosity. Among the latter, the popular tales, the stories drawing their inspiration from scenes of everyday life, and the fables often deal with themes familiar to Bantu folklore. They present a symbolic bestiary and the personages of the human comedy: the wife, the husband, and the simpleton appear just as they do in most oral literatures. Then there are the domestic dramas, like the tale of the 'stubborn husband' in which appetite eventually triumphs over the spirit of discord.

This wealth of learning and literacy was largely overlooked by the early chroniclers. The compiler of the *História* sets the tone when he observes that the people of the Kongo 'have no literature, nor written characters'; and expresses his delight at the zeal they bring to the acquisition of the new learning: 'They are beginning to have schools and to teach reading and writing, which activities they are very partial to.'[9] Pigafetta declares with equal superficiality, 'For want of writing, these people do not preserve the history of their former kings, nor the memory of past centuries'.[10] This was to fail to recognize the vigor of the oral tradition and the extent of the learning which it transmitted. It was also to overlook the difficulties of a modern instruction which lacked teachers and necessarily assumed an initiatory character. Only a minority acquired this education, out of the necessity to ensure communication with the Portuguese and their God. The civilization of the book—and the religion of the book—nevertheless made their appearance toward the middle of the sixteenth century. A Kikongo catechism, the work of Father Gaspar da Conceição, was introduced into the Kongo in about 1555. Another, by Father Mateus Cardoso, followed in 1624; then a Kongo grammar was published in Rome in 1659. Words shifted slowly and imperceptibly from the realm of speech to the magical world of printed symbols. They found a new life, moreover, through the domestication of the words and phrases of the Portuguese language: food, clothing, the home, agriculture and trade, the measurement of time, etc., were so many areas of linguistic innovation after the beginning of the sixteenth century.[11]

In his description of the 'customs' of São Salvador, Pigafetta suggests the comparative refinement of a court culture which was maintained by the entourage of the sovereign. He observes: 'In the court of the king, there are also flutes and fifes which are played with skill; to the sound of these instruments, dances are performed with decorum and dignity. . . . The common people . . . play more crudely than the courtiers.'[12]

He also mentions the large role accorded to the arts of entertainment: 'At festive gatherings and celebrations such as weddings, love songs are sung, the lute is played.'[13] But the capital of the Kongo was above all the place where a modern culture induced, in a sense, by the Europeans was undergoing a painful birth; the devotion of King Afonso I to study was exemplary, and his correspondence, which was edited by Father Antonio Brasio, reveals a desire to construct a civilization invigorated by certain foreign contributions.

From words to the rhythms of music and the dance there was no discontinuity in the traditional society of the Kongo; they were all language, whether of sound or gesture. The drums had a voice; they transmitted messages that were governed by a code. During military operations orders were given to troops by means of signals emanating from drums (ngoma), clapperless bells (ngonge), and transverse horns (mpungi) carved from elephant's tusks.[14] The 'lute' spoke a more agreeable language, and notably that of the heart:

Admirable phenomenon, by means of this instrument, they [the musicians] express their thoughts and make themselves understood so clearly that almost anything that can be said with words they can render with their fingers by touching this instrument. To these sounds they dance, clapping their hands to mark the rhythm of the music.[15]

Pigafetta describes this stringed instrument, which seems to have been modified under the influence of the Portuguese *machete.* The strings 'were made of strong, shiny hairs taken from the tails of elephants', a very fine skin 'like a bladder' covered the resonator, and 'very slender flat pieces of iron and silver' hung from the strings and 'produced different tinklings' according to the manner in which the strings were plucked. To play, 'the musicians tuned the strings of the instrument and, with their fingers, without picks, as one plays a harp, they [produced] a melody or a sound which delighted their ears'.[16]

Dancing rarely took place for pleasure alone. It functioned most often within the framework of veritable ritual dramas. Pupils of the *kimpasi* danced their initiation, members of specialized cults their association with the spirits, chiefs in their headdress their homage to the ancestors with whom they interceded on behalf of the living. The early documents show that because of its sacred implications, power could not be effective without the influence of certain ceremonial dances. The 'principal men' had to perform the 'war dance' which Laurent de Lucques described as a 'military exercise'. During the long (eight-day) annual celebrations which glorified and protected the royalty, certain *mani* received from the hands of their head wives bows and arrows with which they performed a 'secret' dance in her presence. Newly appointed subordinate chiefs, on the other hand, had to demonstrate their obedience by performing a ceremony of which the wife of their *mani* was the witness; thus, in Soyo : 'When he leaves the count's house, [the new chief] goes with a bow and arrows to the house of the countess and begins to dance. . . . After some time, he breaks the bow and finishes with hand-clappings and other rituals.'[17]

Art as Power

In the enclosures of the initiatory schools, dancing was performed for the benefit of supernatural powers which were embodied in sculptured figures or objects which served as snares for 'spirits'. The symbolism of form and of gesture constituted a language and an instrument which bound man to the whole of the Creation. They provided him with roots in the universe and in a past which opened with 'the time of the beginnings'. Pigafetta sheds light on the world of forms constructed by the Bakongo when he discusses the campaign against the traditional religion waged in the reign of Afonso I. This campaign culminated in a gigantic conflagration which destroyed 'idols', 'deviltries', and 'masks'. This brief inventory of the 'abominable images' condemned to the stake at least suggests the richness of the sacred and magical arts. It remains a landmark in those centuries when iconoclastic fury ravaged the works of Kongo sculptors.

Certain pieces, however, have managed to resist the assaults of mankind and of time; these are the stone figurines known as *mintadi* (guardians), carved from chlorite schist, a rock which is 'dense, soft, and silky to the touch', and almost as easy to sculpt as wood. These *matadi dia valua* (carved stones) were already used in the sixteenth century. Afonso I mentions them in a speech to the chiefs of the kingdom whose content he communicated to the king of Portugal in October 1514: 'As for the rocks and wood which you adore, Our Lord gave them to us, the rock to build houses [sic] and the wood for fuel.'[18] The most numerous and the most beautiful of these sculptured figures were collected by Robert Verly on an expedition conducted in the region of Noki, between the Congo and its tributary, the Mpozo. Rock quarried from the south-eastern slopes of the Noki mountains provided the raw material which was used by sculptors from the sixteenth to the late nineteenth century.

The pieces, which are of very different ages, have been found primarily in burial grounds reserved for chiefs of high rank, revered places 'always situated on top of a plateau where there was a forest of full-grown trees'. This is the 'Great Forest of the Ancestors' which Cuvelier mentions in his description of the kingdom of the Kongo.[19] A screen of *mpese-mpese*, the African poplar, set it apart by forming a veritable sacred boundary; and an official gatekeeper, the *mavitu*, saw that prohibitions were respected. Certain very ancient graves were marked only by 'a more or less cubic block of granite or hard rock'. A few still bore objects of value and material symbols honoring the deceased: ancient cannons from the period of the caravels, sixteenth-century sabres, jewels, brass rings, elephants' tusks, signal horns, and brass crucifixes.[20] The stone statuettes often figured among these untouchable riches intended for the commerce of the beyond. Some of these *mintadi* — and this accounts for their preservation—were buried in the ground; the legends held that they walked and talked, playing the role of intermediaries between the world 'above' and the world 'below'. All the figurines were not buried and protected by the secrecy of noble cemeteries; several of them, veritable relics, formed the treasuries of chieftainries and clans, where they stayed beyond the reach of domestic slaves and common people.

The first problem raised by these stone images is that of their function or functions. These were essential ones, for the images multiplied over the centuries, veritable symbols of permanence amid vicissitudes and disasters. Afonso I mentions their existence at the beginning of the sixteenth century; pieces brought to Rome toward the end of the seventeenth century are still found in one of the museums,[21] and numerous pieces of more 'modern' workmanship date from the eighteenth and nineteenth centuries. The style has degenerated, the quality has deteriorated, but they are obviously works of the same nature and purpose. They belong to the category of *biteki* (sculptures) which performed a function of mediation, harmony, and protection. They could not serve magical ends and, still less, insidious aggression.

The majority of the *mintadi* were substitutes for the living but temporarily absent chief, or counterparts of the dead chief; in both cases they were 'living things'; they maintained a vital presence; they provided a mystical continuity which was beneficial to all members of the clan. These stone figures first appeared as 'symbolic portraits' glorifying power, demonstrating the permanence of the chieftainry, and linking the government of the notables with that of eminent ancestors. They were the instruments of the religion of power: they subdued and reassured at the same time. It seems significant in this regard that the sculptured personages symbolized now the chief, now certain dignitaries of his entourage—clanic representatives holding responsibilities and offices in his capital. The *mfumu* (sovereign or chief) was generally caught in a meditative attitude. Sitting cross-legged with his head resting on one hand and his eyes half closed, 'he was thinking of the welfare of his people'.[22] He dwelt in eternity, he enjoyed the life that 'lasts', and guaranteed the support of the spiritual powers. He was the image of power and of the order which this power established. The dignitaries — notables of second rank — were often represented in the attitude of respect which protocol imposed in the presence of persons of high lineage. They knelt with their arms bent, their heads joined, and the palms turned upward. They expressed submission and devotion, whereas the 'royal' *mintadi* expressed majesty. None of these pieces aspired to resemblance. Their truth was located beyond appearances, beyond the ephemeral form assumed by those holding power or authority. The expression of the face was more important than fidelity to the features of which it was composed, the meaning of the gestures more important than respect for the proportions of the body. The symbolic attributes worn by the sculptured personage were not mere accessories: the stylized headdress (*mpu*), the necklace, the 'knife of dignity'—all characterized the office of chief, and appeared because of their significance and not out of a concern for realism. This sculpture, whose expressiveness is based on a simplicity which eliminates unnecessary details and the refinement of forms, possesses an undeniable communicative power. Certain works—those showing the chief in meditation— have even been regarded as 'the first version of The Thinker that the Negro world has produced'.[23]

The work of art is born of the union of an intention and a technique. The second member of the pair is no less important than the first. The technique of the *mintadi* sculptors was that of the direct cut: 'The block of stone chosen was squared off carefully, then the projected work was drawn on the surfaces from the front and from the side, begun with the help of the adze, and finished with suitable small instruments.'[24] The artist, who was respected and attached to the service of the aristocracy, concentrated his labors on the head; he fashioned it with care, finishing it almost completely before tackling the representation of the torso or limbs; he worried less about faults of proportion than he did about faults of expression. He sought the monumental effect, although his works were never over sixty centimeters high; he tried to convey an impression of power and wisdom. This has been remarked: the *mintadi*, 'these crude statues featuring a very pronounced relief, seem animated by an intense, serene, profound life of their own'.[25]

These pieces are distinguished from other products of Negro-African sculpture by their lack of symmetry. The axis of the back is not always vertical, and the head often assumes an oblique position in relation to it. Certain statuettes—notably the *nsona*, or solitary—amaze us by their spiral 'movement', their free and sophisticated composition. Verly describes a seven-teenth-century example: 'With the head turned to the side and resting on the left knee, sitting on the folded right leg, with hands clasped over the knee that supports the head, [the figure forms] a little masterpiece of remarkable style'; its 'classic beauty' recalls the pieces 'found in Benin'.[26] And Verly, while allowing that 'perfection' was alien to the requirements of the Negro artist, brings in Indian statuary and the intervention of 'Hindu fugitives'. If the statuettes are all 'symbolic portraits', and hence subject to a certain conformity, they nevertheless possess singular qualities: qualities expressing the personality of the subject or the talent of the sculptor and his individual style. The Bakongo were capable of showing their admiration for the authors of masterpieces. Even today they are aware of a decline in quality which became apparent during the nineteenth century, a decline that has transformed the revered images into mere graveyard effigies.

The statuettes representing 'motherhood', although of the same workmanship as the *mintadi*, nevertheless occupy a separate position. They are of two kinds: the first kind represents the mother holding a seated but upright child ('mother and child'); the second shows her suckling the newborn child ('nursing mother'). The two types had different functions. The first pieces invoked abundance and ensured the protection of the new generation. The second protected from sterility and promoted the continuity of lineages.[27] Both served fecundity and were part of the rituals designed to encourage it. They also had a supplementary significance; they played a political role. Some of the 'mothers' wore the headdress of chieftainry; they represented the foundresses of the clans; they symbolized feminine power; they were a way of honoring female regents who temporarily replaced deceased chiefs. If the majority of the pieces are 'crudely' made—the sculptor's attention devoted primarily to the head, seat of all wisdom and revelation—a few amaze us by the concern for detail they reveal. The sculptor has reproduced the necklace, the mesh garment that rested on the breastband, the geometrical tattoos on the breast and arms. He anticipates in his art the style of modern artisans who treat similar themes in wood: 'mothers with infants' and 'venerable women'.

These recent works (since the end of the nineteenth century) show the persistence of an aesthetic which combines naturalistic expression with symbolic expression. The material employed—wood—permits physical forms of a more supple nature, a refinement of detail, and an accumulation of decorative elements; the statue becomes a veritable story in sculpture. The finest of these pieces—a 'mother with child' or a kneeling woman—suggest the wealth of the treasure that has been destroyed. Time and the pillagers of 'idols' have reduced it to dust and ashes. The information handed down is precise: noble cemeteries once contained wooden statuettes and terra cotta figurines which were placed on the graves in great numbers; these sculpted 'fetishes' formed an otherworldly society which dominated human society, as the stone image of *Kunya*, one of the most powerful, still attests by having escaped the ravages of time. The ancient accounts note the destruction without revealing the secret of the doomed arts. They mention 'wooden idols' with human or animal forms like *Mavema*, the dog, and moon-shaped masks. The statues and statuettes seem to have been differentiated into: *bimaazi*, effigies of ancestors; *biteki*, images more religious in function; and *binkondi*, images employed primarily for magical purposes.

The inventory is poor, but the wealth of inspiration of artisans of the Kongo is undeniably apparent. In spite of everything, they have managed to preserve forms which express the spirit of their people. They have succeeded in 'Kongolizing the Christian images. In Mbafu a painted grotto has recently yielded an abundant iconography dating from the first evangelization, the one that flourished under the reign of Afonso I. Traditional themes predominate: esoteric writing, animals from the ritual bestiary, characters. But one of the frescoes is dominated by a carefully executed central figure featuring a pectoral ornament and raised on a pedestal bearing the Latin cross; it is a patron saint or prince of the Church. The crucified Christ and the motif of the cross appear in a sequence which seems to reconstruct the story of the conversion.[28] These are the same subjects which artisans—masters of brass, bronze, and steel — have preferred to model since the beginning of the sixteenth century. Their works are not the works of copyists: 'a number of details are peculiarly Negroid—the hair, the eyes, the lips, the frequent prominence of the navel—European methods of stylization have been interpreted'.[29] The influence has its source in fine European pieces made in the fifteenth and sixteenth centuries and imported from Portugal: double reliquary crosses, pectoral crosses (certain solid gold examples are still kept in the treasuries of a few notables), altar crucifixes, and wall crucifixes. The Christian symbolism has, for over four hundred years, been one of the formative elements of Kongo civilization.

According to Robert Wannyn, crucifixes of local workmanship form two groups: pieces resulting from an 'advanced technique which was apparently of foreign inspiration' and pieces 'executed according to increasingly simplified methods'. The first, all in brass, which seem to have been cast by the lost-wax process, reveal 'a somewhat refined naturalism'. The Christ is Africanized with respect to the modelling of the features and certain details; his hair sometimes recalls the aristocratic headdress, but his clothing suggests the short loincloth of slaves. Each arm of the cross often supports small subjects: praying or recumbent figures or 'heads' which suggest miniature masks. The figures are shown in a kneeling or crouching position and treated in the style of the Central African plastic arts. They represent the Apostles, the thieves, or 'God the Father and the Holy Ghost assisting Jesus at the moment of death'.[30] Some of these figurines, differentiated by the long loincloth which was more often a feminine garment, suggest a holy woman or the Virgin. This last interpretation seems to be confirmed by the common Kongo expression for Christ: 'Nkangi Kiditu a Ndona Maria, the Crucified of Lady Mary'.[31] The recumbent figures are divided into several categories: naked persons who have the left hand over the heart and conceal the sex with the right hand; persons with hands clasped and clad in the small loincloth, who symbolize 'man saved by the Redeemer'; figurines holding objects in their right hands, who suggest the sinner and his weaknesses. These interpretations are perhaps too edifying to be perfectly accurate, but there can be no doubt that the crucifix (the Nkangi Kiditu) resembles a mythical account in which Christian themes and traditional themes are combined.

Indeed, its use outside of missionary enclaves unambiguously reveals the process of Africanization. In a great ritual glorifying the ancestors, it had the role of a privileged mediator between the society of men and the 'society of the sacred'. A modern author describes this ancient custom:

239

Every year on the day when all the graves of the village dead (*bakula*) were put in order, when all was completed, the Christ was presented to the assembled village. Then it was washed in palm wine, and when this ceremony was over, it was returned to its place. There followed a [communal] meal in which all took part.[32]

The *Nkangi* 'united' members of the clanic community with a remote God and with the *bakulu* living in their subterranean homes. It also became an attribute of power, regarded in its aspect as arbiter and lawgiver: it was the Christ of the *mbazi a nkanu*, the court of justice. The newly invested chief received it along with the other emblems of his dignity—rings, necklace, headdress, etc.; he raised it at arm's length when he was being presented in all his glory to his assembled subjects, while the drums resounded and the women shouted his praises through their cupped hands.[33] The *Nkangi Kiditu* was the bearer of peace and justice as well as the intercessor with the guardians of the 'lasting life'. These functions did not exclude a magical use with a therapeutic end: healing of the sick body, soothing of the belly of the woman in labor, protection from prowling spirits. The copper of Kongo crucifixes bears the patina of human suffering.

A question arises: by what foreign models have the *Nkangi* decorated with small subjects been inspired? European iconography since the twelfth century reveals the existence of crucifixes enriched by symbolic or allegorical figures. This was the case in Portugal and also in Italy, as a piece preserved in the Cluny Museum recalls. But the relationship has not been established with certainty; the African artisan has multiplied themes which may lend a supplementary richness and a syncretic significance to the Christian symbolism. The more recent crucifixes, undoubtedly cast by the 'open at the top' method after the end of the seventeenth century, differ in quality. They are of cruder workmanship: 'The face of Christ is often distorted, the eyes very large or very small, the lips barely sketched, and the mouth enormous; the treatment of the hair exposes a wide brow. . . . The treatment of the hands and feet is nonexistent, or very sketchy.'[34]

The style is still that of traditional sculpture of the Congo region: it intends to represent allusively and not to describe, it stylizes by simplifying in the extreme. These pieces correspond more closely than the ancient *Nkangi* to the 'celebrated Negroid Christs in brass' mentioned in very diverse accounts.

The religious statuary of the Kongo is known from a small number of examples: statuettes in wood, ivory, brass, lead, and a gray alloy of lead and tin, representing the Virgin and various saints, including the popular Saint Anthony of Padua. Some of these works are crudely fashioned and seem in the outline stage; they are still preserved in the hoards of the chieftainries, but they no longer inspire displays of veneration. Regardless of the material used, the pieces of quality conform to a single style. The artisan followed the European model but simplified the treatment of the face and gave the subject almost canonical proportions; in certain cases, he produced nothing but a 'rather slavish imitation'.[35] The best know statuettes are the *toni malau* (*toni* from Antonio; *lau*, force or vigor in the idiom of São Salvador), the 'Anthony-the-all-powerfuls'. The saint carries the infant Jesus, represented standing or sitting, and his right hand holds a Latin cross which rests against the side of the body. The statuette, which is generally small in size, features a hanging ring on the reverse; it was often used for massage; it acted as an individual talisman, guardian, and fertility charm.[36] Certain pieces of even more modest dimensions, differentiated from the preceding ones by the feminization of the face, the representation of the stole, and the absence of the infant Jesus, have been called *nsundi malau*, from *nsundi* (help) and *lau*. This was the 'helpful power' presented in the form of a virgin or the Virgin. She was solicited by prayer. She banished evil by contact with the body.

Christianity, whether expressed by the unusual images in the grotto of Mbafu or by the arts made to serve religion and magic, has marked the lives of the people of the Kongo from the early sixteenth century. They have assimilated it according to their needs and the rules of their logic. They have appropriated its symbols for ends which the missionaries indignantly condemned. Crucifixes and holy statuettes (the *santu* of the modern era) became snares for benign forces, instruments favorable to fecundity and fertility. Crosses (*kuluzu*) were used in magical operations, especially in rituals ensuring the safety of the hunter and the success of his expedition. Certain pieces consisted of four

Maltese crosses arranged in a cross and mounted on a steel-tipped shaft. Discolored by the blood of animal sacrifices and smoke, they were planted on roads leading to hunting grounds.[37] In Loango the cross was associated with symbols representing the elements, as Christ and the Virgin were associated with *Bunsi*, the divinity of the Earth. It also appeared in homes in the form of 'fetish nails', which had a protective function. In all places it provided a necessary protection against the insidious attacks of sorcerers and the maneuvers of the wandering and vengeful dead.

The motif of the cross appeared in most symbolic figurations. Especially since the eighteenth century, a certain number of *mintadi* 'featured Christian crosses as pendants, either sculpted along with the work, or added with black paint'.[38] The evolution of these stone sculptures is revealing. A certain piece of hybrid form combines the traditional *ntadi* with the cross: the figure, represented standing with his arms apart in a horizontal position, is unfurling a pennant on which the name of the notable so honored is engraved. This funerary monument, which dates from a decadent era (eighteenth century), suggests the Christian symbol by its over-all structure. Another consists of the Latin cross alone, all figures having been eliminated: here the idol-destroying Christianization has found its logical conclusion, but the art of sculpture has disappeared under its thrust. This is the exception, though. The staffs of authority and scepters (*mwala amfumu*) have metallic heads of brass, tin, or an alloy combining lead and tin. This element, which is finely wrought, takes various forms: a simple disc surmounted by a Greek cross, a stylized composition centered around a figure represented in an attitude of submission, a group of human subjects surmounting two facing animals. One feature is common to all: the Greek cross is always present, on the breast of the main figure or crowning the whole.[39] In the eyes of the Bakongo, the emblems of power demonstrate the intimate union of the political and the sacred.

What with modifications of form imposed upon Christian symbolism and changes of meaning, the art of the Kongo has sometimes produced extraordinary works. In addition to the crosses mentioned by chroniclers, hunters used feminine figurines carved out of wood and 'ending in a kind of pointed shaft designed to be planted in the ground'.[40] The figure was in an attitude of meditation, with the hands joined at breast level. A patina was given to it by anointment with *tukula* (the red powder used during initiations) and by the blood of wild animals. This was the *santu* employed principally in Bazombo country, east of São Salvador. Wannyn confirms the existence of wooden statuettes 'representing a misshapen creature of human aspect, with the breasts very developed, the arms outstretched, and the lower part of the body barely suggested'.[41] The position of the arms made it possible to combine the motif of the cross with an object of archaic workmanship whose use remains unknown. Authorities still refer to the 'strange crucifixes' used in now forgotten rituals: 'The Christ figure, fastened to the cross with outstretched arms, is bound with a cord which encircles the body from head to foot';[42] he is truly the bound Christ, the *Nkangi* (from *nkanga*, to be tied) *Kiditu*.

From the earliest times the sovereigns of the Kongo have been, in the solitude of their palaces, in the presence of the spirits and of God. They have sought the support of these spirits in order to strengthen a power founded on conquest and to affirm its legitimacy in the eyes of the conquered peoples. They have enlisted the help of God in order to glorify the unitary nature of royalty and to sanctify their authority. The struggles between the Christian God and the 'savage' God—the ancient *Nzambi Mpungu*—reflect the rivalries among pretenders and the conflict between a tradition closed upon itself and a modernist movement open to outside influence.

Aristocratic art, inspired and stimulated by power, demonstrates the intimate association formed between the government of men and the government of the forces controlling the universe. The political and cultural history of the Kongo are inseparable. Conflicts surrounding sacred figures—burning them, rescuing them, or causing their metamorphosis—mark the past; and when a modern Congo under colonial domination sought rebirth, it was a new mediator of divinity who appeared to claim the role of liberator. The *Nkangi Kiditu*, Christ Bound, was borrowed from Christian tradition to symbolize an aspiration : the recovery of a glorious history that had been wasted and then confiscated by strangers at the end of the nineteenth century.

CHAPTER 10

One God Against Many

The chronicles and the early accounts recognized the powerful influence of the sacred: 'The people of the Congo have a great reverence for their fetishers and priests, whom they called *Ganga*, and obey them in everything, as if God commanded them to do so.'[1] But they present this relationship between man and the invisible, this submission to the forces of the supernatural universe, in a highly critical manner. Some see nothing but superstition, idolatry, and compliance with diabolical operations. Others—like the French missionaries of Loango and Kakongo—find only a vague and flexible religiosity: the Negroes of these kingdoms 'have almost no superstition or religion, no system'.[2] Through fragmentary or slanted descriptions, the system nevertheless appears.

The World of the Spirits

Pigafetta barely mentions the religious pluralism, the rites of worship and offerings composed of 'the most precious things': before the Christianization of the Kongo, 'everyone honored whatever god he pleased, without rule or measure or reason of any sort'.[3] Cavazzi, who devoted three chapters of his *Historical Description* to a presentation of religious ideas and practices, offers a less elementary and more objective documentation. He examines the conception of divinity, ancestor worship, and the rituals associated with the numerous 'fetishes'.

According to him, 'the fundamental dogma of the local idolatry was Nzambi ampungu, from the name attributed to the divinity'.[4] This divinity, conceived as the supreme power, never materialized and ever inaccessible, could not for these reasons be

244

accorded any worship. He alone could be the object of absolute devotion, because he completely eluded the control of men. It was with the 'inferior gods', according to Cavazzi, that men arranged the course of their destinies. After the beginning of the sixteenth century, as all the texts bear witness, the term *Nzambi ampungu* designated both the Supreme Being defined by Kongo religious thought and the God of the Christians. A document published by Felner shows this double interpretation, this identification of the 'Lord of the Sky' with the 'All-powerful creator'.[5] Laman's Kikongo dictionary mentions these aspects and stresses certain attributes of *Nzambi*: his total freedom (he 'does what he thinks right'), his quality of 'great unshakable spirit', so elusive that it was impossible to represent him in material form.[6] Thus the popular theology of the Kongo was less pervaded with anthropomorphism than that of the Christians. As for the term *(a)mpungu*, it indicated that these qualities were possessed in the highest degree; as applied to *Nzambi*, it meant specifically that he was to be identified with the creation, with power and freedom.

Certain proverbs and songs mention the total dependence of the created world and of man upon this unknowable divinity. '*Nzambi* possesses us, he eats us'; or 'It is *Nzambi* who prepares the manioc bread; we men prepare only the seasonings.' Funeral laments repeat, 'He is gone, *Nzambi* has willed it'; or they allude to the path of life and death traced by God alone:

> The great way, is not the work of men;
> The way of death, it is Nzambi who made it.
> The descent is very gentle.[7]

Nzambi saw all and ruled all; in the last analysis, his will was always 'done' and the order of the world continued to conform to his design. He had given men their fundamental laws, and tradition derived all its power from its reference to this age of beginnings. It was his law and his absolute wisdom that underlay the oaths and rituals of loyalty, as well as those the first Jesuit missionaries introduced toward the middle of the sixteenth century.[8] It was he who imposed the gravest punishments, before which man found himself without recourse. He reproved but he did not reward: only the ancestors chose those whom they welcomed after death to their subterranean village.

Christianity tried to orient the whole religious life around *Nzambi ampungu.* It did not succeed, but it introduced new forms of invocation, like this one reported by Cavazzi: *Desu Nghesu fumani,* 'God of Heaven, Lord Jesus'.[9] Above all, it reinforced belief in divine omnipotence and the reverence shown to it. If it made *Nzambi* more present, it nevertheless failed to link him ritually with the religious behavior of the Kongo villager. The Catholic ritual was seen as inseparable from power and from the aristocratic condition, rather than as a relationship between God and the believer. The presence of the missionaries among the powerful and their interventions in local politics contributed to this interpretation, which was all the more compelling since Kongo religious conceptions placed *Nzambi* beyond all knowledge and all communication with men. At least this is what Bishop Manuel Baptista Soares suggests in his report dated 1619: 'They [the people of the capital] are not animated by the sentiment of devotion or virtue, but are moved by a fantastic display. . . . This is why when the chiefs are absent, the servants are also absent.' [10]

Nzambi governed the order of the world and the course of human lives. He was in a certain sense the image of destiny; but the vicissitudes, misfortunes, and chances which affect human existence without altering the general direction of the divine will depended on powers over which man could exert an influence. The Bakongo interpreted the Creation as the system of forces which reveal and support all life. Their genuine vitalism incited them to seek in all things opportunities for reinforcement; it also led them to conceive of animate creatures, including those of primeval times mentioned in myths, as subject to changes of form and not to death. No life could be lost; it merely found another place in a universe perpetually in movement.

The world of the spirits was made up of those forces which *Nzambi* unleashed by his act of creation. In first place there were the *bankita,* creatures of the beginning, 'original ancestors', heroes who had died violent deaths. They were very strong; they intervened during the *kimpasi,* which was essentially consecrated to them; they animated a great number of very powerful 'fetishes'.[11] The *bakulu* (from *nkulu,* the elders) were deceased members of the clan. The earth was their domain; they lived in it near woods and streams, they built villages similar to those of the living where they lived in perfect harmony. The subterranean domain of the *bakulu* was the earth without evil. Cavazzi observes the absence of terror in the face of death: the Mukongo who had always obeyed the rules of the clan believed that he would arrive at the abode of the ancestors, where he would lead another life freed from the burdens of work and pain.[12] Because the clan constituted a permanent unity from the moment of its formation, the *bakulu* were in communication with the living. Though invisible, they remained present; they participated in the undertakings of their descendants, and had the power to promote or oppose their projects. Every fundamental hierarchy in the Kongo was organized with reference to a zero point which was the moment of the beginnings; because they were closer to this point, the *bakulu* enjoyed greater autonomy and power. It was as if, *Nzambi* being the origin of all things, creatures could acquire some attributes of divinity by identifying themselves with the time of origins, or by approaching them. Ancestor worship found here its profoundest justification; pre-eminences within clans and the legitimacy of kings are also explained by this essential conception.

All deceased persons were not included among the ancestors.

At the entrance to the abode of the dead there is a barrier, a bifurcation. Here the ancients judged those who presented themselves and the wicked were not admitted. These wicked then wandered about and frightened the living by apparitions and terrifying dreams. . . . They bewitched men, caused disease, death, failures, bad luck. They became the intermediaries of the sorcerer. . . . [13]

These outcasts were called *matebo* (from *teba*, to glimmer). As Father van Wing remarks, when these spirits were harbored by a material support, they 'were generally used to perform some evil task'.[14]

Obviously the forces at work in the Creation were not associated with human form alone. The operated within the very bosom of nature, and through nature. The *ba-simbi* (from *simba*, to grasp firmly, to seize) could be spirits of the water, of the earth, or of the forests. Dapper mentions a kind of demoniacal agent — *Nkadi Ampemba* — which took the form of 'a bird similar to the owl'. He also alludes, in connection with the king-dom of Loango, to *Kimbo-Bomba*.[15] This is really *Mbumba*, a spirit hidden in the guise of a snake and likened to the rainbow. In Soyo this powerful creature must have corresponded to *Uri*, object of a fertility ritual described by Laurent de Lucques. *Uri* the snake dwelt in a sacred grove in the middle of his field which was 'worked' in a ritual sense; the ceremony which was per-formed under the direction of the 'count' was supposed to bring about rainfall and ensure the abundance of the harvest.[16] Certain animals had a sacred quality: hence, 'the goats with very long beards' worshipped in the south of the kingdom. Others served as distinctive emblems — the leopard was associated with the insignia of power—or as means of differentiating personal rank. For example, Pigafetta points out the existence of 'royal fish'. Dietary prescriptions and prohibitions of a collective and per-sonal nature were based on this symbolic zoology; Father Bernardo de Gallo discovered their force when he struggled vainly against these 'diabolical superstitions'.[17] The evidence is less varied and less precise in the matter of the role of star wor-ship. Pigafetta mentions an 'important' and androgynous god consisting of the sun (male element) and the moon (female element).[18] Monari and Laurent de Lucques say of the moon that 'many people worship it as God', for 'numerous superstitions refer to it'.[19] The solar symbol, a centered disc, was used in the decoration of ceremonial arms and masculine ornaments: it was undeniably linked with the male principle of creation and with virility.[20] This information is only fragmentary, however; it does not help us to evaluate the relative importance of these diverse representations in the cosmology and theology of the Kongo.

All religious and magical techniques were designed to influence these creature-forces. To do so, they made up a kind of trap for 'spirits': an image of wood or stone—privileged sub-stances — which was called *nkisi*; this was the 'fetish' of the fifteenth-century discoverers. A series of misinterpretations, among them Cavazzi's, confused this *instrument* of the sacred with a secondary divinity. Van Wing makes the necessary clari-fication by defining the *nkisi* as an 'artifact containing a spirit controlled by a man'.[21] The Bakongo divided these traps or *nkisi* into two major groups: those that used statues and those that used another method of fixing spirits. This is only a rough classification which implies other more complex categories, for the population of the invisible world was large and varied.

Some of the *nkisi* were widely known, for example, N*kosi* (the lion), regarded as father of the 'fetishes'. He was famous and several seventeenth-century authors mention him. He took the form of a couple; the male lived in a statue representing a man, the female in 'a sack of many ingredients'. He inspired terror and protected from theft of property or souls (sorcery). He intervened in the initiation ritual at the *kimpasi*. Generally speaking, the outward form of 'fetishes' varied according to locality, but their functions appear to have been similar, and were divided into a limited number of categories: protection of health, guarantee of success, maintenance of the fecundity of women and the fertility of the earth, defence against *bandoki* (sorcerers), defence against violence and theft. Cuvelier mentions 'several fetishes' of the eastern region: *Kunya*, of human aspect, protected against 'sorcerers'; *Mpindi*, almost as tall as a man, cured nervous disorders; N*kondi*, in the form of a man 'one meter high', detected thieves; *Mavena*, the image of a dog with 'protruding fangs', drove off seducers; N*tadi* (the guardian), a 'small fetish with a human face', communicated in dreams to warn of danger.[22] The early chronicles emphasize and condemn this devotion to numerous 'idols'. Laurent de Lucques reports with horror the sale of *nkisi* which brought 'a high price, proportional to the virtue which is attributed to them'.[23] In their description of the kingdom of Loango, the French missionaries differentiate between 'idols' associated with the individual and those which, since they depended upon a 'minister', were objects of 'pilgrimages'. The latter involved prohibitions. The former acted as personal guardians, or talismans:

They [the people of Loango] almost all wear some little idol hanging from their side. This is ordinarily a human figure crudely carved out of wood or ivory. . . . They have larger, sometimes life-size figures, which they do not appear to worship in a public and regulated manner. . . . There are certain of these idols, located in out-of-the-way places, to which the Negroes sometimes make pilgrimages, especially when they are planning to assume a responsibility or marry. On such occasions the ministers of these idols simulate oracles which forbid these pilgrims the use of certain foods and certain garments for the rest of their lives.[24]

This multiform influence over the forces that condition all existence was not completely successful: as evil, illness, disorder, and death itself bore witness. If the designs of *Nzambi* and the will of the ancestors defined the limits of human possibility, it was evident nevertheless that, according to Kongo ideas, man might counteract the influence of certain forces. By so doing he disturbed the established order, spread misfortune, sterilized nature. These were manifestations of sorcery, or *kindoki*: an inverted action which brought back chaos and cancelled the progress of civilization. It is significant, moreover, that the sorcerer (*ndoki*) was conceived as a man capable of altering his appearance, of indiscriminately taking the form of a human being or an animal, of destroying the boundaries between civilization and nature. And the anomaly, the accident, the state of crisis, were attributed to operations of sorcery which had to be counteracted. An abnormal drought, a fire, a death by lightning, an epidemic, and so forth were the work of *bandoki*, as Dapper has observed.[25] Disturbances resulting from the Portuguese conquest and the spread of Christianity were interpreted by this same logic: 'innovations are leading the land to ruin: *nsi ifwidi*'; the modernist party could only be that of the sorcerers. Even before Dom Afonso had taken the throne, a campaign conducted by his rival and the traditionalists presented him as 'a secret malefactor':

They came to say [to the king] that by means of magic spells which the Christians use, Dom Afonso was flying through the air at night, indulging in debauchery, and returning home in the same manner. They added that he was drying up the rivers, stopping the rainfall, and thus destroying the crops and cutting off the king's income in order to seize the kingdom. . . . The Christians were accused of using evil powers.[26]

The accusation was made in the language of sorcery because the 'modernists' threatened the established order, and because the struggle for power first used indirect methods. The hunting down of sorcerers served both political ambition and conservatism, in the Kongo and elsewhere.

The Village of the Ancestors

The *História* devotes a few vague lines to ancestor worship : 'They [the people of the Congo] bury their dead on the mountains in cool and pleasant places which they call *infindas*. The children and close relatives go at each new moon for many years to weep on the grave. After these lamentations they leave wine and food.'[27]

The Loango missionaries are not much more explicit, but they do mention the etiquette which honored and appeased the dead: 'The extraordinary and expensive honors they pay to the dead, and the often excessive fear they feel that the spirits of deceased persons will harm them, prove that they are convinced that the soul survives the body.'[28]

Death (*lufwa*) was caused by the departure of the sensitive spirit—double, shadow, and principle of perception. The corpse (*mvumbi*) was not just a dead body: it still carried the soul (*mo-oyo*). It was the vehicle which enabled the deceased to return to the village of the ancestors. It would be abandoned in the grave once the dead person had himself become a *nkulu*; that is, an ancestor, a white-shaped creature which retained its rank and personality from its earthly life.

These conceptions explain the long-drawn-out process which led up to the burial ceremony of dignitaries. After the mortuary toilet, the corpse was wrapped in cloths and blankets—the number depended on the social status of the deceased—and exhibited in a special hut where fires released a heavy smoke that contributed to its mummification. The widows and certain other women came permanently, and clan members and relatives by marriage came a few at a time to honor the deceased in his temporary habitation. The women wept and sang 'songs of the house of the dead' or 'songs of tears'; the men performed funeral songs, or *mbembo*, accompanied by drums, hammered iron bells, and ivory horns. For one month, while the body dried out and the matter of succession was settled, these demonstrations continued in the bereaved village.[29] The treatment of the dead person en route to the village of the ancestors and the funeral ceremony followed the same principles in Loango:

251

Singing and dancing enter into all their [the inhabitants']
ceremonies . . . when some member of their family dies, they
exhibit him in a large hut, move into smaller huts around, and
spend a good part of the day and night with the corpse; now and
they they weep. The period of mourning lasts six to eight
months, and sometimes a year.[30]

The grave was dug, as the *História* notes, on a hill. A cortege
carried the body, which was laden with new riches—blankets,
loincloths, fabrics, and rugs — for the occasion. The more
numerous and valuable the goods, the greater was the satisfaction of the deceased. The body—lowered into the grave, accompanied in the case of a chief by one or more sacrificed slave
women, and covered with personal articles and money—could
now negotiate the subterranean voyage of the deceased. Close
relatives offered a viaticum of palm wine and a message: 'You
who are going, bear our tidings to the ancestors, that we who
stay may be prosperous.'[31] The end of the voyage was the land
of the ancestors; the goal, acquisition of 'the lasting life'. The
dead were 'the living par excellence'; they lived outside of time
and surrounded by riches; they possessed a power which enabled
them to control nature and men. From their villages, which were
situated under river beds or lake bottoms, they could emerge to
mingle with the living (without being seen) and direct the course
of events.

Cavazzi shows the importance of this 'underground society'
of the *bakulu* where men lived a new life free from poverty,
disease, or death, but where they retained their positions in the
hierarchy. He describes this real life without suffering or misery;
this never-ending holiday amid an abundance of women, money,
luxury, game, and palm wine. He brings out the constant intervention of the ancestors in human affairs, and describes the
ritual practices required by this 'vital' relationship between dead
and living members of the clan.[32]

He suggests the parallel hierarchies governing the succession
of ancestors, the society of the *bakulu*, and the groups formed
within the clanic unit. The rule governing this order is obvious;
it was based, as we have seen, on a kind of dynamism of vital
forces; the ancestors closest to the beginnings were the most
powerful, the living persons closest to the ancestors were the

most effective intercessors. These included the elders of the clans and lineages. But the true priest of the ancestor cult was that dignitary to whom early authors referred as 'chief of the land'. Father Zucchelli is very careful to distinguish 'two classes of fetishers': 'The first are fetishers in the true sense of the term, the second are the chiefs of the land [*capi della terra*]';[33] the first act through 'fetishes', the second through the ancestors. Cavazzi makes a similar distinction. And Laurent de Lucques notes the moral prestige which the priest-chiefs enjoyed by virtue of their familiarity with the *bakulu*: 'These chiefs give the benediction, predict the future, have great authority. . . . Those who live in the same village as one of these great chiefs must tell him everything they do or intend to do, and he on his side indicates when a given thing must be done.'[34]

This religious power, which was clearly differentiated from political power, may be explained by the decisive role the ancestors played at every moment, and by the necessity in which each clan stood of acting in harmony with the *bakulu*. The latter were honored regularly: one of the four days of the week was consecrated to them. Their orders were solicited, above all in dreams. Their support was sought in every great undertaking, and especially on the occasion of the hunt. They were asked to pacify the village when discord and death struck. At solemn and magnificent ceremonies they received the homage of all their adult descendants together with their husbands and wives. No Mukongo could imagine living, surviving, apart from his land and his dead; a proverb reminded him, 'Where your ancestor does not live, you cannot build your house.'

The Holy Land

The *bakulu* and the Europeans who landed in the Kongo in the late fifteenth century seemed to be related by an extraordinary kinship. They were incorporated into a single landscape, a single symbolic universe. The newcomers came from the water (their caravels were compared to whales) and had the white color of relatives who had gone to the village of the dead. They arrived bearing riches and armed with instruments which demonstrated their power. They came to speak of God and lands unknown. The analogy seemed obvious: these Whites, these *mundele*, were emissaries who heralded the return of the ancestors. They were going to build the 'society of below' on earth, to divulge the secret of the true life, of power and abundance. Upon this colossal misunderstanding, of which no one was aware, the first Christianization was founded. It was doomed: its vicissitudes are familiar; they began with the missionaries being driven out of the capital after 1495.

With Afonso I, Christianity was re-established and the royal power became stronger and altered its organization. The church became an ally and a symbol of power, and suffered attacks resulting from political conflicts. Despite the efforts of the missionaries, whose 'service was troubled and scattered', Christianity affected only a slim minority. For the majority of the people of the Kongo, its ceremonies, its symbolism, its churches, and its clergy were less pretexts for belief than occasions for imitation. It left a lasting impression only where it managed to become associated with traditional usages. In trying to reach the people, it became an instrument of syncretism. Father Laurent de Lucques observes this to his indignation:

The fetishers corrupt the faith we preach. They also try to persuade the people that what we say is untrue. . . . So that the people will lose confidence in us, they themselves sprinkle water with the aspergillum as we do on Sunday. If we make use of diverse ornaments, they do so too. In short, they imitate us in everything and in this way deceive the poor, who are devoid of intelligence.[35]

This same witness mentions more than once the abuse of Christian symbols: combined use of the crucifix, the rosary, and 'wooden idols'; identification of statues of saints with these same idols; use of the cross in conjunction with hunting 'fetishes'. Under the name of *kuluzu* (distortion of the Portuguese *cruz*) or *ngubu santu*, the cross became one of the most celebrated 'fetishes'; fashioned on a small scale from palm stalks, it was even used as a talisman against the assaults of wandering spirits.[36]

The advance of syncretism and the growing resistance to Christianity led to the exposure of a second misunderstanding. The Bakongo did not believe that direct communication with God was possible; it was not only impossible, but inconceivable. Their theology allowed them only two forms of religious action: upon the ancestors and upon the forces harbored by the *nkisi*. The Christian ritual and the instruments of the liturgy tended to be classed in the second of these two categories. They belonged, according to Kongo logic, to the order of the *nkisi*. They furnished the most powerful of these, but their vigor did not suffice to render them exclusive of all the others. What was involved was one of the laws of the dynamism of vital forces: the strong *nkisi* drove out the weak *nkisi*, but not all the *nkisi* in existence. This explains why the first missionaries were able to bring about the destruction of the instruments of 'idolatry' without much difficulty. This happened at the beginning of the reign of Afonso I, according to Pigafetta:

It is remarkable that in less than a month the idols, deviltries, masks, and all the objects that were worshipped and regarded as gods were brought to the court. . . . The king had collected all these abominable images from several houses in the capital. At the very place where he had recently fought and defeated his brother's troops, he ordered that each man bring a load of wood so as to make a great pile, on which were thrown the idols, images, and all the objects which the people had formerly regarded as sacred. Fire was applied and everything burned. After that he called together all the people and, in place of the idols, he distributed crosses and images of saints brought by the Portuguese.[37]

This passage reports the facts with an edifying motive; but it nevertheless reveals the mechanism of substitution that operated. The Christian *nkisi*, which were recognized as more effective, replaced certain of the ancient 'fetishes'. Syncretism made its appearance, but it was vulnerable, fluid by nature, and antagonistic to any totalitarian organization of the sacred.

Alongside a Christianity which was weakly established and in constant danger, the traditional religious pluralism and the syncretic cults oriented the religious life of the people of the Kongo from the sixteenth century on. This coexistence slowly prepared the way for more profound changes. They appeared abruptly during the last years of the seventeenth century, and then took the form of the 'heresy' known as Antonianism. A crisis of exceptional gravity accounted for this revolution in the realm of the sacred: it was the consequence of the total defeat suffered by the Kongo armies at Ambouila at the hands of the Portuguese—and their allies, the redoubtable Yak warriors—on October 25, 1665. Jadin recalls the significance of this tragic event:

The royal power, weakened by this defeat, was never again to recover its glory. . . . Factions were to contend for the throne and pretenders, ruined by the commitments of their electoral campaigns, would have a precarious authority. The opposition of their competitors would leave them only a nominal authority, outside of their native territories or chieftainries.[38]

This collapse of the royalty created instability and gave free rein to civil wars, which compounded the destruction: 'For more than thirty years, the pretenders would try in vain to reconquer the hegemony and to restore peace with the unity of the kingdom.'[39] After 1667 there were three kings, established in three different regions of the country: in the north (Bula), in the center (São Salvador) and in the south (banks of the Ambriz). The capital itself was eventually abandoned.

Toward the end of the century, when the political structure had dissolved and misery had become universal, a series of movements combining mysticism with realism caused the awakening of the Kongo. A revealed religion was born at the same time that, under the impetus of its founders, the rebirth of the political unity was being prepared. The daring of a few visionaries aroused national feeling and sustained hope for a better future. Christianity had provided the means for a liberation and restoration of the kingdom; it became the instrument of a salvation which was not the one its teachings foretold. Premonitory signs and minor prophets prefigured the event. A woman received a message from the Virgin informing her of Christ's indignation at the conditions existing in the Kongo; her recommendation was to recite the *Ave Maria* three times and to invoke the divine mercy three times at nightfall. Then a young man announced that God would punish the people of the Kongo unless they rebuilt the capital. In 1704, an old woman named Ma-Futa claimed to have found the head of Christ 'all disfigured by the wounds the wickedness of men had inflicted'—in reality, a stone worn by the Ambriz River—and to have received a vision of the Madonna. The latter predicted the catastrophes that would befall the Kongo unless the king set off for São Salvador. The 'rumor that the old woman was a saint' spread, the queen and the people credited her with miraculous cures, and the legal sovereign protected her from the justice of the missionaries.[40]

These were merely annunciations. The true foundress of the national religion was a young Mukongo of aristocratic rank named Kimpa Vita, or Dona Beatriz. She had been a 'priestess' of the cult of Marinda before having the experiences that revealed her 'saintliness' to her, before curiously repeating the adventure of Joan of Arc: like her, she was called a heretic and undertook the mission of correcting the evils of the kingdom. A drawing by Bernardo de Gallo, in which she wears a golden crown and is clad in green garments,[41] and a few lines from Laurent de Lucques provide her portrait:

This young woman was about twenty-two years old. She was rather slender and fine-featured. Externally she appeared very devout. She spoke with gravity, and seemed to weigh each word. She foretold the future and predicted, among other things, that the day of Judgment was near.[42]

It was during the year 1704 that Dona Beatriz obtained recognition of her spiritual royalty. In São Salvador, where she later taught, she received numerous evidences of veneration from the highest dignitaries: when she ate, the 'lords . . . offered her the ends of their capes as mantillas or tablecloths'; her believers fought over food or drink from her hand; when she travelled, the roads were cleared 'by the noblest ladies'. This rapid ascension was explained by the popular conviction that the Christian God was finally responding to the long anguished waiting of the people of the Kongo. Dona Beatriz was his representative; she partook of his power. She had power over nature—it was said that twisted or fallen trees straightened up at her passing—and worked miracles; she permitted the Bakongo to have 'their saints' —that is, the spokesmen of a remodelled and Africanized Christianity. She heralded a new age. It all began in the manner of the great initiations: a death and a rebirth, a sacred possession, an exceptional power placed at the service of the collective welfare. An interview with Dona Beatriz conducted by Father Bernardo de Gallo shows this clearly:

The event occurred in this manner, she said. When she was sick and on the point of death, at the last gasp, a brother dressed as a Capuchin appeared to her. He told her he was Saint Anthony, sent by God through her person to preach to the people, hasten the restoration of the kingdom, and threaten all those who tried to oppose it with severe punishments. She died, because in place of her soul, Saint Anthony had entered her head; without knowing how, she felt herself revive. . . . She arose then and calling her parents, explained the divine commandment to go and preach, teach the people, and hasten the departure toward São Salvador. So as to do everything properly, she began by distributing the few things she possessed, renouncing the things of this world, as the apostolic missionaries do. Having done this, she went up into the Mountain (Mount Kibangu) and in complete liberty fulfilled her duty, as God had commanded her to do, and with great success.[43]

Thus the religious tradition of the Kongo and the Christian tradition were combined: the Catholic saint replaced the ancient 'possessor' spirits; the symbolic death, the revelation of the divine plan, and the renunciation of possessions were inspired by initiatory procedures. How did Saint Anthony—who was deeply revered in Portugal, the place of his birth—come to be the center of the mystical adventure of the young Kongo woman? He was one of the three saints worshipped in the old kingdom and in Angola. Statuettes sculpted or cast in the style already described represented him carrying the Infant Jesus; they showed him to be a privileged intercessor. Dona Beatriz praised him and identified herself with him for this same reason. She claimed that Saint Anthony was the 'second God' and that he 'held the keys to heaven'. She described him as compassionate and eager to restore the earthly kingdom. Through him she associated individual salvation with the salvation of the Kongo. It was from this central symbol that the religious movement took the name of Antonianism, or the 'sect of the Antonians'.

Dona Beatriz tried, however, to revive symbolically the beginnings of Christianity, to bring about a second birth of this religion in order to make it directly available to the people of the Kongo. She imitated the death of Christ: she was 'in the habit of dying every Friday'; she went up to heaven to 'dine with God and plead the cause of the Negroes, especially the restoration of the Kongo'; she 'was born again on Saturday'.[44] She imitated the Virgin and longed to bring into the world a son who would become the Saviour of the people, a son born of the intervention of the holy spirit: she wished 'to be regarded as chaste'. A male child was born, of whom she said, 'I cannot deny that he is mine, but how I had him, I do not know. I know, however, that he came to me from Heaven.'[45] This was 'the irremediable misfortune' which would eventually lead to her ruin.

In less than two years the young 'heretic' nevertheless succeeded in creating a dogma and a doctrine, establishing a rudimentary church, and causing a political revival. She emphasized the essential difference between the Blacks and the Whites: the latter 'were originally made from a certain soft stone called *fama* [*fuma*, clayey rock]'; the former 'came from a tree called *musenda* [*nsanda*, a species of fig]'. Her believers wore garments made from the bark of this tree, the real cloth of negritude, and their chiefs were distinguished by the wearing of a crown made of the braided fibers of this same *nsanda*, badge of their faith and emblem of their power. Moreover, Dona Beatriz taught that the Kongo was the true Holy Land and that the founders of Christianity belonged to 'the Negro race'. She maintained that Christ was born in São Salvador (Bethlehem) and received baptism in Nsundi (Nazareth), that the Virgin 'was born of a slave or servant woman of the marquis Nzimba Npanghi', and that Saint Francis belonged 'to the clan of the marquis of Vunda'.[46] She substituted the sacred places of the Kongo for those that had provided the setting for the Christian revelation. She changed this revelation to the advantage of the people of the Kongo; she raised messianic hope; she predicted a golden age. The revived and repopulated capital would contain all covetable goods; the roots of fallen trees would change into gold and silver; the reconstructed ruins would reveal mines of precious stones and metals; the 'rich objects of the Whites' would come to all those who believed in the new faith and contributed to the rebirth of the kingdom. Father de Gallo, after recalling these promises and denouncing their falsity, mentions the 'frauds' of the prophetess: 'To lend credence to all this, she secretly had some of the local currency, that is, certain sea shells, buried in different parts of the ruined cathedral, and then publicly revealed the location of the caches and had the aforesaid shells dug up.'[47]

This detail has a purely anecdotal interest. It is of small importance in comparison with the expectation of wealth, power, and a new social order that was apparent in Antonianism as in all messianic or revolutionary movements.

The doctrine of Dona Beatriz was modelled on that of the missionaries. She 'proved to be the enemy of vices, superstitions, fetishism, and other things of this kind', which 'caused the ignorant Blacks to regard her as a saint'. She adapted certain Catholic songs, the *Ave Maria* and the *Salve Regina*, which glorified the 'intentions' of the faithful by eliminating the sacraments and works. She tried to organize a church; she founded a hierarchy; she 'sent her ambassadors into all parts of the kingdom' and 'even began to make nuns'. The imitation of Christianity did not exclude opposition to the missionaries and their work of evangelization. On the contrary, disciples were exhorted 'not to worship the cross because it was the instrument of the death of Christ'. The fundamental prescriptions of Catholicism —baptism, confession, prayer—were rejected in the form that the Church taught them, and with them the sacred character of marriage, which restored a 'legal' status to polygamy. Foreign priests were driven out and threatened. They were accused of having monopolized the revelation and the secret of wealth associated with it to the exclusive advantage of the Whites, and of opposing the work of salvation of the 'black saints'. The Christian ferment aroused national sentiment. The new religion expressed this sentiment, as well as the profoundly felt need for a reconstruction of Kongo society.

The very success of the Antonian movement bears witness to the importance of its aims; despair turned into hope. The Capuchin missionaries noted the vigor of a debate 'that destroyed the Catholic faith' and a certain order of relations between the Kongo and Europe. They denounced the mystical violence practiced by spokesmen — 'little Anthonys' — who predicted the catastrophes and punishments to overtake those who opposed the new revelation. Disobedience to the law of the foundress specifically entailed the risk of being swept away by the deluge or being reduced to an animal state.[48] The coercion introduced by Dona Beatriz was justified by the desire to restore the kingdom to its greatness and build a society free of evil and misery, similar to the one the ancestors had built in the world 'below'. The anticipated kingdom would revive past glories and realize a radiant future. The project of the young Kongo mystic had a political significance which the opposing parties could not ignore. Dona Beatriz acquired one of the royal emblems—the 'purse known as *sanctissimo sacramento*'—at Bula, and went to restore the ruined capital:

Thus it came about that São Salvador was rapidly populated, for some went there to worship the pretended saint, others to see the rebuilt capital, some to see friends, others attracted by the desire to recover their health miraculously, others still out of political ambition and to be the first to occupy the place. In this manner the false saint became the restorer, ruler, and lord of the Congo.[49]

This quotation from Bernardo de Gallo clearly demonstrates the multiple meanings of Antonianism: mystical movement, religion of salvation, renascent nationalism. In this last form it played a political role of prime importance. The two lineages pretending to the throne—Ki-Malaza, to which King Pedro IV belonged, and Ki-Mpanzu—fought insidiously and tried to divert or utilize the national religion, which was fervent and very widespread. After a long period of indecision, Pedro IV yielded to the pressure of the Capuchin missionaries, all the more readily because Dona Beatriz seemed to have adopted the opposing party. He had her arrested during the early months of the year 1706, a time when the child whom she had just brought into the world invalidated her claim to sanctity. Indeed, the first question put to the prisoner was, 'How does Saint Anthony beget children?' The king remained undecided, however; he was afraid to oppose popular sentiment by condemning Dona Beatriz to death; he considered sending her 'to the bishop of Angola, in Loanda', which would give her opportunity to be liberated by her followers along the way. At this point the Capuchins, motivated 'solely by zeal for the glory of God', stepped in. The royal council pronounced 'a sentence of death by fire on the false Saint Anthony and his guardian angel'. The execution of the verdict took place July 2, 1706. Fathers Bernardo de Gallo and Laurent de Lucques witnessed this drama, which they had brought about, in the hope of 'helping the souls' of the condemned and 'making them publicly abjure their errors'. In the tenth of his *Relations*, Laurent de Lucques reports the final scene which consigned Beatriz to the stake and the fury of the crowd:

Two men with bells in their hands . . . went and stood in the middle of this great multitude and gave a signal with their bells, and immediately the people fell back and in the middle of the empty space the *basciamucano*, that is, the judge, appeared. He was clad from head to foot in a black mantle and on his head he wore a hat which was also black, a black so ugly that I do not believe its like for ugliness has ever been seen. The culprits were led before him. The young woman, who carried her child in her arm, now appeared to be filled with fear and dread. The accused ones sat on the bare ground and awaited their death sentence.

We understood then that they had decided to burn the child along with his mother. This seemed to us too great a cruelty. I hastened to speak to the king to see whether there was some way to save him. . . .

The *basciamucano* made a long speech. Its principal theme was a eulogy of the king. He enumerated his titles and gave proofs of his zeal for justice. Finally he pronounced the sentence against Dona Beatriz, saying that under the false name of Saint Anthony she had deceived the people with her heresies and falsehoods. Consequently the king, her lord, and the royal council condemned her to die at the stake, together with her infant. . . . They were led to the stake. The woman did all she could to recant, but her efforts were vain. There arose such a great tumult among the multitude that it was impossible for us to be of assistance to the two condemned persons. They were quickly led to the stake. . . . For the rest, all we can say is that there was gathered there a great pile of wood on which they were thrown. They were covered with other pieces of wood and burned alive. Not content with this, the following morning some men came again and burned the bones that remained and reduced everything to very fine ashes.[50]

Like Joan, Beatriz died 'with the name of Jesus on her lips'. Bernardo de Gallo reports this fact, adding a short (and cynical) epitaph: 'The poor Saint Anthony, who was in the habit of dying and rising again, this time died but did not rise again.'[51] The observation proved false, however: hope survived in the hearts of the living. The Antonians spread the word that the place where their saints had been sacrificed 'was transformed into two deep wells and that in each of these there appeared a very beautiful star'. They collected fragments of bone 'to save as relics'. They claimed that Beatriz had disappeared only in one of her forms.[52] The king's party did not triumph as soon as the ashes of the stake had cooled. Two years later, in 1708, Pedro IV had to raise an army 'of close to twenty thousand men' to put down his adversaries and the heresy that inspired their ardor.[53] In the final analysis, his victory was, paradoxically, the victory of the young Mukongo. Her goal was attained: the disunited kingdom temporarily recovered its vigor. Over two centuries afterwards, in a colonized and modernized Congo, the mystical heirs of Dona Beatriz would rediscover, without even knowing her name, the road to the ideal kingdom of liberty and fullness of life.

Notes

PART ONE. THE FAILURE OF THE KINGS

CHAPTER 1. THE BLACKSMITH KING

1. J. Cuvelier, *L'Ancien Royaume de Congo*, Brussels, 1946, pp. 45–49. With a summary of the symbols and of the inscription: 'It shows the arms of the king of Portugal with five escutcheons, a triangle surmounted by a cross, and the motto: *Aqy chegaram os navios.* . . . The names of Diogo Cão, Pedro Anes, Pedro da Costa, and others of the principal members of the expedition are here inscribed.'
2. H. M. Stanley, *Five Years in the Congo*, 1879–1884 (French translation), Brussels, n.d., pp. 169, 174, 175.
3. K. E. Laman, *Dictionnaire ki-kongo-français*, Brussels, 1936, Foreword.
4. L. van de Velde, 'La Région du Bas-Congo et du Kwilu Niadi. Usages et coutumes des indigènes,' *Bulletin de la Sociéte royale belge de Géographie*, 1886, 10th year.
5. K. E. Laman, *The Kongo*, Vol. I, Uppsala, 1953.
6. R. L. Wannyn, *L'Art ancien du métal au Bas-Congo*, Champles (Belgium), 1961.
7. L. M. Jordão de Paiva Manso, *História do Congo, Documentos 1492–1722*, Lisbon, 1877, p. 60.
8. O. Dapper, *Description de l'Afrique, contenant les noms, la situation et les confins de toutes ses parties* (translated from the Flemish), Amsterdam, 1685.
9. J. Cuvelier and L. Jadin, *L'Ancien Congo d'après les archives romaines (1518–1640)*, Brussels, 1954, pp. 14–16.
10. Cuvelier, *L'Ancien Royaume de Congo*, p. 72.
11. Cuvelier and Jadin, *L'Ancien Congo*, Document 18, p. 137.
12. J. Cuvelier, *Relations sur le Congo du père Laurent de Lucques (1700–1717)*, Brussels, 1953, p. 257.
13. Paiva Manso, *História do Congo*, p. 266. This author mentions that the 'natives' of the conquered land 'were Ambundu of another race' (according to A. Oliveira de Cadornega).
14. The name 'Motino-Bene' (Ntinu Wene) appears in the *História do Reino do Congo* (cited by A. de Alburquerque Felner); 'Motinu Nimi' (Ntinu Nimi) in Paiva Manso; and 'Mutinu Lukeni' in Cavazzi.
15. Cf. Cuvelier, *L'Ancien Royaume de Congo*, pp. 251–252, note 2.

16. G. da Montesarchio, *Viaggio dal Congo*, manuscript, Montughi Archives, Florence. Quoted by Cuvelier, *L'Ancien Royaume de Congo*, p. 251, note 1.
17. Cuvelier, *L'Ancien Royaume*, pp. 12–14.
18. J. van Wing, *Études bakongo, histoire et sociologie*, Brussels, 1921, pp. 80–81. The most important section of Chap. 3 is entitled 'Origine et première immigration'.
19. *Ibid.*, p. 89.
20. According to the *História do Reino do Congo* (cited by Felner), there were 'six princes' between the founder and Nzinga a Nkuwu. Paiva Manso and Cavazzi regard the latter as the fifth sovereign. Similarly, in a modern document, Ravenstein retains only three kings between the founder and the first Catholic king; see E. G. Ravenstein, *The Strange Adventures of Andrew Battell of Leigh in Angola and Adjoining Regions*, London, 1901.
21. G. A. de Montecucullo Cavazzi, *Istorica descrizione degli tre regni Congo, Angola e Matamba*, Bologna, 1687, p. 237.
22. Description of 'a very skilful artisan' from whom the kings of the Kongo were descended appears in *Archives congolaises*, published by the *Revue congolaise*, January 1914; for mention of his attribute of inventor of the art of metal, see Cavazzi, *Istorica descrizione*, p. 136.
23. Cuvelier, *Relations sur le Congo de Laurent de Lucques*, p. 140.
24. Cuvelier, *L'Ancien Royaume*, p. 11.
25. Text from Cuvelier, *L'Ancien Royaume*, p. 11, after Cavazzi, *Istorica descrizione*, Book I, No. 234.
26. See G. Dumézil, *Mitra-Varuna*, Paris, 1940, Chap. 2, 'Celeritas et Gravitas,' and Chap. 3, the Numa-Romulus antithesis. It all begins in the Kongo as at Rome: Ntinu Wene, like Romulus, leaves his original society because he does not accept not reigning there; he, too, has the 'thirst for power'.
27. Van Wing, *Études bakongo*, p. 94.
28. Cuvelier, *L'Ancien Royaume*, pp. 15–16.
29. Document 38 (dated November 25, 1595), in Cuvelier and Jadin, *L'Ancien Congo*, pp. 199, 200. This document is also found in A. Brasio, *Monumenta Missionaria Africana*, Lisbon, 1953, and in a study by Théophile Simar in *Mélanges Moeller*, Louvain, 1914, Vol. II.
30. Paiva Manso, *História do Congo*, Document 103, dated 1624; quoted by Cuvelier, *L'Ancien Royaume*, p. 253.
31. Van Wing, *Études bakongo*, p. 138.
32. Laman, *Dictionnaire*; see article on *ntotila*.
33. Cuvelier and Jadin, *L'Ancien Congo*, Document 18, p. 134.

CHAPTER 2. THE CHRISTIAN KING

1. On the composition of the missionary expedition of 1490, see Cuvelier, *L'Ancien Royaume*, pp. 266 ff., note 22. The principal sources of information are compared.

2. Cuvelier, *L'Ancien Royaume*, p. 63.

3. *História do Reino do Congo* manuscript, National Library, Lisbon; also mentioned by various chroniclers: G. de Resende (1622), J. de Barros (1706), Rui de Pina (1792). See Cuvelier, *L'Ancien Royaume*, p. 265.

4. Cuvelier, *Relations sur le Congo de Laurent de Lucques*, p. 149.

5. The Portuguese caravels arrived at Pinda March 29, 1491; the baptism of the *mani* Soyo took place on the third of April. It seems impossible that a 'messenger' could have covered, both ways, the *three-hundred-odd* kilometers that separated the seat of the province of Soyo from the capital of the Kongo.

6. Cuvelier, *L'Ancien Royaume*, p. 71.

7. The date of the baptism of Mbemba Nzinga, the future Afonso I, is the subject of debate. J. de Barros holds it to be after the baptism of the 'queen'. The *História do Reino do Congo* gives the same date for both baptisms.

8. *História do Reino do Congo*, Chap. 22. The whole controversy regarding the location of the rebel tribes is meticulously examined by Cuvelier in *L'Ancien Royaume*, pp. 277–279.

9. Cuvelier, *L'Ancien Royaume*, p. 83.

10. *Ibid.*, p. 81.

11. *História do Reino do Congo*, Chap. 23.

12. Van Wing, *Études bakongo*, p. 36. More recent scholarship gives 1506 as the date of the death of the first Christian king.

13. Paiva Manso, *História do Congo*, p. 11; cf. Cuvelier, *L'Ancien Royaume*, p. 284. Saint James, the performer of the 'miracle', was known as patron saint of the Portuguese army.

14. Dom Afonso's execution of his mother is related by G. Monari da Modena in *Viaggio al Congo* (p. 129 of the partial edition of Father Evaristo Gatti, Parma, 1931). It is described by Msgr. Manuel Alves da Cunha in *Os primeiros bispos negros*, Luanda, 1939, from a document dated January 1782. Since the terms *mother* and *maternal line* are denoted by the same word, *ngudi*, an error in translation must be considered. The ritual described implied a symbolic rupture with the lineage (and probably the execution of a material relative or of a slave of this relative), but not the execution of the mother of the new king. Unless it is a question of the mother of the defeated and executed pretender, who was also mother, in the classificatory sense, to Dom Afonso.

15. Pedro V (1855–1891). See J. H. Weeks, *Among the Primitive Bakongo*, London, 1914, p. 36.

16. See especially L. de Heusch, 'Aspects de la sacralité du pouvoir en Afrique,' in *Le Pouvoir et le Sacré*, Institut de Sociologie Solvay, Brussels, 1962.

17. See especially, F. Pigafetta and D. Lopes, *Description du Royaume de Congo et des contrées environnantes* (French translation by W. Bal), Louvain, 1963, and Cavazzi, *Descrizione storica*. A document in the Vatican Library cited by J. Cuvelier (*L'Ancien Royaume*, p. 284) mentions the duty of constructing and maintaining the churches entrusted to 'a certain noble'.

18. An example is given by C. R. Boxer in his short study, 'The Old Kingdom of the Congo,' in R. A. Oliver, *The Dawn of African History*, New York, 1961.

19. Translation given by Cuvelier, *L'Ancien Royaume*, pp. 158–160; cf. Brasio, *Monumenta*, Vol. I, p. 361.

20. From a letter from Bras Correa to Msgr. Vives. (See Cuvelier and Jadin, *L'Ancien Congo*, p. 440.) The expression 'Apostolo do Congo' occurs in *História do Reino do Congo*, Chap. 24.

21. Placide Tempels, *La Philosophie bantoue*, Paris, 1949, pp. 32 ff.

22. Cuvelier, *L'Ancien Royaume*, p. 124.

23. Brasio, *Monumenta*, Vol. I, p. 361.

24. Letter from Afonso I, 1526.

25. Cuvelier and Jadin, *L'Ancien Congo*, p. 17.

26. *Ibid.*, p. 18.

27. Damião de Goes, *Chronica do felicissimo rey Dom Manuel*, Lisbon, 1619, Part II, Chap. 30, and Part III, Chap. 4.

28. Cuvelier, *L'Ancien Royaume*, p. 125.

29. Van Wing, *Études bakongo*, p. 33.

30. Cuvelier, *L'Ancien Royaume*, p. 326, note 57.

31. 'Report by Bishop Manuel Baptista Soares on His Diocese of the Congo and Angola'; cf. Cuvelier and Jadin, *L'Ancien Congo*, Document 112, p. 391.

32. Van Wing, *Études bakongo*, p. 37.

33. *Ibid.*, p. 38.

34. From the Introduction, Cuvelier and Jadin, *L'Ancien Congo*, p. 35.

35. For information on São Tomé, consult the excellent studies by Francisco Tenreiro; *Descriçao de Ilha de São Tomé no secule XVI*, Lisbon, 1952, and *As Ilhas de São Tomé e Principe*, Lisbon, 1956. Also, the *Description de la côte occidentale d'Afrique* by Valentim Fernandes (French translation), Bissau, 1951.

36. Cuvelier, *L'Ancien Royaume*, pp. 139–140.
37. Letter by E. Pacheco (dated March 1536) in Paiva Manso, *História do Congo*.
38. Cuvelier, *L'Ancien Royaume*, p. 249.

CHAPTER 3.   THE RIVAL KINGS

1. See Ravenstein, *The Strange Adventures of Andrew Battell*; this author refers to the matrilinear system (p. 101) and later indicates that matrilinear royal succession was interrupted for a period, without specifying when.
2. See Van Wing, *Études bakongo*, p. 23.
3. Cuvelier and Jadin, *L'Ancien Congo*, p. 19.
4. *Ibid.*, p. 20.
5. In *Études bakongo* (p. 41), Father van Wing notes: 'According to a clause in this agreement, the merchants of São Tomé could trade only with tribes who were subject to the king of São Salvador, and in return the kingdom of the Congo was open to all Portuguese merchants, and exclusively to the Portuguese. This agreement was observed by neither of the two parties.'
6. V. Baesten, *Les Anciens Jésuites au Congo, 1548–1648*, Brussels, 1898.
7. *Ibid.*
8. Cuvelier and Jadin, *L'Ancien Congo*, p. 20.
9. Van Wing, *Études bakongo*, p. 43.
10. Cuvelier and Jadin, *L'Ancien Congo*, p. 21. See also the work of V. Baesten.
11. Van Wing, *Études bakongo*, p. 44.
12. Passage quoted in the French edition of Cuvelier and Jadin (*L'Ancien Congo*, p. 125) after a compilation at the Vatican Library which draws heavily on the Lopez-Pigafetta version. The latter, which was published by Pigafetta and became famous, is the principal source of information on the kingdom of the Kongo at the time of Alvaro I.
13. Van Wing, *Études bakongo*, p. 45.
14. Passage quoted in Cuvelier and Jadin, *L'Ancien Congo*, pp. 128–129.
15. *Ibid.*, p. 129.
16. T. Simar, *Le Congo au XVIe siècle d'après la relation de Lopez-Pigafetta*, Brussels, 1919, p. 18.
17. 'Summary of the Instructions carried to Rome by Dom Antonio Manuel' (June 29, 1604); French text: Document 52 in Cuvelier and Jadin, *L'Ancien Congo*, p. 261.

18. *Ibid.*, p. 263.
19. *Ibid.*
20. *Ibid.*, pp. 264–265. The gist of the 'instructions' is found in several other documents published by Cuvelier and Jadin; see Documents 56, 57, 58, and 80.
21. Cuvelier and Jadin, *L'Ancien Congo*, Document 97.
22. The manuscript of the account, which was printed in 1634 at Haarlem with alterations, is preserved at Leyden. See J. Cuvelier's article, 'L'Ancien Congo d'après Pierre van den Broecke (1608–1612), '*Bulletin des Séances de l'Académie royale des Sciences Coloniales*, Nos. 1–2, Brussels, 1955.
23. Van Wing, *Études bakongo*, p. 53.
24. Cuvelier and Jadin, *L'Ancien Congo*, p. 31.
25. Van Wing, *Études bakongo*, p. 54.
26. See the 'instructions' given by Alvaro II to the ambassador Don Antonio Manuel. See also A. de Albuquerque Felner, *Angola, apontamentos sóbre a occupação e início do estabelecimento dos portugueses no Congo, Angola e Benguela*, Coimbra, 1933, p. 177.
27. Paiva Manso, *História do Congo*, p. 201.
28. R. A. Oliver, *The Dawn of African History*, New York, 1961, plate 6.
29. Van Wing, *Études bakongo*, pp. 24–25.
30. A. de Oliveira de Cadornega, *Historia geral das guerras angolanas*, 3 vols., Lisbon, 1940–1942.
31. Cuvelier, *Relations sur le Congo de Laurent de Lucques*, pp. 58 ff. Description of the wars with Soyo in Girolamo Merolla, *Relazione del viaggio nel regno di Congo*, Naples, 1692, pp. 79 ff.
32. Van Wing, *Études bakongo*, pp. 70–71.
33. This result is mentioned in A. Zucchelli, *Relazioni del Viaggio e Missione di Congo*, Venice, 1712, Vol. I, No. 19, pp. 336–337.
34. Cuvelier, *Relations sur le Congo de Laurent de Lucques*, No. 11 (December 1707), pp. 278–279.
35. *Ibid.*, No. 15 (June 1709), pp. 287 ff.
36. *Ibid.*, No. 21 (December 1714), p. 323.
37. J. H. Pirenne, 'Les éléments fondamentaux de l'ancienne structure territoriale et politique du bas Congo,' *Bulletin des Séances de l'Académie royale des Sciences Coloniales*, Brussels, Vol. V, No. 3 (1959), p. 561.
38. Van Wing, *Études bakongo*, p. 76.
39. Cuvelier and Jadin, *L'Ancien Congo*, p. 36.
40. *Ibid.*, p. 35.
41. Brasio, *Monumenta*, Vol. II, pp. 311–313.

42. Paiva Manso, *História do Congo,* Document 38.
43. Cuvelier, *Relations sur le Congo de Laurent de Lucques,* p. 63.
44. Translation given by Cuvelier in *L'Ancien Royaume,* p. 230.
45. Cuvelier and Jadin, *L'Ancien Congo,* p. 91, note 1.
46. 'Assembly of the Council of Portugal' (March 31, 1607), appended document, in Cuvelier and Jadin, *L'Ancien Congo.*
47. Cuvelier, *L'Ancien Royaume,* p. 243.
48. Pigafetta, *Description du Royaume de Congo,* pp. 103–104.

PART TWO

CHAPTER 4. THE FORGE AND THE PALM

1. Pigafetta, *Description du Royaume de Congo,* p. 77.
2. Cavazzi, *Descrizione storica,* p. 33.
3. Pigafetta, *Description du Royaume de Congo,* p. 78. The modern name of the tree is *mungyengye.* This tree is still used for its fruit, and its architectural use also persists, notably in Mayombe.
4. *Ibid.,* p. 77.
5. J. Cuvelier, *Documents sur une mission française au Kakongo, 1766–1776,* Brussels, 1953, p. 51.
6. J. Koechlin, 'Sur quelques usages de plantes spontanées de la région de Brazzaville,' *Bulletin de l'Institut d'Études Centrafricaines,* Brazzaville, Vol. II, 1951.
7. Pigafetta, *Description du Royaume de Congo,* p. 76.
8. Cuvelier and Jadin, *L'Ancien Congo,* Document 18, pp. 117–118; Cavazzi, *Descrizione storica,* p. 26.
9. Cavazzi, *Descrizione storica,* p. 26.
10. K. E. Laman, *Dictionnaire ki-kongo-français,* Brussels, 1936, p. 712.
11. Pigafetta, *Description du Royaume de Congo,* p. 76.
12. Cavazzi, *Descrizione storica,* p. 33.
13. Cuvelier and Jadin, *L'Ancien Congo,* Document 18, p. 117.
14. J. Cuvelier, quoted by W. Bal in his Note (246) commenting on Pigafetta's *Description du Royaume du Congo,* 1963 edition.
15. Cuvelier, *Relations sur le Congo de Laurent de Lucques,* pp. 200–201.
16. Cuvelier, *Documents sur une mission française,* pp. 47, 50.
17. Cf. the very fine study by A. Raponda-Walker and R. Sillans, *Les Plantes utiles du Gabon,* Paris, 1961, p. 460.
18. Cavazzi, *Descrizione storica,* p. 27.

19. Cf. M. A. de Morais Martins' useful inventory in *Contacto de culturas no Congo português*, Lisbon, 1958, p. 27.
20. Cuvelier, *Relations sur le Congo de Laurent de Lucques*, No. 7 (January 1704), pp. 79–80.
21. H. Nicolai, *Luozi. Géographie régionale d'un pays du Bas-Congo*, Brussels, 1961, p. 39.
22. K. E. Laman mentions these ancient 'gardens' in *The Kongo*, p. 117.
23. Cuvelier, *Relations sur le Congo de Laurent de Lucques*, No. 8 (January 1705), pp. 109–112.
24. See Cuvelier, *Relations sur le Congo de Laurent de Lucques*, p. 146; Zucchelli, *Relazioni del Viaggio e Missione*, pp. 173, 185–186; also Cavazzi, *Descrizione storica*.
25. Cavazzi, *Descrizione storica*, p. 94.
26. Pigafetta, *Description du Royaume de Congo*, p. 54.
27. *Ibid.*, pp. 53 and 55.
28. Cuvelier, *Relations sur le Congo de Laurent de Lucques*, p. 145.
29. *Ibid.*, pp. 128–129.
30. *Ibid.*, p. 244.
31. *Ibid.*, p. 332.
32. Pigafetta, *Description du Royaume de Congo*, pp. 29–30.
33. Cuvelier, *Relations sur le Congo de Laurent de Lucques*, pp. 114–115.
34. Van Wing, *Études bakongo*, 2nd ed., Brussels, 1959, p. 290.
35. *Ibid.*, pp. 462–464. Also F. Ngoma, *L'Initiation bakongo et sa signification*, unpublished thesis, 1963, p. 82.
36. Cuvelier, *Relations sur le Congo de Laurent de Lucques*, pp. 115–118.
37. Pigafetta, *Description du Royaume de Congo*, p. 59.
38. Cuvelier and Jadin, *L'Ancien Congo*, Document 38, p. 197.
39. *Ibid.*, Document 18, p. 120.
40. J. Cuvelier, 'L'Ancien Congo d'après Pierre van den Broecke 1608–1612),' *Bulletin des Séances de l'Académie royale des Sciences Coloniales*, Brussels, 1955, Nos. 1–2, p. 188.
41. Cuvelier, *Documents sur une mission française*, p. 51.
42. Cuvelier, *Relations sur le Congo de Laurent de Lucques*, p. 77.
43. *Ibid.*, p. 338.
44. *Ibid.*, p. 140.
45. J. de Heinzelin, 'Métallurgie primitive du fer dans le région de la Basse-Semliki,' *Bulletin des Séances de l'Académie royale des Sciences Coloniales*, Brussels, 1959, pp. 686–692.
46. Wannyn, *L'Art ancien du métal*, p. 59.
47. Pigafetta, *Description du Royaume de Congo*, p. 67.

48. Cavazzi, *Descrizione storica*, p. 111, and illustrated insert, p. 301.
49. Laman, *The Kongo*.
50. Cuvelier, *Relations sur le Congo de Laurent de Lucques*, pp. 139–140.
51. *Ibid.*, p. 149.
52. Wannyn, *L'Art ancien du métal*, p. 60.
53. *Ibid.*, p. 61.
54. *Ibid.*, p. 62.
55. *Ibid.*, p. 58.
56. *Ibid.*, p. 30.
57. *Ibid.*, p. 48.
58. *Ibid.*, p. 82 note to plate 29.
59. See Laman, *The Kongo*.
60. Cuvelier, *Relations sur le Congo de Laurent de Lucques*, p. 121.
61. Cuvelier, *Documents sur une mission française*, p. 52.
62. Pigafetta, *Description du Royaume de Congo*, pp. 36–37.
63. Cavazzi, *Descrizione storica*, especially pp. 111 and 113.
64. Cuvelier, *Relations sur le Congo de Laurent de Lucques*, p. 56.
65. Cuvelier, *Documents sur une mission française*, p. 47.
66. Wannyn, *L'Art ancien du métal*, p. 18.
67. Pigafetta, *Description du Royaume de Congo*, p. 83.
68. Cuvelier and Jadin, *L'Ancien Congo*, Document 18, p. 122.
69. Cavazzi, *Descrizione storica*, p. 100.
70. Quoted by E. Gatti, *Sulle terre e sui mari*, Parma, 1931, p. 172.
71. Pigafetta, *Description du Royaume de Congo*, p. 29.
72. Cuvelier, *Relations sur le Congo de Laurent de Lucques*, p. 121.
73. *Ibid.*, p. 54.
74. *Ibid.*, p. 118.
75. *Ibid.*, pp. 83–84.
76. *Ibid.*, pp. 133–134.
77. *Ibid.*, p. 213.
78. *Ibid.*, p. 66.
79. Van Wing, *Études bakongo*, 2nd ed., pp. 148–149.
80. Pigafetta, *Description du Royaume de Congo*, pp. 41–42.
81. *Ibid.*, p. 43.
82. *De la situation du royaume de Congo*, Document 38 in Cuvelier and Jadin, *L'Ancien Congo*, pp. 198–199; passage also in Brasio, *Monumenta*, Vol. III, pp. 505–510.
83. *História do Reino do Congo*, Document 18 in Cuvelier and Jadin, *L'Ancien Congo*, p. 136.
84. *Ibid.*, pp. 141, 143. See also Pigafetta, *Description du Royaume de Congo*, p. 70.
85. Cuvelier and Jadin, *L'Ancien Congo*, p. 121.

86. Wannyn, *L'Art ancien du métal*, pp. 59–60.
87. Pigafetta, *Description du Royaume de Congo*, p. 43.
88. *Ibid.*, p. 42.
89. Van Wing, *Études bakongo*, 2nd ed., pp. 148–149.
90. Report by Father Bernardo de Gallo (1710), published by L. Jadin in *Le Congo et la secte des Antoniens*, in *Bulletin de l'Institut historique belge de Rome*, Vol. XXXIII, 1961, pp. 411–614.
91. Cuvelier, *L'Ancien Royaume*, pp. 306–312, notes.
92. Cuvelier and Jadin, *L'Ancien Congo*, Document 18, pp. 133–134.
93. Pigafetta, *Description du Royaume de Congo*, p. 25; and numerous other sources, such as Cuvelier and Jadin, *L'Ancien Congo*, pp. 142, 263, 381; and especially Vol. IV, pp. 536–545, of Brasio's *Monumenta*.
94. See Édouard Darteville's very fine study, *Les 'Nzimbu,' monnaie du royaume de Congo*, Brussels, 1953.
95. Cuvelier, *L'Ancien Royaume*, pp. 306–312, note on 'finances'.
96. *Ibid.*, documentation quoted from Paiva Manso, *História do Congo*, p. 21.
97. Cuvelier and Jadin, *L'Ancien Congo*, pp. 264–265, note 2.
98. Quoted by Cuvelier in *L'Ancien Royaume*, p. 311.
99. Cuvelier and Jadin, *L'Ancien Congo*, Document 18, p. 135.
100. Pigafetta, *Description du Royaume de Congo*, p. 71.
101. Wannyn, *L'Art ancien du Métal*, pp. 19–20.
102. *Ibid.*, p. 19.
103. Cuvelier and Jadin, *L'Ancien Congo*, Document 18, pp. 152–153. Much information also contained in the description by O. Dapper.
104. Morais Martins, *Contacto de culturas*, p. 96.
105. Van Wing, *Études bakongo*, 2nd ed., p. 149.
106. Cf. Cuvelier, *Documents sur une mission française*, pp. 21, 34. See also L. B. Proyart, *Histoire de Loango, Kakongo et autres royaumes d'Afrique*, Paris and Lyons, 1776.
107. See Cuvelier, 'L'Ancien Congo d'après P. van den Broecke.'

CHAPTER 5. THE FRAGILE TOWNS

1. Cuvelier and Jadin, *L'Ancien Congo*, Document 18, pp. 120–121.
2. Cavazzi, *Descrizione storica*, p. 90.
3. Cuvelier, *Relations sur le Congo de Laurent de Lucques*, p. 80.
4. Cuvelier, *Documents sur une mission française*, pp. 23–24.

5. Cuvelier, *Relations sur le Congo de Laurent de Lucques*, pp. 80–81.
6. *Ibid.*, p. 169.
7. *Ibid.*, p. 213.
8. Cavazzi, *Descrizione storica*, p. 89.
9. Note by W. Bal, p. 118 of the appendix to his edition of Pigafetta's *Description du Royaume de Congo*.
10. Cavazzi, *Descrizione storica*, p. 95.
11. Cuvelier, *Relations sur le Congo de Laurent de Lucques*, p. 55.
12. Cuvelier and Jadin, *L'Ancien Congo*, Document 18, p. 120.
13. Cuvelier, *Documents sur une mission française*, p. 23.
14. Cavazzi, *Descrizione storica*, p. 95.
15. Quoted by Cuvelier, *L'Ancien Royaume*, pp. 303–304.
16. Cuvelier, *Documents sur une mission française*, p. 25.
17. Cuvelier, *Relations sur le Congo de Laurent de Lucques*, p. 149.
18. *Ibid.*, p. 149.
19. *Ibid.*, pp. 149–150.
20. *Ibid.*, pp. 119–120.
21. Cuvelier and Jadin, *L'Ancien Congo*, Document 51, p. 258.
22. Pigafetta, *Description du Royaume de Congo*, p. 74.
23. Hyacinthe de Bologne (?), *Pratique missionnaire*, p. 99, quoted by Cuvelier.
24. J. Cuvelier, 'L'Ancien Congo d'après Pierre van den Broecke, 1608–1612),' *Bulletin des Séances de l'Académie royale des Sciences coloniales*, Brussels, 1955, Nos. 1–2, pp. 183 ff.
25. Marcellino d'Atri, *Giornate apostoliche fatte . . . nelle missioni dei regni d'Angola e Congo (1690–1703)*, manuscript, quoted by Cuvelier, *L'Ancien Royaume*, pp. 342 ff. See especially the recent French edition published by *Cahiers Ngonge*, No. 5, 1960.
26. Cuvelier, *L'Ancien Royaume*, pp. 72–74.
27. Letter published in Brasio, *Monumenta*, Vol. II, pp. 493–512.
28. See and compare description of the towns and palaces of Benin in P. Mercier, *Civilisations du Bénin*, Paris, 1962, Chap. 6.
29. Pigafetta, *Description du Royaume de Congo*, pp. 75–76, 78.
30. Cuvelier and Jadin, *L'Ancien Congo*, Document 18, p. 137.
31. Cuvelier, *L'Ancien Royaume*, pp. 326–327.
32. Cuvelier, *Relations sur le Congo de Laurent de Lucques*, pp. 246, 251, 255, 256–257. Compare the old descriptions of São Salvador with that of the German explorer A. Bastian, in *Ein Besuch in San Salvador, der Haupstadt des Königreichs Congo*, Bremen, 1859.

NOTES

CHAPTER 6. THE FABRIC OF DAILY LIFE

1. Cuvelier, *Relations sur le Congo de Laurent de Lucques*, p. 150.
2. See Morais Martins, *Contacto de culturas*, p. 138.
3. Cuvelier, *Relations sur le Congo de Laurent de Lucques*, pp. 144–145.
4. Pigafetta, *Description du Royaume de Congo*, p. 65.
5. See E. Torday, 'Dualism in Western Bantu Religion,' *Journal of the Royal Anthropological Institute*, Vol. LVIII, 1933.
6. Quoted by Van Wing, *Études bakongo*, 2nd ed., p. 297.
7. K. E. Laman, *Dictionnaire ki-kongo-français*, Brussels, 1936; article on *ntangu*, p. 787.
8. See Cuvelier, *Relations sur le Congo de Laurent de Lucques*, pp. 109–112; Cavazzi, *Descrizione storica*, Book I, § § 235–236; Monari, *Viaggio al Congo*, E. Gatti, *Sulle terre e sui mari*, pp. 142 ff.
9. Cuvelier, *Documents sur une mission française*, pp. 112–113.
10. Cuvelier and Jadin, *L'Ancien Congo*, Document 38, p. 197.
11. Cavazzi, *Descrizione storica*, p. 36.
12. Cuvelier, *Relations sur le Congo de Laurent de Lucques*, pp. 77, 200–201.
13. Cuvelier, *Documents sur une mission française*, p. 50.
14. N. Diederich, in C. van Overbergh, *Les Mayombé*, Brussels, 1907, pp. 108–109.
15. E. de Wildeman, *A propos de médicaments indigènes congolais*, Brussels, 1935.
16. Cuvelier, *Relations sur le Congo de Laurent de Lucques*, p. 168; Zucchelli, *Relazioni del Viaggio e Missione*, p. 223.
17. Cavazzi, *Descrizione storica*, p. 94.
18. Cuvelier, *Relations sur le Congo de Laurent de Lucques*, p. 76.
19. Cuvelier and Jadin, *L'Ancien Congo*, Document 18, p. 132.
20. *Ibid.*, p. 141.
21. Cuvelier, *Relations sur le Congo de Laurent de Lucques*, pp. 118–119.
22. Cuvelier and Jadin, *L'Ancien Congo*, Document 18, pp. 119–120.
23. Dapper, *Description de L'Afrique*; Proyart, *Histoire de Loango*; and especially J. Fourneau and L. Kravetz's good article, 'Le Pagne sur la Côte de Guinée et au Congo du XVᵉ siècle à nos jours,' *Bulletin de l'Institut Études Centrafricaines*, Brazzaville, Nos. 7–8, 1954.
24. Dapper, *Description de l'Afrique*, quoted in Fourneau and Kravetz, 'Le Pagne sur la Côte de Guinée et au Congo,' p. 7.
25. Pigafetta, *Description du Royaume de Congo*, p. 119.

275

26. Cuvelier, *Relations sur le Congo de Laurent de Lucques*, p. 78.
27. Pigafetta, *Description du Royaume de Congo*, p. 118.
28. Fourneau and Kravetz, 'Le Pagne sur la Côte de Guinée et au Congo,' p. 10.
29. Pigafetta, *Description du Royaume de Congo*, p. 119.
30. Cuvelier, *L'Ancien Royaume*, pp. 293–294.
31. See the chapter entitled 'Insignes profanes et parures' in Wannyn, *L'Art ancien du métal*.
32. Letter from Father G. Simoes (1575) in Brasio, *Monumenta*, Vol. III, p. 133.
33. See Laman, *The Kongo*.
34. Cuvelier, *Relations sur le Congo de Laurent de Lucques*, p. 142.
35. F. Ngoma, *L'Initiation bakongo et sa signification*, unpublished thesis, 1963, p. 192.
36. Van Wing, *Études bakongo*, 2nd ed., pp. 142, 147, 184–186.
37. See Cuvelier and Jadin, *L'Ancien Congo*, p. 205, note 1.
38. Pigafetta, *Description du Royaume de Congo*, pp. 32, 122.
39. Quoted by Havelock Ellis in Vol. I of his *Studies in the Psychology of Sex*, pp. 42–43.
40. Van Wing, *Études bakongo*, 2nd ed., pp. 144, 161–163, 177–179, 192.
41. Cuvelier, *Relations sur le Congo de Laurent de Lucques*, p. 89.
42. *Ibid.*, pp. 136–138; certain aspects of this description are confirmed in Monari, *Viaggio al Congo*.
43. Cuvelier and Jadin, *L'Ancien Congo*, Document 38, p. 200.
44. Cuvelier, *Documents sur une mission française*, p. 52. Proyart refers to these facts in his *Histoire de Loango*.
45. Dapper, *Description de l'Afrique*, p. 97.
46. J. Cuvelier, 'L'Ancien Congo d'après Pierre van den Broecke 1608–1612),' *Bulletin des Séances de l'Académie royale des Sciences Coloniales*, Brussels, 1955, Nos. 1–2, pp. 183 ff.
47. Cuvelier, *Relations sur le Congo de Laurent de Lucques*, p. 125.
48. Vereycken, 'La Région des cataractes,' *Le Congo illustré*, Elisabethville, 1895, p. 138.
49. Cuvelier, *Relations sur le Congo de Laurent de Lucques*, p. 81.
50. *Ibid.*, p. 113.
51. Vereycken, 'La Région des cataractes,' p. 138.
52. Zucchelli, *Relazioni del Viaggio e Missione*, p. 302.
53. Cuvelier, *Relations sur le Congo de Laurent de Lucques*, pp. 66–67.
54. *História do reino do Congo*, Document 18 in Cuvelier and Jadin, *L'Ancien Congo*, p. 133.
55. Dapper, *Description de l'Afrique*, cf. pp. 536–537, p. 579 of the 1676 edition (quoted by J. van Wing).

CHAPTER 7. MASTER AND SLAVE

1. Cuvelier and Jadin, *L'Ancien Congo*, Document 18, p. 123.
2. Cuvelier, *Documents sur une mission française*, pp. 51–52.
3. *Ibid.*, p. 49.
4. Van Wing, *Études bakongo*, 2nd ed., pp. 85–86.
5. *Ibid.*, pp. 48–49.
6. Cuvelier, *L'Ancien Royaume*, p. 143.
7. Cuvelier, *Relations sur le Congo de Laurent de Lucques*, p. 138.
8. Quoted in Cuvelier, *L'Ancien Royaume*, p. 299.
9. Van Wing, *Études bakongo*, 2nd ed., p. 98.
10. Cuvelier, *Relations sur le Congo de Laurent de Lucques*, p. 148.
11. *Ibid.*, pp. 336–337.
12. *Ibid.*, pp. 138–139.
13. Cuvelier, *Documents sur une mission française*, p. 51.
14. *Ibid.*, p. 51.
15. See, among others, the account by Bishop Manuel Baptista Soares in Cuvelier and Jadin, *L'Ancien Congo*, p. 400, and Felner, *Angola*, p. 473.
16. Frei Luís de Sousa, *Historia de S. Domingos*, Lisbon, 1662, Book VI, p. 244.
17. Pigafetta, *Description du Royaume de Congo*, p. 34.
18. Cuvelier and Jadin, *L'Ancien Congo*, Document 18, p. 135.
19. Van Wing, *Études bakongo*, 2nd ed., p. 102.
20. Cuvelier, *Documents sur une mission française*, p. 52.
21. Pigafetta, *Description du Royaume de Congo*, p. 107.
22. Cuvelier, *Documents sur une mission française*, p. 82.
23. Cuvelier, *L'Ancien Royaume*, p. 175.
24. Cuvelier and Jadin, *L'Ancien Congo*, p. 85.
25. Proyart, *Histoire de Loango*, p. 158.
26. Cuvelier, *L'Ancien Royaume*, p. 223.
27. *Ibid.*, pp. 141–142.
28. Cuvelier and Jadin, *L'Ancien Congo*, Document 18, p. 135.
29. Cuvelier and Jadin, *L'Ancien Congo*, p. 452, note 2.
30. *Ibid.*, p. 89.
31. Reference to the 'princess of Soyo in Cuvelier, *Relations sur le Congo de Laurent de Lucques*, p. 49.
32. Cuvelier, *L'Ancien Royaume*, pp. 99–100.
33. Dapper, *Description de l'Afrique*, 1685 ed., p. 355.
34. See Cuvelier, *Relations sur le Congo de Laurent de Lucques*, p. 337.

35. See Part II, Chap. 4, 'The Forge and the Palm," pp. 89-138.
36. For a fuller analysis, see Cuvelier, *Relations sur le Congo de Laurent de Lucques*, pp. 109–112, 114–122, 124–125.
37. Proyart, *Histoire de Loango*, p. 129.
38. Dapper, *Description de l'Afrique*, 1685 ed., p. 229.
39. *Ibid.*, p. 97.
40. *Ibid.*, pp. 536-537.
41. Cuvelier, *Documents sur une mission française*, p. 48.
42. J. Mertens, *Les Chefs couronnés chez les Bakongo orientaux*, Brussels, 1942.
43. The edition of this document was prepared by L. Jadin; see partial prepublication in his 'Aperçu de la situation du Congo et rite d'élection des rois en 1775, d'après le P. Cherubino da Savona, missionnaire au Congo de 1759 à 1774,' in *Bulletin de l'Institut historique belge de Rome*, Vol. XXXV, 1963.
44. Brasio, *Monumenta*, Vol. I, pp. 528–529.
45. Cuvelier and Jadin, *L'Ancien Congo*, p. 200, note 1.
46. Van Wing, *Études bakongo*, 2nd ed., p. 42.
47. Ravenstein, *The Strange Adventures of Andrew Battell*, p. 104.
48. Account by Bernardo de Gallo, in Jadin, *Le Congo et la secte des Antoniens*, p. 64.
49. See L. Jadin, 'Aperçu de la situation du Congo,' p. 405.
50. Cuvelier, in *L'Ancien Royaume*, recalls these facts and mentions the chief sources of information: Chap. 10 and annotations, pp. 252, 298, and 302.
51. Jadin, 'Aperçu de la situation du Congo,' pp. 398 ff.
52. See F. Bontinck, 'Les Armoiries de l'ancien royaume de Congo,' in *Antennes: Chroniques culturelles congolaises*, No. 12, 1963.
53. Jadin, 'Aperçu de la situation du Congo,' pp. 401–402.
54. *Ibid.*, p. 402.
55. J. F. Lafitau, *Histoire des découvertes et conquests des Portugais dans le Nouveau Monde*, Paris, 1734, Vol. I, p. 75.
56. Cf. Cuvelier and Jadin, *L'Ancien Congo*, Document 112, p. 339.
57. Jadin, 'Aperçu de la situation du Congo,' p. 404.
58. *Ibid.*
59. Dapper, *Description de l'Afrique*, 1685 ed., p. 202.
60. Van Wing, *Études bakongo*, 2nd ed., p. 43.
61. Proyart, *Histoire de Loango*, p. 120.
62. See A. Ihle, *Das alte Königreich Kongo*, Leipzig, 1929, pp. 201 ff.
63. Cuvelier, *Relations sur le Congo de Laurent de Lucques*, pp. 112–114.

PART THREE. THE MAKING OF MEN

CHAPTER 8. EDUCATION

1. F. Ngoma, *L'Initiation bakongo et sa signification*, unpublished thesis, 1963, p. 39.
2. Pigafetta, *Description du Royaume de Congo*, p. 31.
3. Account published in Jadin, *Le Congo et la secte des Antoniens*, p. 43.
4. *Ibid.*, p. 43.
5. Cuvelier, *Relations sur le Congo de Laurent de Lucques*, pp. 136 ff.
6. Cavazzi, *Descrizione storica*, pp. 67–68.
7. Translation of Cavazzi by Father J. B. Labat, *Relation historique de l'Éthiopie occidentale*, Paris, 1732, Vol. I, pp. 296 ff.
8. Ngoma, *L'Initiation bakongo*, p. 70.
9. For a detailed description of the *kimpasi* see Ngoma, *L'Initiation bakongo*, pp. 63–86; and van Wing, *Études bakongo*, 2nd ed., pp. 426–508.
10. Van Wing, *Études bakongo*, 2nd ed., p. 475.
11. Dapper, *Description de l'Afrique*, 1676 ed., pp. 176–177 (quoted by van Wing).
12. Cuvelier, *Relations sur le Congo de Laurent de Lucques*, p. 123.
13. *Ibid.*, p. 134.
14. See Jadin, *Le Congo et la secte des Antoniens*, p. 43.
15. *Ibid.*, p. 44.
16. Cavazzi, *Descrizione storica*, pp. 63–69.
17. Pigafetta, *Description du Royaume de Congo*, pp. 122–123.
18. Cuvelier, *Relations sur le Congo de Laurent de Lucques*, p. 131.
19. *Ibid.*, p. 131.
20. *Ibid.*, pp. 131–132.
21. Cuvelier, *L'Ancien Royaume*, pp. 325–326.
22. Cuvelier, *Relations sur le Congo de Laurent de Lucques*, p. 141.
23. *Ibid.*, p. 332.
24. 'Relation de Bernardo de Gallo,' (December 1710), in Jadin, *Le Congo et la secte des Antoniens*, p. 52.
25. *Ibid.*, pp. 52–53.
26. Cuvelier, *Relations sur le Congo de Laurent de Lucques*, p. 132.
27. For valuable observations on the blacksmith, see ibid., pp. 139–140.
28. Van Wing, *Études bakongo*, 2nd ed., p. 226.
29. Cuvelier, *Relations sur le Congo de Laurent de Lucques*, p. 56.

30. *Ibid.*, pp. 67–68.
31. Cuvelier and Jadin, *L'Ancien Congo*, Document 18, p. 131.
32. J. Cuvelier, 'L'Ancien Congo d'après Pierre van den Broecke (1608–1612),' in *Bulletin des Séances de l'Académie royale des Sciences Coloniales*, Brussels, 1955, Nos. 1–2, p. 183.

CHAPTER 9. LANGUAGE AND ARTS

1. Cavazzi, *Descrizione storica*, p. 56.
2. See, for example, Morais Martins, *Contacto de culturas*, pp. 117–129.
3. F. Ngoma, *L'Initiation bakongo et sa signification*, unpublished thesis, 1963, pp. 52–55.
4. Van Wing, *Études bakongo*, 2nd ed., p. 65.
5. 'Free' reconstruction by Cuvelier, in *L'Ancien Royaume*, p. 172.
6. Van Wing, *Études bakongo*, 2nd ed., pp. 482–483 : documents on the *kimpasi* compiled at the beginning of the century, which illustrate observations made by Cavazzi and several missionaries.
7. *Ibid.*, p. 265; many other examples of *mbembo* on pp. 263–278.
8. I. Struyf, *Les Bakongo dans leurs légendes*, Brussels, 1936.
9. Cuvelier and Jadin, *L'Ancien Congo*, Document 18, p. 135.
10. Pigafetta, *Description du Royaume de Congo*, p. 121.
11. See the lists of 'Kongolized' expressions drawn up by Morais Martins, *Contacto de culturas*, pp .125–150.
12. Pigafetta, *Description du Royaume de Congo*, p. 122.
13. *Ibid.*, p. 121.
14. *Ibid.*, p. 42.
15. *Ibid.*, p. 121.
16. *Ibid.*
17. Cuvelier, *Relations sur le Congo de Laurent de Lucques*, pp. 113–114.
18. Brasio, *Monumenta*, Vol. I, p. 299.
19. Cuvelier, *L'Ancien Royaume*, p. 113.
20. R. Verly, 'La Statuaire de pierre du Bas-Congo,' in *Zaïre*, Brussels, May 1955, p. 482.
21. Museum of Prehistory and Ethnography, information supplied by V. L. Grottanelli.
22. Statement made by Verly's informants.
23. H. Lavachery, *Statuaire de l'Afrique noire*, Brussels, 1954, p. 33.
24. Verly, 'La Statuaire du Bas-Congo', p. 473.

25. Jean Jacques Maquet, *Afrique: Les Civilisations noires*, Paris, 1962, p. 110.
26. Verly, 'La Statuaire du Bas-Congo,' p. 510.
27. *Ibid.*, p. 511.
28. G. Mortelmans and M. Monteyne, 'La Grotte peinte de Mbafu, témoignage iconographique de la première évangélisation du Bas Congo,' *Annales, Sciences humaines*, No. 40, Tervuren, 1962, pp. 457–486.
29. Wannyn, *L'Art ancien du métal*, p. 30.
30. *Ibid.*, p. 33.
31. Tata Nsiesie, 'Notes sur les christs et statues de l'ancien Congo,' *Brousse*, Leopoldville, No. 3, 1939.
32. *Ibid.*, p. 33.
33. *Ibid.*
34. Wannyn, *L'Art ancien du métal*, p. 35.
35. O. de Bouveignes, 'La Statuette no. L.E. 89-S du Musée,' *Brousse*, Leopoldville, 1945 (only issue), p. 25.
36. See Wannyn, *L'Art ancien du métal*; O. de Bouveignes, 'Saint Antoine et la pièce de vingt reis,' *Brousse*, Leopoldville, Nos. 3–4, 1947, pp. 19–20.
37. Reproduction in Wannyn, *L'Art ancien du métal*, plate 23.
38. Verly, 'La Statuaire du Bas-Congo,' p. 499.
39. Wannyn, *L'Art ancien du métal*, p. 44.
40. *Ibid.*, p. 37.
41. *Ibid.*
42. *Ibid.*

CHAPTER 10. ONE GOD AGAINST MANY

1. Cuvelier and Jadin, *L'Ancien Congo*, Document 18, p. 122.
2. Cuvelier, *Documents sur une mission française*, p. 26.
3. Pigafetta, *Description du Royaume de Congo*, p. 97.
4. Cavazzi, *Descrizione storica*, p. 60.
5. Quoted in Felner, *Angola*.
6. K. E. Laman, *Dictionnaire ki-kongo-français*, Brussels, 1936; article on *nzambi*, p. 821.
7. See van Wing, *Études bakongo*, 2nd ed., p. 300.
8. *Ibid.*, p. 302.
9. Cavazzi, *Descrizione storica*, p. 61.
10. Cuvelier and Jadin, *L'Ancien Congo*, Document 112, p. 395.
11. Van Wing, *Études bakongo*, 2nd ed., p. 292.
12. Cavazzi, *Descrizione storica*, p. 88.

13. Cuvelier, *L'Ancien Royaume*, p. 115.
14. Van Wing, *Études bakongo*, 2nd ed., p. 291.
15. Dapper, *Description de l'Afrique*, 1676 ed., pp. 176–177.
16. Cuvelier, *Relations sur le Congo de Laurent de Lucques*, pp. 111–112.
17. 'Relation de Bernardo de Gallo' (December 1710), in Jadin, *Le Congo et la secte des Antoniens*, pp. 49–52.
18. Pigafetta, *Description du Royaume de Congo*, p. 65.
19. Monari, *Viaggio al Congo*, in Gatti, *Sulle terre e sui mari*, p. 190; Cuvelier, *Relations sur le Congo de Laurent de Lucques*, pp. 144–145
20. Wannyn, *L'Art ancien du métal*, p. 53.
21. Van Wing, *Études bakongo*, 2nd ed., p. 383.
22. Cuvelier, *L'Ancien Royaume*, pp. 325–326.
23. Cuvelier, *Relations sur le Congo de Laurent de Lucques*, p. 147.
24. Cuvelier, *Documents sur une mission française*, pp. 53–54.
25. Dapper, *Description de l'Afrique*, 1676 ed., p. 527.
26. Cuvelier, *L'Ancien Royaume*, p. 88.
27. Cuvelier and Jadin, *L'Ancien Congo*, Document 18, p. 123.
28. Cuvelier, *Documents sur une mission française*, pp. 54–55.
29. Van Wing, *Études bakongo*, 2nd ed., pp. 242 ff.
30. Cuvelier, *Documents sur une mission française*, p. 54.
31. Van Wing, *Études bakongo*, 2nd ed., pp. 247–250.
32. See Cavazzi, *Descrizione storica*, Book I, Chap. 5; résumé in Morais Martins, *Contacto de culturas*, pp. 64–67.
33. Zucchelli, *Relazioni del Viaggio e Missione*, pp. 173, 185–186.
34. Cuvelier, *Relations sur le Congo de Laurent de Lucques*, p. 146.
35. *Ibid.*, pp. 130–131.
36. Morais Martins, *Contacto de culturas*, p. 118.
37. Pigafetta, *Description du Royaume de Congo*, pp. 97–98.
38. Jadin, *Le Congo et la secte des Antoniens*, p. 13.
39. *Ibid.*
40. *Ibid.*, 'Relation de Bernardo de Gallo,' pp. 84–85.
41. *Ibid.*, plate 1, p. 118.
42. Cuvelier, *Relations sur le Congo de Laurent de Lucques*, pp. 231–232.
43. 'Relation de Bernardo de Gallo,' in Jadin, *Le Congo et la secte des Antoniens*, p. 91.
44. *Ibid.*, pp. 109–110.
45. Cuvelier, *Relations sur le Congo de Laurent de Lucques*, p. 229.
46. 'Relation de Bernardo de Gallo,' in Jadin, *Le Congo et la secte des Antoniens*, p. 107.
47. *Ibid.*, p. 108.
48. *Ibid.*, p. 99.

49. Ibid., pp. 96–97.
50. Cuvelier, Relations sur le Congo de Laurent de Lucques, pp. 235–238.
51. 'Relation de Bernardo de Gallo,' in Jadin, Le Congo et la secte des Antoniens, p. 116.
52. Ibid., pp. 116–117.
53. Ibid., p. 121.

Bibliographical Suggestions

ACCOUNTS AND COLLECTIONS OF EARLY TEXTS

Antonio Brasio, Monumenta Missionaria Africana, Vols. I–IX, Lisbon, 1953–1960; 2nd series, Vols. I–III, Lisbon, 1963.

António de Oliveira de Cadornega, Historia geral das guerras angolanas, Luanda, 1681; new ed., 3 vols., Lisbon, 1940–1942.

Giovanni Antonio de Montecucullo Cavazzi, Descrizione storica dei tre regni Congo, Matamba e Angola, modern ed., Tivoli, 1937. Originally published as Istorica descrizione degli tre regni Congo, Angola e Matamba, Bologna, 1687.

Jean Cuvelier, Relations sur le Congo du père Laurent de Lucques (1700–1717), Brussels, 1953.

Jean Cuvelier, Documents sur une mission française au Kakongo, 1766–1776, Brussels, 1953.

Jean Cuvelier and Louis Jadin, L'Ancien Congo d'après les archives romaines (1518–1640), Brussels, 1954.

Olfert Dapper, Description de l'Afrique, contenant les noms, la situation et les confins de toutes ses parties (translated from the Flemish), Amsterdam, 1685.

Alfredo de Albuquerque Felner, Angola, apontamentos sôbre a ocupação e início do estabelecimento dos portugueses no Congo, Angola e Benguela, Coimbra, 1933.

Louis Jadin, Aperçu de la situation du Congo et rite d'élection des rois en 1775, d'après le P. Cherubino da Savona, missionnaire au Congo de 1759 à 1774, Brussels, 1963.

Levy Maria Jordão, Visconde de Paiva Manso, História do Congo, Documentos 1492–1722, Lisbon, 1877.

Filippo Pigafetta and Duarte Lopes, Description du Royaume de Congo et des contrées environnantes (French translation by W. Bal), Louvain, 1963. Originally published as Relazione del reame di Congo, Rome, 1591.

Liévain Bonaventure Proyart, *Histoire de Loango, Kakongo et autres royaumes d'Afrique*, Paris and Lyons, 1776.

E. G. Ravenstein, *The Strange Adventures of Andrew Battell of Leigh in Angola and Adjoining Regions*, London, 1901.

Jean François de Rome, *La Fondation de la mission des Capucins au royaume de Congo* (French translation and notes by F. Bontinck), Louvain and Paris, 1964.

Antonio da Grandisca Zucchelli, *Relazioni del Viaggio e Missione di Congo*, Venice, 1712.

MODERN STUDIES

Jean Cuvelier, *L'Ancien Royaume de Congo*, Brussels, 1946.

Alexander Ihle, *Das alte Königreich Kongo*, Leipzig, 1929.

Louis Jadin, *Le Congo et la secte des Antoniens; restauration du royaume sous Pedro IV et la 'saint Antoine' congolaise (1694–1718)*, Brussels, 1961.

Louis Jadin, 'Aperçu de l'histoire du royaume du Congo (1482–1718),' in *Bulletin du Faculté des Lettres de Strasbourg*, March 1964.

Manuel Alfredo de Morais Martins, *Contacto de culturas no Congo português*, Lisbon, 1958.

Théophile Simar, *Le Congo au XVIe siècle d'après la relation de Lopez-Pigafetta*, Brussels, 1919.

Jan Vansina, 'Notes sur l'origine du royaume du Congo,' *Journal of African History*, Vol. IV, No. 1, 1963.

Robert Verly, 'La Statuaire de pierre du Bas-Congo,' *Zaïre*, May 1955.

Robert L. Wannyn, *L'Art ancien du métal au Bas-Congo*, Champles (Belgium), 1961.

ETHNOLOGICAL REFERENCES

Georges Balandier, *Sociologie actuelle de l'Afrique noire*, 2nd ed., Paris, 1963.

Karl E. Laman, *The Kongo*, 2 vols., Uppsala, 1953 and 1957.

Joseph van Wing, *Études bakongo, histoire et sociologie*, Brussels, 1921; 2nd ed., 1959.

Index

Afonso I, King (Dom Afonso Nzinga Mbemba), 22, 23, 29, 45, 48-59, 61-6, 78, 79, 81-4, 119, 127, 131, 138, 150-2, 189, 191, 197, 200, 226, 232-5, 238, 250, 254, 255; Afonso II, King, 67.

Afonso, Dom, 55.

Africa, 7-9, 12, 13, 19ff., 30, 37f., 48, 50, 84, 85, 137, 158, 172ff., 186, 236, 239f., 257.

Alvares, Gaspar, 192.

Alvaro I, King, 68-72, 189; Alvaro II, King (Mpanzu a Nimi), 64, 71, 73, 84, 198; Alvaro III, King, 73, 198; Alvaro IV, King, 73; Alvaro V, King, 73; Alvaro VI, King, 74, 198.

Alvaro, Frei, 84.

Ambouila, Battle of, 19, 75, 85, 128, 131, 198, 199, 256.

Ambundu, 29-31.

America, 9, 93.

Angola (Ndongo), 7-9, 11, 19, 20, 22, 29, 36, 62, 69, 71-5, 79, 81, 85, 91, 92, 123, 130, 132, 161, 169, 192, 206, 261.

Anna, Dona (Queen), 167.

Antonian Movement, 13, 21, 83, 255ff.

António I, 75, 85, 220.

Antonio, Dom Pedro, 70.

Anzika (Bateke), 29, 188, 190.

Bakongo, 7, 8, 10, 11, 19, 20, 24, 31, 64, 75, 90-5, 99, 102, 107-8 111-13 118, 122f., 141, 148, 154-7, 160, 163, 169-70, 230, 233, 237, 242, 246, 248, 254, 257.

Bamba, 102, 146; Dukes of, 77.

Bambata, 188.

Bampangu, 188.

Bantu, 67, 99, 231.

Baptista, Bishop Manuel, 83, 125, 170, 202.

Barroso, Dom Antonio, 109.

Basolongo, The, 157.

Bata (Province), 68, 146.

Bateke (Anzica), 11, 27, 28, 67, 134, 188.

Batta, 134; Dukes of, 40, 77, 175, 201.

Bazombo, 137, 243.

Bayaka, 8, 10.

Beatriz, Dona (Kimpa Vita), 21, 152, 257-63.

Bengo, River, 29, 75, 82, 95.

Bernardo I, King (Nzinga Mbemba), 45, 67.

The Book of Marco Polo, 22.

Brazil, 62, 81, 180, 226.

Breton, André, 19.

Bula, 75, 256, 261.

Cadornega, 132.

Cahir d'un retour au pays natal, 19

Camoes, 19.

Cao, Diogo, 19, 27.

Caporale, Fransesco, 165.

Capuchins, The, 22, 74, 76, 79, 161, 167, 220, 258, 260-2.

Cardoso, Father Mateus, 231.

Carmelites, 79, 147.

Catholicism, 8, 50-3ff., 73f., 79ff., 217, 225, 246, 258-60.

Cavazzi Giovanni Antonio, 22, 35-7, 90, 93, 95, 99, 106-8, 115, 117, 140, 142, 143, 147, 157, 158, 160, 161, 168, 217, 219-21, 227, 230, 244-8, 252, 253.

Central Africa, 9, 93, 102, 239.

Césaire, Aimé, 19.

Chimpazu, 198.

Christianity, 13, 19, 21, 27, 35, 42-52, 54-8, 60, 62, 64ff., 71-2, 77, 79-85, 136, 154, 166, 173, 180, 187, 192, 197-9, 201, 202, 206, 207, 221, 225-7, 238-46, 250, 254-60.

Congo, States of, 7-14, 19-20, 24, 39, 53, 56, 57, 70, 71, 76-8, 92, 93, 100, 106, 111, 117, 119, 121, 130, 144, 148, 160, 170, 217, 240, 243, 244, 251, 261, 263.

Congo, River, 7-10, 19, 24, 27-30, 32, 34, 35, 45, 55, 68, 78, 91, 102, 105, 118, 136, 137, 174, 234.

Correa, Bras, 94, 102, 165.

Correa, Da Silva, 168.

Cuvelier, Msgr Jean, 21, 22, 30, 32, 38, 43, 44, 46, 54, 56, 58, 60, 81, 93, 106, 108, 128-30, 146, 148, 183, 185, 189-91, 198, 222, 234, 249.

Da Concesçao, Father Gaspar, 231.

D'Aguiar, Rui, 42, 43, 46, 48.

Da Modena, Father Giuseppe Monari, 118.

Da Montesarchio, Father Girolamo, 32, 127, 185, 218.

DAILY LIFE IN THE KINGDOM OF THE KONGO

Dapper, Olfert, 23, 29, 30, 111, 122, 129, 151, 163, 164, 166, 175, 179, 196, 200, 204, 205, 215, 219, 220, 247, 250.
Da Savona, Father Cherubino, 139, 199.
Da Silva, Simáo, 57.
D'Atri, Marcellino, 132, 148.
De Brito, Domingos do Abreu, 131.
De Bry, Brothers, 21.
De Buffon, Georges, 103.
De Busseto, Father, 139.
De Cadornega, António de Oliveira, 75.
De Gallo, Father Bernardo, 21, 215, 216, 221, 223, 248, 257, 258, 260-2.
De Gouvea, Dom Francisco, 68.
De Lucques, Father Laurent, 21, 30, 44, 76, 77, 80, 81, 90, 94-6, 100-4, 106, 107, 109, 115, 119-21, 140-2, 144, 152, 153, 157-65, 167, 169, 170, 173, 176-9, 184, 186, 187, 193, 194, 207, 216, 221-3, 225, 233, 248, 249, 253, 254, 257, 262.
De Melo, Fernão, 61
De Novais, Governor Dias, 71.
Descourvières, J. J., 175.
Description de l'Afrique, 111.
De Sousa, Gonçalo, 42.
De Sousa, Rui, 42, 43, 46, 48.
Diogo I, King (Dom Nkumbi Mpudi a Nzinga), 64-7, 85, 203.
Dominicans, 42-66, 69, 79.
Dumézil, Georges, 37.
Dunga, 134-5.

Eastern Africa, 107, 113, 150, 195.
Enchus, Marquises of, 77.
England, 70, 73, 81.
Equimoloza (also Ki-Nlaza), 77.
Esikongo, 123, 126.
Études Bakongo, 127.

Felner, Alfredo de Albuquerque, 22, 245.
Fernandes, Diego, 61.
France, 21, 72, 73, 91, 106, 114, 125, 132, 140, 178, 181, 185, 195, 244, 249.
Franciscans, 42, 57.
Francisco, Dom (Mpudi a Nzinga Mbemba), 64, 65.
Frobenius, Leo, 19.

Gabon, 8, 29, 61, 95, 99.
Garcia I, King, 73; Garcia II, King, 73, 75.
Giornate, 148.

Gomes. Diogo, 65, 66.
Great Forest of the Ancestors, The, 234.

Henrique I, King, 68.
Henrique, 'Prince' (Bishop of Utica), 52, 55-7, 58.
História do Reino do Congo, 35, 43, 46, 48, 93-5, 106, 117, 127, 129, 133, 136, 139, 141-3, 151, 156, 157, 162, 163, 169, 172, 180, 187, 188, 190, 191, 205, 226, 231, 251, 252.
Historical Description, 244.
Holland, 73, 74, 81, 121, 125, 138, 166, 178.
Horses, Isle of the, 68, 118, 189.

Jadin, Father Louis, 22, 56, 60, 81, 256.
Jesuits, 66, 79, 82, 85, 149, 226.
Joan of Arc, 13, 152, 257, 263.
João I, King, 35, 45, 48, 49, 58, 190; João II, King, 42.
João I, King (Portugal), 45; João II, King (Portugal), 42; João III, King (Portugal), 62, 66, 82, 197; João IV, King (Portugal), 131.

Kakongo, Kingdom of, 21, 29, 34, 91, 95, 106, 114, 116, 128, 132, 133, 157-9, 164, 166, 181, 185, 187, 189, 244.
Kasavubu, Joseph, 12.
Kibangu, 75; Mount, 258.
Kikongo, 24, 28, 67, 94, 115, 130, 180, 183, 197, 203, 214, 228, 231, 245.
Ki-Malaza, 198, 261.
Kimbangu, Simon, 13.
Ki-Nlaza (also Ne-Nlaza), 75, 77.
Kinshasa, 7, 8, 11.
Kongo, Kingdom of, historical background, 7-14; Introduction, 19-24; early exploration, 27-31; founder, 31; clans and lineage, 31-5; first sovereign, 35-41; missionaries and arrival of Christianity, 42-9; Afonso I defeats adversaries, becomes King, 49-52; reign of Afonso I, 52-62; Afonso I dies, 63; struggles for power, 64-75; battle of Ambouila—António I killed, 75; breakdown of political unity, 75-9; progress and effects of Christianization, 79-85; uses of palm tree, 89; agriculture, 90-99; hunting, 99-102; fishing, 102-6; breeding of animals, 106; high posi-

tion of ironwork profession, 107-9; work of the blacksmith, 109-12; rings and bracelets, 112; other crafts and industries, 112-16; communications and transport, 116-18; making war, 118-28; economy and slavery, 128-36; European merchants, 136-8; towns and villages, 139-52; daily life, 153-6; diet, 156-63; dress, 163-9; sexual behaviour, 169-76; etiquette, 176-9; social relationships, 180-8; enslavement, 188-93; royalty, 193-209; education, 213-15; rites and initiation, 215-26; language and learning, 227-32; music and dancing, 232-3; sculpture, 234-8; religious art, 238-43; idolatry, 244-51; death, 251-3; resistance to Christianity, 253-6; Dona Beatriz tries to revive the beginnings of Christianity, 257-63.

Kongo dya Ntolita, 24.
Kwango, 136, 137; River, 8, 10, 28, 29, 32.

Labat, Father J. B., 217.
Lafitau, J. F., 202.
Laman, Carl, 40, 153, 164, 245.
L'Ancien Congo d'après les archives romaines, 22.
Lau, *mani*, 40.
Leo X, Pope, 52.
Lisbon, 13, 24, 42, 51, 55, 72, 209.
Loanda, 11, 69, 73-5, 79, 82, 95, 102, 129-31.
Loango, Kingdom of, 11, 21, 29, 78, 134, 138, 140, 143, 155, 158, 164, 172, 175, 179, 185, 187-9, 195, 197, 205, 206, 219, 220, 242, 244, 248, 249, 251, 261.
Lopes, Alvaro, 57.
Lopes, Duarte, 21, 70, 91, 150.
Lukeni lua Mbemba, 68.
Lumumba, Patrice, 12.
Lunda, Empire of, 8, 9, 11, 130; River, 30.
Lunga, 134-5.
Lusiads, 19.

Mabambala, Chief, 36.
Ma-Futa, 256.
Manso, Levy Maria Jordão de Paiva, 22, 31, 40, 49, 53, 74.
Manuel, King of Portugal, 56, 61, 62, 200.

Manuel, Antonio, 165.
Maquela do Zombo, 112.
Marinda, cult of, 257.
Masongo, *mani*, 110.
Matamba, 8, 29, 74.
Mbamba, 73, 76, 116, 122, 124, 142, 159, 161, 208; Duke of, 76.
Mbanza (Province), 142.
Mbanza Kongo (*see also* São Salvador), 19, 30, 32, 37, 44-6, 48, 53, 55, 57, 58, 62, 66, 70, 79, 92, 108, 122, 146, 148, 150, 182, 183, 190, 191, 199, 226.
Mbanza, Mbata, 139.
Mbanza Mpangu, 139.
Mbanza Soyo, 147, 148, 193, 226.
Mbata (Province), 11, 29, 32, 39, 57, 76, 132, 134, 137, 175, 199, 206.
Mbata, *mani*, 45, 124, 162, 200, 202, 203.
Mbata, Chief Nsaku of, 46.
Mboma, 183.
Merolla, 142.
Merovingian period, 54.
Mfulana Nsaku, 229.
Mobutu, General, 12.
Mocicongo, 123, 126, 165.
Monari, 147, 222, 248.
Monumenta Missionaria Africana, 22, 115.
Mpangala, 36, 44.
Mpangu (Province), 29, 33-5, 48, 50, 57, 58, 132, 134, 157, 182, 183, 188, 228.
Mpanza, *mani*, 48, 50.
Mpemba (Province), 19, 28, 29, 76, 206, 218.
Mpinda, 27, 42, 55, 62, 65, 76, 94, 118, 135, 147.
Mukongo, 22, 24, 90, 153, 159, 167, 176, 181, 184, 188, 189, 214, 224, 227, 228, 247, 253, 257, 263.

Negrillos, 219.
Negroes, 19, 59-60, 106, 176, 226, 236, 244, 249, 259; slave trade in, 9-10, 20, 56, 81ff., 118, 166, 180ff.
Ngombela, 148.
Ngoyo, 29, 34, 128.
Nkusu, 29, 35, 50.
Noki, 234.
Nsaku, 38-9, 94, 199, 205, 229.
Nsaku Lau, 39, 199-200, 206.
Nsanga, 45, 46.
Nsimba (Inkisi), 34, 136.

Nsundi (Province), 29, 32, 45ff., 73ff., 108, 109, 124, 132, 134, 148, 206, 259.
Ntinu (founder of Kongo—also Wene, Nimi, Lukeni), 35-9, 149, 199.
Ntinu, King Nkuwu a, 40.
Nunho, Father, 61.
Nzambi, 230, 244, 247, 250.
Nzimba Mpanghi, Marquis, 259.
Nzinga, 183.
Nzinga, Mpanza a, 48-50.

Ovando, dukes of, 77.

Pancheco, Manuel, 62.
Pangala, mani, 120, 144f.
Paul V, Pope, 72.
Pedro I, King (Nkanza Mbemba), 64; Pedro II, King, 73, 200; Pedro IV, King, 76, 78, 124, 139, 152, 261, 263.
Pemba (Province), 30, 146.
Pereira, Duarte Pacheco, 129.
Philip III, King (Portugal), 83f.
Pigafetta, Filippo, 21, 22, 42, 70, 89-93, 99ff., 106, 108, 114ff., 123ff., 130, 133-4, 139f., 146, 150, 155, 157, 160f., 163-72, 179, 188f., 192, 199, 206, 215, 221, 228, 231-3, 244, 248, 255.
Pratique Missionaire, 147.
Proyart, Father Liévain, 21, 141, 148, 163, 166, 205.

Quime, mani, 120, 144f.
Quimpanzo (Ki-Mpanzu), 77, 198, 261.

Ravenstein, 198.
Relations (of de Lucques), 115, 160, 262.
Relazione del reame di Congo, 70.
Relazioni del Viaggio e Missione di Congo, 76.
Ribeiro, Father, 81.
Rodrigo, 55, 62.
Rome, 20, 56, 67, 70-4, 80, 165, 203, 231, 235.

Sabastião, King Dom (Portugal), 68.
Santo Elói, College of, 24, 79.

São Salvador (see also Mbanza Kongo), 20, 68, 71, 73, 75-7, 80, 84, 94, 127, 132, 134-8, 145-8, 151-2, 193, 198, 208, 219, 232, 241, 243, 256-9, 261.
São Tomé, island of, 59-61, 66, 68, 81, 137, 189.
Simoes, Father Garcia, 168.
Soares, Bishop Manuel Baptista, 59, 246.
Sogno, 76, 78.
Soyo (Province), 27, 29, 34, 42-5, 73-7, 94ff., 100, 103ff., 110, 115, 119-22, 128, 132, 141f., 144-7, 155, 157, 160-2, 167, 173ff., 178, 184, 193-5, 197, 205-7, 216, 225f., 233, 248, 257.
Soyo, mani, 43-5, 77, 145-7, 167, 175, 193, 207.
Spain, 62, 69ff.
Stanley, Sir H. M., 28.
Stanley Pool (Mpumbu), 7, 10, 11, 23, 27, 28, 135, 136.

Tempels, Placide, 54.

Van den Broecke, Pieter, 73, 91, 100, 106, 147, 175, 226.
Van Wing, Father Joseph, 31ff., 48, 51, 58-9, 76, 80, 104, 127, 137, 170, 182ff., 188, 190, 198, 247f.
Vatican, the, 72, 143.
Verly, Robert, 234, 237.
Viaggio al Congo, 147.
Vives, Msgr., 73.
Vunda, mani, 40, 199-203, 205.
Vunda, António Manuel ne, 72.
Vunda, Marquis of, 259.
Vunda, Nsaku ne, 38-9, 42.
Vungo, mani, 144.

Wannyn, Robert, 108, 111, 116, 134, 239, 243.
Weulersse, Jacques, 27.

Yaka, the, 67f., 73, 82, 94, 124, 127, 189, 256.